THE POWER FORMULAS
PART ONE

THE BOOK OF MORMON AND THE POWER FORMULAS

(Prequel to *SUPER POWER*)

Copyright ©1993, Revised 2014

Craig A. McManama

For Heber Jentzsch

ACKNOWLEDGEMENTS

Thank you to all those who have contributed to my understanding through the years. A special thanks to my parents, Robert and LaRae McManama. Thank you for your teachings and example.

Thank you to those whose thoughts or writings have been quoted in this book. Thank you to Joseph Thacker for his words of blessing, inspiration and encouragement. Thank you to Eric Korb, whose words kindled the idea for this book. Thanks to him and his wife who taught my wife Karla and I and befriended us.

Thank you to my wife, Karla, and to my children, Cassie Belle, Sarah Jean, Joseph Craig and Megan Kathleen, for their patience and for their love.

Thank you to Barbara Stott and to my father for working and re-working the manuscripts. Thank you also to Kay Williams for editing and bookmaking of the revised edition in 2014. Thank you to Kris Humphries for her ideas which helped produced the Title and cover for this book.

Finally, thank you, the readers, who use a portion of your valuable time to consider these ideas. May Heavenly Father bless you all

ABBREVIATIONS

Book of Mormon (BofM)
Doctrine and Covenants (D&C)
New Testament (NewT)
Old Testament (OldT)
Pearl of Great Price (PofGP)

"MAKE A RECORD"

The Power Formula

The American author, L. Ron Hubbard, wrote of a series of actions, which could be used to transfer power from one person to another. He called these actions the **Power Formula**. His **Power Formula** speaks of the need to **"Make a Record"**:

1) The first law of the condition of power is, **don't disconnect**. You can't just deny your connections, what you have got to do is take ownership and responsibility for your connections....
2) The first thing you've got to do is **make a record** of all its lines, and that is the only way you'll ever be able to disconnect. So on a condition of power, the first thing you have to do, is **write up your whole post. You have made it possible for the next fellow in to assume the state of power change**. If you don't write up the whole post, you're going to be stuck with a piece of that post, since time immemorial and a year or so later somebody will still be coming to you and asking you about the post which you occupied.
3) The responsibility is to **write the thing up, and get it into the hands of the guy [or gal] who is going to take care of it.**
4) Do all you can to make the post occupiable[1] (emphasis added).

"MAKE A RECORD"

The Book of Mormon

Nephi, The first record keeper of *The Book of Mormon*, began his account with these words:

I, Nephi, having been born of goodly parents, therefore I was taught somewhat in all the learning of my father; and...having been highly favored of the Lord in all my days; yea, having had a great knowledge of the goodness and the mysteries of God, therefore I **make a Record** of my proceedings in my days (*BofM: 1 Nephi* 1:1; emphasis added).

Mormon, the author who compiled and abridged *The Book of Mormon* records, began his book with these words:

And now I, Mormon, **make a record** of the things which I have both seen and heard, and call it *The Book of Mormon* (*BofM: Mormon* 1:1; emphasis added).

The Book of Mormon is actually God's Record and **Power Formula** for us. This truth is evidenced by these words revealed to Mormon's son, Moroni who was the final record keeper:

And I exhort you to remember these things; for the time speedily cometh that ye shall know that 1 lie not, for ye shall see me at the bar of God; and the **Lord God will say unto you: Did I not declare my words unto you, which were written by this man**, like as one crying from the dead, yea, even as one speaking out of the dust? (*BofM: Moroni* 10:27; emphasis added).

THE BOOK OF MORMON RECORD FULFILLED BIBLICAL PROPHECY

After Moroni finished engraving his final words on the golden plates which contained *The Book of Mormon* Record, he buried them in a stone box.

Moroni was the final Record Keeper and survivor of a fallen nation known as the Nephites. His people had existed upon the American continent, but they were eventually destroyed because of wickedness and war.

Approximately 1400 years later, Moroni returned to earth as an angelic messenger. He was sent by God to reveal the Record to a modern prophet, Joseph

"MAKE A RECORD"

Smith. Joseph removed the plates from out of the ground. He was literally taking up a Record of God's prophets who were thus "crying [speaking] from the dead." Also, this Record came "out of the dust". The Old Testament prophet Isaiah foretold of the falling away from the truths which Jesus Christ had taught in the Holy Bible and of the coming forth of *The Book of Mormon*. Isaiah also prophesied of the restoration of the fullness of the gospel of Jesus Christ, which he called "a marvelous work and a wonder". Here are Isaiah's prophecies:

> Isaiah 29:4 And thou shalt be brought down, and shalt speak out of the ground, and thy speech shall be low out of the dust, and thy voice shall be, as of one that hath a familiar spirit, out of the ground, and thy speech shall whisper out of the dust.
> 9 Stay yourselves, and wonder; cry ye out, and cry: they are drunken, but not with wine; they stagger, but not with strong drink.
> 10 For the Lord hath poured out upon you the spirit of deep sleep, and hath closed your eyes: the prophets and your rulers, the seers hath he covered.
> 11 And the vision of all is become unto you as the words of a book that is sealed, which men deliver to one that is learned, saying, Read this, I pray thee: and he saith, I cannot; for it is sealed:
> 12 And the book is delivered to him that is not learned, saying, Read this, I pray thee: and he saith, I am not learned.
> 13 Wherefore the Lord said, Forasmuch as this people draw near me with their mouth, and with their lips do honour me, but have removed their heart far from me, and their fear toward me is taught by the precept of men:
> 14 Therefore, behold, I will proceed to do a marvellous work among this people, even a marvellous work and a wonder: for the wisdom of their wise men shall perish, and the understanding of their prudent men shall be hid.
> 18 And in that day shall the deaf hear the words of the book, and the eyes of the blind shall see out of obscurity, and out of darkness.

TABLE OF CONTENTS

Preface..Page 13

Chapter 1..Page 19
The Book of Mormon and The Power Formulas

Chapter 2..Page 31
Nephi Makes a Record

Chapter 3..Page 47
Jacob Followed Nephi's Instructions and Example, Thereby Accomplishing the Action Now Described as Power Change

Chapter 4..Page 55
Enos, The Third Record Keeper: An Example of Caring for Others and of the "Dynamics"

Chapter 5..Page 65
Jarom, Omni, Amaron, Chemish, Abinadom and Amaleki: Men Who Preserved the Record in Very Difficult Times

Chapter 6..Page 73
King Benjamin and the Power Formula

Chapter 7..Page 97
King Mosiah^2 and Power Change

Chapter 8..Page 107
Alma^2 And the Sons of Mosiah: From the Spiritual Conditions of Confusion and Treason to a Condition of Power

Chapter 9..Page 139
Bridges

Chapter 10..Page 167
Alma Passed the Record to His Son Helaman^2, Teaching that God Shows His Power Through the Record

TABLE OF CONTENTS

Chapter 11 ....Page 175
    Helaman and His Sons Tried to Bring Their People Out of Danger

Chapter 12 ....Page 187
    Nephi² Gave "Charge Unto His Son," Nephi 3, Who "Did Keep the Records in His Stead"

Chapter 13 ....Page 201
    Nephi's Account of the Visit and Teachings of Jesus Christ to the People of Ancient America Are the Heart of *The Book of Mormon* Record

Chapter 14 ....Page 231
    Nephi⁴, Amos¹, Amos² and Ammaron Recorded a Period of Spiritual Power and Then Decline

Chapter 15 ....Page 235
    Mormon was Chosen to "Make a Record" for Us

Chapter 16 ....Page 251
    Moroni Finished the Record of His Father

Chapter 17 ....Page 273
    Moroni's Farewell Advice to Us: Become "Perfect in Christ" and "Deny Not His Power"

Appendix I ....Page 287
    Power Formulas and Record Transfers Between *The Book of Mormon* Record Keepers

Appendix II ....Pagge 313
    A Proclamation on the Family

References ....Page 315

Preface

Power (pou'er), n.   1) Ability to do or act; capability of doing or accomplishing something...12) often powers of deity; divinity...23) to give power to; make powerful[2] (emphasis added).

What do we think of when we hear or read the word power? Many images come to mind. Some of these images are positive and some are not. Of the thirty-two definitions of power in the dictionary, these three define power as used in this book.

Definition 23 speaks of transferring or giving power to someone else. The **Power Formula** is a formula for transferring power to others. Here is where the first definition comes in, because the **Power Formula** is actually a formula for transferring "the ability to do or act," and "the capability of doing or accomplishing something" to others.

The **Power Formula** can be applied to any type of activity. One example would be a transfer of leadership within a business organization. However, the powers that we are most interested in understanding are the powers of deity..., mentioned in definition 12 above.

The Lord's powers encompass and supercede all other powers. We are narrowing down the meaning of power as used in this book. We will focus upon the "powers of deity," and upon how His abilities or powers to accomplish good and powers that can be transferred to us.

L. RON HUBBARD AND THE POWER FORMULAS

The title for this book comes from the writings of the American author, L. Ron Hubbard. Mr. Hubbard was a very prolific writer. He wrote many books of science fiction. He also wrote a great deal about other topics including the human mind, survival, ethics, behavior and management. His most widely known work is the book "Dianetics." He also founded the Church of Scientology, International.[3]

My first awareness of his writings came in 1988, while taking a business management course. The content for this course came from L. Ron Hubbard's writings. Specifically, the information studied in this course was called the **Conditions Formulas**. Mr. Hubbard identified a number of **Conditions**, or operating states, which

PREFACE

could be applied to any individual or group.

The Conditions Formulas contain a series of actions, which people and organizations can take to improve their Conditions.

The highest **Condition** discussed in this course is named **Power**. When one achieves this **Condition**, he or she has an obligation to prepare the way for successors. L. Ron Hubbard identified a series of steps designed to help others obtain this **Condition of Power**. He named these steps the **Power Formula**.

The steps of the **Power Formula** were listed prior to this preface. One of these steps is to "make a record." This record teaches those who are ascending to a **Condition of Power** how to gain the "capability of doing or accomplishing" like their predecessor.

L. Ron Hubbard also described a series of actions to be followed by those who are succeeding the one in power.

He called these actions the **Power Change Formula**. The essence of this **Formula** is to **follow the predecessor in such a way that you "don't change anything..."**[4].

Our Heavenly Father and His Son Jesus Christ Use Principles Like Those of the Power Formulas

The Father and the Son have made a record for us, so that we can follow Their example. *The Book of Mormon* is a record and **Power Formula** from God for our lives. This is the primary subject of *Part One* of *The Power Formulas*.

In *The Power Formulas, Part Two, Our Father in Heaven, His Son Jesus Christ and Their Power Formulas,* we will review another of **God's Power Formula Records** for us: **The Holy Bible**. Also in *Part Two,* the line of power flow will be illustrated. Briefly this line starts with our Father in Heaven. The Father trained and empowered His son Jesus Christ. The Savior in turn trains and empowers us through the Holy Ghost, His servants, the apostles and prophets, and through His Church. A diagram of this flow of God's Power through a series of **Power** and **Power Change Formulas** is included later in *The Power Formulas Part Three*.

In preparing His Son, it could be said that the Father took actions like those of the **Power Formula**. He trained and prepared his Son, Jesus Christ, to be our Savior "...from before the foundation of this world..."[5].

Jesus Christ followed His Father's will and example in all things. In the New Testament the Savior taught:

> The Son can do nothing of Himself but what He seeth the Father

do: for what thingsoever He doeth, these also the Son does likewise (*NewT: John* 5:4).

In following His Father, the Savior used actions like those described in the **Power Change Formula**. As a result of His preparation and obedience, Jesus was able to declare:

....all power is given unto me in heaven and in earth (*NewT: Matthew* 28:8).

Jesus Christ, in turn, has used actions like those of the **Power Formula** for us. He has prepared a record for us and has gotten it into our hands. He has done everything He can do to help us. These actions are the same as the steps of the **Power Formula**.

In following Him, we are also using actions like those of the **Power Change Formula**. As we follow Jesus Christ, we receive the "...power to become the sons [heirs] of God...".

But as many as received him, to them gave he power to become the sons [and daughters] of God, even to them that believe on his name (*NewT: John* 1:12).

The scriptures teach that God uses a law of witnesses. This law is that:

...in the mouth of two or three witnesses every word may be established (*NewT: Matthew* 18:16).

The Holy Bible and *The Book of Mormon* are two of God's Records, or "witnesses" for us. Through His modern prophets and apostles, God has given us a third Record and witness. This Record is contained in *The Doctrine and Covenants of The Church of Jesus Christ of Latter-day Saints*, and in *The Pearl of Great Price*.

Among the topics reviewed in *Part Three* is one of these modern scriptural records from God to us. Also, we will consider the **Power Formula**-like actions of the Savior in establishing His Church.

Finally, in **Super Power** we will look at how the Lord had made the blessings of His Gospel or **Power Formula** available to all people, including those who have died without hearing it. We sill also consider the important role of the Lord's priesthood authority and of His Temples in His **Power** and **Super Power Formulas** for us.

The Power Formulas, Part Two, Part Three, and Super Power, answers these questions: What is the power of God; what is its source; how can we receive it;

PREFACE

how much of it can we receive; and what can we do with His power?

To finish this series, *The Power Formulas, Part Three: Jesus Christ and The Church of Jesus Christ and the Power Formulas* and *Super Power* have been completed. These books are now available online through Amazon Kindle books, and in printed form through the same publisher.

By now, you realize my perspective is that of a member of The Church of Jesus Christ of Latter-day Saints. Some people call this church the "Mormon Church," because of the Church's acceptance of *The Book of Mormon* as, "...a volume of Holy Scripture comparable to *The Holy Bible*." Indeed, the Latter-day Saints believe ***The Book of Mormon*** is **Another Testament of Jesus Christ**.[6]

You may be asking yourself this question: Why would a Latter-day Saint write a book about *The Book of Mormon* and the **Power Formulas**? The best way to answer this question is to cite statements from Latter-day Saint apostles and prophets regarding the search for truth. Joseph Smith, the first prophet and president of The Church of Jesus Christ of Latter-day Saints taught that:

> One of the grand fundamental principles of "Mormonism" is to receive truth, let it come from whence it may.[7]

Brigham Young, who succeeded Joseph Smith as the Prophet and President of the Church taught:

> For me, the plan of salvation must...circumscribe [contain all] the knowledge that is upon the face of the earth, or it is not from God. Such a plan incorporates every system of true doctrine on the earth, whether it be ecclesiastical, moral, philosophical, or civil: it incorporates all good laws that have been made from the days of Adam until now; it swallows up the laws of nations, for it exceeds them in all knowledge and purity: it circumscribes the doctrines of the day, and takes from the right and the left, and brings all truth together in one system, and leaves the chaff to be scattered hither and thither.[8]

James E. Talmage, an apostle of the Church during the early part of the twentieth century, also commented on the search for truth. He was a dedicated scientist, educator, and a noted author. One of his works, *Jesus the Christ,* is, perhaps, the finest book ever written about the Savior's life and mission.

James E. Talmage taught that:

> Within the gospel of Jesus Christ there is room and place for every truth thus far learned by man, or yet to be made known.[9]

PREFACE

My study and life experiences have convinced me that the principles contained in the **Power Formulas** are among these truths. Indeed, there is ample scriptural evidence that our Father in Heaven and His Son Jesus Christ, operate using principles like those described in the **Power Formulas**.

It is my hope that this work will be especially valuable to those who already accept the teachings of L. Ron Hubbard. Mr. Hubbard brought the idea of a **Power Formula** to our attention. Our goal is to now identify the **Records** which contain the **Power Formula of God**, so that each of us may receive it and follow it. *The Book of Mormon* is one of these records. In fact, these three great records: *The Holy Bible, The Book of Mormon* and books of latter-day scripture revealed to the prophet Joseph Smith are actually the "two or three witnesses" which God has provided of His Gospel and His Power Formula for us!

The Power Formulas Part One Overview

In Chapter 1, you will find a brief description of the two main topics of this book. These topics are:

1) *The Book of Mormon*, and
2) The **Conditions Formulas**, especially the last two: **Power Change** and the **Power Formula**.

It should be noted that it is not my claim to be an expert in **either** of these topics. However, study has shown correlations and points of agreement **between** *The Book of Mormon* and the **Conditions Formulas**. What follows in *Part One: The Book of Mormon and the Power Formulas* is an effort to describe these correlations. It is freely acknowledged that both myself and these books are imperfect.

A brief word of explanation about the appendix[1] at the end of this book. The appendix brings together the **Power Formulas** and record transfers between the ancient prophets who wrote *The Book of Mormon*. Appendix[2] contains an inspired document written by living apostles and prophets about the importance of the family. This document is titled: *A Proclamation on the Family*. Also, while researching and writing this book, many examples were noted of internal evidences of the truthfulness of *The Book of Mormon*. The original plan was to include these evidences in a second appendix. However, so many evidences were found, that this section became too long for an appendix. Therefore, these evidences will be made available as a separate volume, titled: *Internal Evidences of the Truthfulness of the Book of Mormon*.

A glossary was also planned. Because of its length, this glossary will be made available, published separately as: *A Glossary of The Book of Mormon*.

Although no glossary is included, you will find many references to dictionary

PREFACE

definitions throughout this book. L. Ron Hubbard taught that finding the meaning of words, which are not understood, is of vital importance in study. He wrote:

> One of the biggest barriers to learning a new subject is its nomenclature, meaning the set of terms used to describe the things it deals with. A subject must have accurate labels, which have exact meanings before it can be understood and communicated...
>
> A student comes along and starts to study something and has a terrible time of it. Why? Because he or she not only has a lot of new principles and methods to learn, but a whole new language as well. Unless the student understands this, unless he or she realizes that one has to "know the words before one can sing the tune," he or she is not going to get very far in any field of study or endeavor.
>
> Now I'm going to give you an important datum: *The only reason a person gives up a study or becomes confused or unable to learn* is *because he or she has gone past a word that was not understood.*
>
> The confusion or inability to grasp or learn comes AFTER a word that the person did not have defined and understood.
>
> Have you ever had the experience of coming to the end of a page and realizing that you didn't know what you had read? Well, somewhere earlier on that page, you went past a word that you had no definition for...
>
> This datum about not going past an undefined word is the most important fact in the whole subject of study. Every subject you have taken up and abandoned had its words, which you failed to get defined...
>
> ...If the material becomes confusing or you can't seem to grasp it, there will be a word just earlier that you have not understood. Don't go any further, but go back to BEFORE you got into trouble, find the misunderstood word and get it defined...[17]

Things Learned While Writing This Book

The summation of my experiences while writing has been an assurance that ***The Book of Mormon* is a scriptural witness of Jesus Christ, and a record of His teachings and instructions for our lives**. *The Book of Mormon* is a record from God, and thus it is a **Power Formula** from Him to us.

The Book of Mormon teaches us to have faith in the Savior and His power. In *The Book of Mormon*, the Savior instructed us to pattern our lives after His. He taught

> ...the works that ye have seen me do, that shall you also do (*BofM: 3 Nephi* 27:20)

PREFACE

This is the central principle of the **Power Change Formula.**

Why is This Book Titled The Power Formulas?

The **Power Formula** and **Power Change Formula** are both necessary if a transfer of power is to occur. One Formula describes the actions of the power giver, and the other describes the actions of the one who is being empowered. For a transfer of power, which is the "capability to do or accomplish something," to occur, both principles are needed. This is the reason why the title of this book is *The Power Formulas*, rather than *The Power Formula*.

The Gift

We have been given a great gift by the Lord. This gift is His record and **Power Formula** for this life and for eternity. What are we to do with this gift? Through the prophet Joseph Smith, the Lord taught this important lesson about His gifts:

> For what doth it profit a man if a gift is bestowed upon him, and he receive not the gift? Behold, he rejoices not in that which is given unto him, neither rejoices in him who is the giver of the gift (*D&C* 88:33).

May you receive the gift, and come to love both the gift and the Giver. In doing so you will find joy. You will also find power through learning to love as the Father and the Son love. It is by gaining perfect love and sharing that love through service that we will find true and lasting power.

THE POWER FORMULAS

Chapter 1

The Book of Mormon and The Power Formulas

Purpose

My primary purposes in writing this book are to encourage you to read *The Book of Mormon* and to "Come unto Christ, and be perfected in Him..." (BofM, Moroni 10:31). Please obtain a copy of *The Book of Mormon* and keep it with you as you read this book. You can obtain a copy of *The Book of Mormon* by contacting the local Church of Jesus Christ of Latter-day Saints, or from most libraries. You will want to refer to it often. **In fact, it is my hope that you become so interested in *The Book of Mormon* that you lay this book aside, and read *The Book of Mormon* instead, for it truly is "Another Testament of Jesus Christ"!**

Why should you read *The Book of Mormon*? It is God's record and His **Power Formula** for our lives. This is an amazing claim. If this statement is true, then *The Book of Mormon* is one of the most important books that we can read and follow. The Prophet Joseph Smith, who translated the Record, gave this appraisal of the value of *The Book of Mormon*:

> ...I told the brethren that *The Book of Mormon was the most correct of any book on earth*, and the keystone of our religion, *and a man would get nearer to God by abiding by its precepts, than by any other book* (BofM Introduction, emphasis added).

Think for a minute about the meaning of the phrase "...nearer to God..." in this quote. What does this mean? One possible answer is to become closer to His actual presence, as in proximity to God. However, the phrase "...nearer to God..." means more than this. It also means becoming *more like Him* in our attributes. This includes, the attributes of having His Power. In this way, *The Book of Mormon* truly functions as a **Power Formula** from God to us.

The Conditions Formula

As the title of this book, *The Power Formulas, Part One, The Book of Mormon and the Power Formulas*, would indicate, this book has been written with a particular perspective. It has been written primarily to those people who have an understanding of, and an agreement with the **Conditions Formulas**.

THE POWER FORMULAS

The similarity of concepts in *The Book of Mormon* and the **Conditions Formulas** came to my attention in 1988 while studying these **Conditions Formulas** and reading *The Book of Mormon*.

What are these **Conditions Formulas**? This chapter will try to give an introductory answer to this question. The other topic of this chapter is an introduction to *The Book of Mormon*.

The **Conditions Formulas** are a series of **actions**, which can be used to improve our **Condition**. The principles advocated in the **Conditions Formulas** were being taught and used by the Record Keepers of *The Book of Mormon*.

The Book of Mormon

The Book of Mormon is a book of scripture dealing with a three groups of peoples who migrated anciently from the Eastern to the Western hemispheres. The group mentioned most prominently left Jerusalem at about 600 B.C. Jerusalem was soon to be destroyed. Its inhabitants would either be killed or taken captive to Babylon. The people of Jerusalem were being warned by their prophets of this impending danger.

However, most of the people did not believe the warnings of the prophets. One of these prophets was Lehi. Lehi was instructed by the Lord to flee with his family into the wilderness. The Lord wanted Lehi and his family to escape capture or death. He also had special plans for their settlement in the Americas.

Lehi was inspired to travel through the wilderness to the shore of the Red Sea. Here, his son, Nephi, with the assistance of his brothers, built a ship. These people were directed to sail the ship to a "...land of promise..." (*1 Nephi* 2:20). According to the prophet Joseph Smith, they landed a little south of the Isthmus of Darien [Panama].[12,13]

After arriving in their new home, these people soon divided into two groups. This division actually started at the time that the family left Jerusalem. Nephi, the fourth son, had great faith in the Lord, and in his prophet/father, Lehi. Nephi's two oldest brothers did not believe their father's prophecies. These two men, Laman and Lemuel, went reluctantly into the wilderness. Soon they began to murmur and conspire against Lehi.

Laman and Lemuel wanted to return to their home and their possessions. While traveling in the wilderness, they were visited by an angel, who convinced them, at least temporarily, to follow Lehi and Nephi.

While they were camped in the wilderness, Lehi was inspired to send his sons back to Jerusalem to obtain the scriptural record available at that time. This record was engraved on brass plates and contained the writings of Moses and other Old Testament prophets. Later, the brothers also made another return visit to Jerusalem to invite another family to come with them. This family had a number of children, who eventually became the spouses for Lehi's children.

These families lived in the wilderness, along the shore of the Red Sea for about nine years. As previously mentioned, they eventually built a ship and sailed to the new world.

Soon after arriving on the Western Hemisphere, Nephi, his family and those who believed in God, and in Jesus Christ, as he did, were forced to separate themselves. This was because Laman and Lemuel would have destroyed Nephi and his followers. The people who followed Laman became known as the "Lamanites." Those who followed Nephi became known as the "Nephites."

Unfortunately, the contentions, which began with the early rebellions of Laman and Lemuel, increased. This led to many wars between the descendants of these groups.

The general **Conditions** of these groups were, for many years a reflection of the **Spiritual Condition** of their leaders. Those who followed Nephi were, for the most part, a more prosperous, industrious and spiritual people. At times they enjoyed a condition of national power and individual spiritual power.

Those who rebelled, like Laman and Lemuel, generally became less enlightened. However, there were periods when some groups of Lamanites were living better lives than their contemporary Nephite peoples.

Some of the Lamanite leaders were aggressive. Also, many power-seeking Nephite traitors formed alliances with the Lamanites in order to make war on their own people. Thus, the Nephites were often required to fight in defense of themselves and their families.

Actions Like Those Described in the Power and Power Change Formulas Were Used by *The Book Of Mormon* Record Keepers

The Record of these peoples covers the period from 600 B.C. to 420 A.D. It is amazing that for over 1000 years the spiritual leaders in ancient America were inspired to "make a record." These prophets had a common desire for their records to be preserved and passed on, for the benefit of others. This desire to help those who would come later, is what the **Power Formula** is all about.

When their time as the Record Keeper was nearly over, they would give a "charge," or strict instruction, to the next writer to preserve the Record and to add to it. They would then turn the Record over to their successor. These actions included all the steps of what we now call the **Power Formula**. Also, the Record Keepers admonition to their successors to **do as I have done** is the essence of the **Power Change Formula**.

A word of explanation about the names of these Record Keepers. In the course of the Record, certain names appear more than once. For example: there are three Helaman's, four Nephi's, two Moroni's and two Alma's mentioned in the Record. Therefore, to avoid confusion about which Record Keeper is being referred to a small number is placed above his name. An example of this would be Alma[1].

This distinction is used at the beginning of chapters and at other places where the reader might become confused about the Record Keeper's identity. This notation system is the same as that used in the index in *The Book of Mormon*.

God's Power Formula

The Book of Mormon is the finest example of the application of **Power Formula** and **Power Change Formulas**. The **Power Formula** in *The Book of Mormon* is **not** the Formula of a man. While it is true that prophets recorded the words, it was the Lord who was teaching the principles.

***The Book of Mormon* is actually God's Power Formula for us**. Therefore, we should learn and follow the principles taught in this **Power Formula**. We can do **Power Change** with the Lord as we live by these principles.

Christ and Christians in Ancient America

It is interesting to note that these prophets, most of who lived hundreds of years before the coming of Jesus Christ, recorded many prophesies of the Savior. They were Christians. These prophets taught the principles of faith in Jesus Christ, repentance and baptism for the remission of sins.

The Savior actually appeared to the people on this continent. *The Book of Mormon* recounts that after His resurrection, Jesus Christ appeared to the people of the western hemisphere. He taught them His gospel. He also established His Church among these people. The effect of His visit was so powerful that for 200 years the people lived in peace and prosperity.

Two of *The Book of Mormon's* foremost purposes are to be a witness of Jesus Christ, and to bring us to Him. The reason why it is so important that we accept and follow Jesus Christ is because only He can bring us back into the presence of our Father in Heaven. The Savior taught:

> *...I am the way, the truth, and the life; no man cometh unto the Father, but by Me* (*NewT: John* 14:6; emphasis added).

The Book of Mormon stands together with *The Holy Bible* as 'Another Testament of Jesus Christ'.

> And the angel spake unto me, saying: These last records, which thou hast seen among the Gentiles, shall establish the truth of the first, which are of the twelve apostles of the Lamb, and shall make known the plain

and precious things which have been taken away from them; and shall make known to all kindreds, tongues, and people, that *the Lamb of God is the Son of the Eternal Father, and the Savior of the world; and that all men must come unto him, or they cannot be saved* (*BofM: 1 Nephi* 13:40, emphasis added).

Jesus Foretold of His Visit to His "Other Sheep"

You may be wondering: Why didn't Jesus tell His disciples in the Holy Land of this other group of people, that He would be visiting? Actually, He did tell of this other group. While in the Holy Land, He taught his disciples that He was the Good Shepherd. He also taught that, as the Good Shepherd, He had more than one flock to visit.

> I am the good shepherd, and know my sheep, and am known of mine.
> As the Father knoweth me, even so know I the Father: and I lay down my life for the sheep.
> **And other sheep I have, which are not of this fold: them also I must bring, and they shall hear my voice; and there shall be one fold, and one shepherd** (*NewT: John* 10:14-16; emphasis added)

When the Savior appeared to His ancient American followers, He told them:

> **Ye are they of whom I've said, Other sheep I have which are not of this fold and they shall hear my voice** (*BofM:3 Nephi* 5:2).

Why the Record Was Named *The Book of Mormon*

After the 200 years of peace produced by the Savior's visit, contentions and wars began to occur again. There were a number of prophets among the people. One of them was a man named Mormon. He also became the military leader of the Nephite nation at a very young age.

Mormon obtained the Records, which had been written by other inspired teachers down through the centuries. He then made an abridgment of earlier Records onto thin plates of gold, which were held together by rings. This final Record told the story of the people since the time they had left Jerusalem at about 600 B.C., until Mormon's time, approximately 400 years after Christ.

The Book of Mormon was named after Mormon because he was the one who edited or abridged the many different books, and put them together into a set of plates. Unfortunately, the Nephite nation became so corrupt and weakened that they began to lose many battles to the Lamanites. Mormon was injured in one of these battles. He told his son, Moroni that he should take the plates and keep them safe. Eventually, Mormon died, trying to defend his people in a final battle.

Moroni lived a number of years after this great battle. He was alone, and his people had been destroyed. During these lonely years, Moroni struggled to survive and to safe-guard the plates. He also added two books to the Record.

Moroni also wrote the title page of the Book. He appropriately named it after his father, *"The Book of Mormon"*. Moroni's love and respect for his father are reflected in the title he gave to the completed work: *"The Book of Mormon"*.

When he had finished engraving on the plates, Moroni made a box of stone and cement. He then buried the plates in a hill. In this way, the Record was preserved for about fourteen centuries.

The Translation of the Record

The translation of the plates of *The Book of Mormon* into the English language occurred during the years 1827-1829. To understand how this translation took place, we need to first review briefly the story of the translator. In 1820, Joseph Smith was a fourteen-year-old boy living with his family in the upper part of New York.

Although he believed in Jesus Christ, Joseph did not belong to a church. He was diligently trying to decide which church to join. During this time Joseph was reading in *The Holy Bible*, and he came across this passage in the book of James:

> If any of you lack wisdom, let him ask of God, that giveth to all men liberally, and upbraideth not; and it shall be given him (*NewT: James* 1:5).

This scripture provided the way for him to find out which church was right. Joseph decided that he would use this promise from James. He would pray and ask God which church he should join. Joseph went to a grove of trees near his home and, early on a beautiful spring day, he knelt in prayer.

In answer to his prayer, a pillar of light appeared above his head, and in this light he saw two Persons. One of Them said, pointing to the other: "This is my beloved Son, hear Him." Joseph Smith was visited by God the Father and his Son, Jesus Christ!

Joseph asked Jesus which church he should join. He was told that he should join none of them.[14] Joseph Smith later became the instrument through which the true Church, and the power of Jesus Christ were restored to the earth. Thus was the calling of a modern prophet. Through the prophet Joseph Smith, the Savior restored His gospel, which is His Power Formula for us.

Part of that restoration came in the form of the ancient record of *The Book of Mormon*. Joseph was personally instructed by an angel to go to a hill, not far from his home. Near the top of this hill, he was directed to lift a large stone covering the stone box. Inside the box he found the golden plates, which comprised *The Book of Mormon* records.

It's interesting to realize that the angel who appeared to Joseph, and who showed him the location of the golden plates, was this same Moroni, who had buried the plates anciently. Joseph matured, and received yearly visitations and instructions from Moroni. Four years after Moroni's first visit, Joseph was allowed to remove and translate the plates by the gift and power of God.

A Question to Ask Yourself While Reading *The Book of Mormon*

Please keep something in mind as you read *The Book of Mormon*: In the 1820s, when the Record was translated, Joseph Smith was only in his early twenties. He had very little formal education. As you read *The Book of Mormon*, ask yourself this question: Is it possible that a young man, with little educational background, could have written this book?

Perhaps an even better question would be: Could any person, or any group of people, have written this record? This book must be inspired. It was impossible for Joseph Smith, or any individual or group to have written *The Book of Mormon*.

Further information about this subject, is found in *Internal Evidences of the Truthfulness of The Book of Mormon*, which is briefly mentioned earlier in this book.

More About The Conditions Formulas

As mentioned above, in 1988, while re-reading *The Book of Mormon* and studying management principles called the **Conditions Formulas**, it became apparent to me that principles like those of the **Conditions Formulas** were being used by the inspired Record Keepers who wrote *The Book of Mormon*.

Here is a list of these **Conditions** from the highest to the lowest:

Power	Non Existence
Power Change	Liability
Affluence	Doubt
Normal	Enemy
Emergency	Treason
Danger	Confusion[15]

The determination of which **Condition** an individual or a group is in can be made by looking at a graph of their statistical trends. However, these **Conditions** are not just related to statistics. L. Ron Hubbard taught that these **Conditions** represented levels of ethics, as well.[16]

The **Condition** of any group, or individual, determine their present potential for survival. Activities, which produce a **Condition** of high survival ability, for oneself and others, are considered ethical. Those actions, which endanger survival are considered to be unethical. L. Ron Hubbard defined ethics in this way: "The reason and contemplation of optimum survival..."[17].

For instance, a declining statistical trend would indicate a **Danger Condition**, in terms of survivability. An increasing trend would indicate an **Affluence Condition** and a good potential for survival. A trend, which is nearly level, but slightly increasing, is called a **Normal Condition**.

The survival potential of an organization in a **Normal Condition** is better than that of one in a **Danger Condition**. Also the survival potential of an organization, which is operating in a **Normal Condition** is not as good as one whose statistical performance would indicate a **Condition of Affluence**.

In a group situation, each individual has his own personal **Condition** level, related to how well he or she is carrying out his or her responsibilities to the group.

Starting with **Non Existence** and above, these **Conditions** are positive, in that something **good or of value** is being accomplished. **Non Existence** really means beginning to exist or function. It means coming out of a non-existent state in regard to an activity or a position.

For example, as a person begins a new job, he starts by learning his duties, as defined by the policies of the organization he is working for. Next, he begins to perform these duties. The higher on this scale he goes, the greater the potential for survival in his group.

As this person learns his job, he begins to perform better. However, he must still continue to improve. If he does not improve, he becomes a **Liability** and is at risk of losing his position.

Those **Conditions** below **Non Existence** are negative, in that the actions of people, groups or nations in these **Conditions** are counter productive, and counter survival. As noted above, if someone were to accept a position, but never really learned to do his job, he would then become a **Liability** to the organization.

Furthermore, if this person fails to accept responsibility and to make the needed corrections, he could begin to have a **Doubt** about the organization. If he still fails to make change, he would begin to consciously oppose the purposes of the group. This opposition can be either open (**Enemy**), or covert (**Treason**).

Remember also, that L. Ron Hubbard taught that each of these **Conditions** has a set of actions or a **Formula** for improving up to the next **Condition**. We could review examples of actions like each of these **Conditions Formulas** in *The Book of Mormon*. However, the **Conditions** we are most interested in discussing are those at the top of the scale: **Power and Power Change. Most of our attention will be focused on the principles of Power and Power Change, as they relate to *The Book of Mormon*.**

Examples of the Power and Power Change Formulas in *The Book of Mormon*

The Book of Mormon contains an account of the teachings and the reigns of a king Benjamin and his son, and successor, king Mosiah. The stories of king Benjamin and king Mosiah, offer great examples of principles of the **Power** and **Power Change Formula**. The prophet record keepers of *The Book of Mormon* routinely followed these principles.

Perhaps the best example of the **Power** and **Power Change Formula** principles in *The Book of Mormon* is seen in Christ's appearance to the Nephites. Among His teachings to these people was this injunction to do as He had done:

> Verily, verily, I say unto you, this is my gospel; and **ye know the things that ye must do in my church; for the works which ye have seen me do that shall ye also do; for that which ye have seen me do even that shall ye do** (*BofM: 3 Nephi* 27:2; emphasis added).

Here, the Savior taught a principle of **Power Change**. The central action taught by L. Ron Hubbard in his **Power Change Formula** is to:

> ....don't change anything...go through the exact same routine every day that your predecessor went through....[18]

The Savior also taught some of these Nephites that they could become:
> ...even as I am, and I am even as the Father... (*BofM: 3 Nephi* 28:0).

Becoming "even as" the Father and the Son, is **Power Change** on the highest possible level. As we become "even as" They, we receive power "even as" Theirs! What could possibly be a greater challenge than this? This is what our Father and our Savior want for us! They want to empower us. They want us to become like They are. **This is why they have prepared a record for us!** *The Book of Mormon* **is that record.**

The Book of Mormon is not the Lord's only record for us. As mentioned previously, God has also inspired the prophets and writers of both *The Old* and *The New Testaments*. However, *The Book of Mormon* is "the most correct" record that we have *because* it was not only written by prophets of God, it was also translated by a prophet of God.

Although *The Book of Mormon* does not include all of the Lord's revealed principles, it contains the truths necessary to prepare us to receive additional truth. The prophet Mormon taught:

> ...if it so be that they shall believe these things [*The Book of Mor-*

THE POWER FORMULAS

mon] then shall the greater things be made manifest unto them (BofM: 3 Nephi 26:9).

Among those additional revelations that are made available to those who read and believe *The Book of Mormon* are these modern scriptural records: *The Doctrine and Covenants* and *The Pearl of Great Price*.

Cycles of Action of Prophets

As we review the writings of the Record Keepers we shall see that *The Book of Mormon* was produced by a series of prophets who made a record, and who then passed the Record on to a successor. The next Record Keeper was given instructions to do the same. These prophets each followed then a cycle of action by doing **Power Change**, and then a **Power Formula** for the person who was to follow them.

A List of Purposes and Truths

The purposes of this book were stated at the beginning of this chapter. These purposes are to encourage you to read *The Book of Mormon* and to "...come unto Christ...". As you do so, you will also gain good insight into many important truths. Among the truths are those listed below.

1. Our Bridge to eternal life is Jesus Christ through His powers to atone for our sins and to resurrect our bodies.[19]
2. *The Book of Mormon* provides a bridge between Scientology and Christianity.[20]
3. The gospel of Jesus Christ is God's **Power Formula** for our lives.[21]
4. The Lord's **Power Formula** is contained in the scriptural records of the *The Holy Bible*, *The Book of Mormon,* and books of modern revelation*: The Doctrine Covenants of the Church of Jesus Christ of Latter-day Saints,* and *The Pearl of Great Price.*[22]
5. *The Book of Mormon* is "...the most correct of any book on earth...," and we can get "nearer to God by abiding by its precepts than by any other book."[23]
6. Jesus Christ has the power to heal us emotionally, physically and spiritually.[24]
7. The process of spiritual rebirth through coming unto Christ is the most effective way to raise our emotional Tone Level.[25]
8. The central message of *The Book of Mormon* is that "...JESUS IS THE CHRIST, the ETERNAL GOD."[26]
9. We should all "come unto Christ and be perfected in Him."[27]
10. We need to acknowledge the power of Jesus Christ before we can be perfected by His power.[28]
11. As we learn and live by His gospel and **Power Formula**, we will be doing **Power**

Change with the Savior. This means that with the Savior's help we can eventually become like Him, and like our Father in Heaven.[29]

12. Each of us can come to a revealed, personal knowledge of these truths through revelation from God, and "...by the power of the Holy Ghost..."[30].

Chapter 2

Nephi Makes a Record

The first realization of examples of **Power Formula** and **Power Change** in *The Book of Mormon* came while studying both *The Book of Mormon* and the **Conditions Formulas**. It was amazing to see a remarkable example of the use of principles like those of the **Power** and **Power Change Formulas** in the story of two of *The Book of Mormon* kings.

King Benjamin, had grown old, and was ready to pass the power of his kingdom to his son, Mosiah. The way in which power was transferred between Benjamin and Mosiah fulfilled perfectly the actions that L. Ron Hubbard described for the **Power** and **Power Change Formulas**.

After seeing how king Benjamin had used principles like these **Power Formulas**, it caused me to wonder: could there be other such examples in *The Book of Mormon*? It was not necessary to search far to find the answer to this question. *All that was necessary was to read the first verse of the Book*. The first prophet and Record Keeper to engrave upon the plates, which would become *The Book of Mormon*, was a man named Nephi. Here is Nephi's opening statement:

> I, Nephi having been born of goodly parents, therefore I was taught somewhat in all the learnings of my father; and having seen many afflictions in the course of my days, nevertheless, having been highly favored of the Lord in all my days; having a good knowledge of the goodness and the mysteries of my God, therefore I **make a record** of my proceedings in my days (*BofM: Nephi* 1:1; emphasis added).

Nephi began by making himself known. He then explained why he was going to make a record. He made other references to making a Record in verses 2 and 3. Here are those statements:

> Yea, I **make a record** of the language of my father, which consists of the learning of the Jews and the language of the Egyptians.
> And I know that the **Record that I make is true: and I make it with mine own hand and I make it according to my knowledge** (*BofM: Nephi* 1:2-3; emphasis added).

You will recall that in his **Power Formula**, L. Ron Hubbard stated: "...the first thing you have to do is to **make a record**..."

Why are Nephi's words so much like the **Power Formula**? Is this just a coincidence? In the coming pages, we will review many indications that these

Nephi Was in a Condition of Spiritual Power

Nephi prefaced his statement about making a record with these words:

> **...having been highly favored of the Lord in all my days; yea, having had a great knowledge of the goodness and the mysteries of God,** *therefore* **I make a record** of my proceedings in my days...(*BofM: 1 Nephi* 1:1; emphasis added).

If we analyze these statements, we see that Nephi was telling us, in a humble way, that he was in a highly favored condition in regards to his knowledge of the things of God. If we were to classify Nephi's **Spiritual Condition** according to the **Condition** levels used by L. Ron Hubbard, he was in a **Condition of Spiritual Power**. Therefore, Nephi was making a Record because he was in the **Condition of Spiritual Power**.

By making a Record for us, Nephi was endeavoring to help us also become "highly favored of the Lord." Also, through studying his Record, we can gain "great knowledge of the goodness and mysteries of God."

Not only was Nephi's language similar to that of the **Power Formula**, his motivation also paralleled that of someone completing a **Power Formula**. Nephi wanted others to benefit from his knowledge and experience (see *BofM: 2 Nephi* 33:1-4).

Modern leaders of the Church continue to teach and use similar principles. Elder Spencer J. Condie, one of the General Authorities of the Church of Jesus Christ of Latter-day Saints, has taught:

> Long before his martyrdom, the Prophet Joseph [Smith] was diligently training those who would continue to lead the kingdom after he was gone. Here is another important lesson of leadership: **Leaders are duty bound and obligated to prepare others to take their place** at some future time. Brothers and sisters, the cemeteries are filled with leaders who thought they were indispensable (emphasis added).[31]

This statement illustrates that the prophet Joseph Smith also used principles like those of the **Power Formula**.

Nephi's Record is an example of this principle at work. In later verses he explained his purpose in making the Record. Please note that Nephi was also training future Record Keepers. Nephi gave the future Record Keepers this standard to use in determining the content of their writings:

For the fullness of mine intent is that I may persuade men to come unto the God of Abraham, and the God of Isaac, and the God of Jacob, and be saved.

Wherefore, the things which are pleasing unto the world I do not write, but the things which are pleasing unto God and unto those who are not of the world.

Wherefore, I shall give commandment unto my seed, that they shall not occupy these plates with things which are not of worth unto the children of men (*BofM: 1 Nephi* 6:4-6; emphasis added).

Nephi's Two Records

Nephi actually started two sets of plates. One set was initially meant to contain a more secular history. The other, a smaller set of plates, was meant to contain the spiritual teachings of these people. In a video presentation entitled *The Things of My Soul*, Elder Boyd K. Packer, a member of the Church's Council of Twelve Apostles, explained the distinctions between Nephi's two sets of plates. Speaking first of the large plates of Nephi, Elder Packer taught:

> ...They were largely a secular history handed down through the lineage of the kings. They are for the most part, written in the third person. He [Nephi] wrote [that] "upon the other plates should be engraven an account of the reign of the kings, and the wars and contentions of my people" (*BofM:1 Nephi* 9:4). The large plates were many in number. In fact, there were many plates and records mentioned in the book which we do not now have. "And now there are many records kept of the proceedings of this people, by many of this people, which are particular and very large, concerning them..." (*BofM:Helaman* 3:13). "But behold, there are many books and many records of every kind, and they have been kept chiefly by the Nephites. And they have been handed down from one generation to another by the Nephites..." Nephi faithfully kept the secular history on the large plates. Thereafter, they were kept by the kings. No doubt they contained a great resource of historical information, but they were by no means the most valuable record (*BofM: Helaman* 3:15-16).

Elder Packer also explained how the small plates differed from the more secular, large plates of Nephi:

> For Nephi was commanded to keep another account, not a secular history this time, but a record of their ministry—the small plates of Nephi. The purpose of the small plates was best explained when Nephi gave the Record to his brother Jacob. For they were to remain with his

seed.

Notice that they are written in the first person.

> And he gave me, Jacob, a commandment that I should write upon these [small] plates a few of the things which I consider to be most precious; that I should not touch, save it were lightly, concerning the history of the people...For he said that the history of his people should be engraven upon his other [large] plates and hand them down unto my seed, from generation to generation. And if there were preaching which was sacred, or revelation which was great, or prophesying, that I should engraven the heads of them upon these [small] plates, and touch upon them as much as it were possible, for Christ's sake, and for the sake of our people (*BofM:Jacob* 1:2-4).

Did you notice that he was not to touch, save it were lightly, on the history of the people, but he was to touch upon the sacred things as much as possible.

Nephi made this clear statement on the relative value of the two histories:

> And it mattereth not to me that I am particular to give a full account of all the things of my father, for they cannot be written upon these [small] plates, for I desire the room that I may write of the things of God. For the fullness of mine intent is that I may persuade men to come unto the God of Abraham, and the God of Isaac, and the God of Jacob, and be saved. Wherefore, the things which are pleasing unto the world I do not write, but the things which are pleasing unto God and unto those who are not of the world. Wherefore, I shall give commandment unto my seed, that they shall not occupy these plates with things which are not of worth unto the children of men (*BofM: 1 Nephi* 6:3-6).
>
> ...This I do that the more sacred things may be kept for the knowledge of my people...I do not write anything upon the plates save it be that I think it be sacred (*BofM:1 Nephi* 19:5-6).[32]

The Prophet Mormon Also Wrote of Making a Record

Mormon, was a prophet and a military commander. He was also the compiler and abridger of the Records. He lived about 900 years after Nephi. Like Nephi, Mormon made two records. One of these was his personal record, the other was an abridgment and a compilation of the writings of many other prophets.

Mormon named his first-hand account of his personal experiences *The Book of Mormon*. Later, his son, Moroni, named the rest of the book after Mormon.

Moroni did so because Mormon had abridged, and added inspired commentary to the writings of many others. Mormon had also assembled these records into a set of plates. It was Mormon's son, Moroni, who finished and buried the Record.

Mormon's First Verse

How did Mormon begin his Record? Mormon's very first words were:

> And now I, Mormon, **make a record** of the things which I have both seen and heard, and call it *"The Book of Mormon"* (*BofM: Mormon* 1:1; emphasis added).

Did you note the similarity of Mormon's opening statement to Nephi's? Both of these men began by introducing themselves and telling us that they were going to **"make a record"**.

Like Nephi, Mormon was Chosen to Make a Record Because of His High Spiritual Condition

In the second verse of his personal Record, we learn why Mormon was chosen to be a Record Keeper. Again, note the similarity to Nephi's words.

> And about the time that Ammaron hid up the Records unto the Lord, he came unto me, (I being about ten years of age, and **I began to be learned somewhat after the manner of learning of my people and Ammaron said unto me: I perceive that thou art a sober child, and art quick to observe** (*BofM: Mormon* 1:2; emphasis added).

Mormon humbly acknowledged his high **Spiritual Condition**, as the reason he was chosen to receive the Record. He was "learned somewhat," "and he was a sober child," and "quick to observe". All of the qualities were evident in Mormon by the time he was about ten years of age!

By the time Mormon was 15, he had been "...visited of the Lord..." Here is his account of this experience:

> And I, being 15 years of age, and **being somewhat of a sober mind, therefore I was visited of the Lord, and tasted and knew of the goodness of Jesus** (*BofM: Mormon* 1:15; emphasis added).

As with Nephi's self-assessment, Mormon was very humble in describing his high **Spiritual Condition**.

THE POWER FORMULAS

Mormon Also Wrote of Making a Record as He Abridged the Writings of Others

We might inquire as to whether Mormon also made reference to making a Record, as he compiled his abridgements. Would it surprise you to learn that he made reference to Record making **eighteen** other times while he abridged the writings of others?

These verses include some of the last ones engraved by Mormon before he passed the Record to his son Moroni. Please note in these verses that Mormon made many references to **making a record**. Here are these references to record making that Mormon engraved as he abridged the writings of the other prophets:

> Therefore I have **made my record** of these things according to the Record of Nephi, which was engraven on the plates, which were called the plates of Nephi. [He was abridging this collection of records.]
>
> And behold, I do **make the Record** on plates, which I have made with mine own hands.
>
> Behold, I am a disciple of Jesus Christ, the Son of God. I have been called of him to declare his word among his people, that they might have everlasting life.
>
> And it hath become expedient that I, according to the will of God, that the prayers of those who have gone hence, [previous Record Keepers whose writings Mormon was abridging] who were the holy ones, should be fulfilled according to their faith, should **make a record** of these things which have been done—
>
> Yea, a small record of that which hath taken place from the time that Lehi left Jerusalem, even down until the present time.
>
> Therefore I do **make my record** from the accounts, which have been given by those who were before me, until the commencement of my day;
>
> And then I do **make a record** of the things, which I have seen with mine own eyes.
>
> And I know **the Record, which I make** to be a just and **a true record**; nevertheless there are many things, which, according to our language, we are not able to write (*BofM: 3 Nephi* 5:10-11, 13-18; emphasis added).
>
> And now I, Mormon, being about to deliver up **the Record which I have been making** into the hands of my son Moroni, behold I have witnessed almost all the destruction of my people, the Nephites.
>
> Wherefore, I chose these things, to **finish my record** upon them, which remainder of **my record** I shall take from the plates of Nephi; and I cannot write the hundredth part of the things of my people.

And now I, Mormon, proceed to **finish out my record**, which I take from the plates of Nephi; and I make it according to the knowledge and the understanding which God has given me (*BofM: Words of Mormon* 1:1, 5, 9; emphasis added).

Also, in *3rd Nephi* 5:10-18, Mormon referred to his record and record making eight more times. In total, Mormon referred to the record he was making at least 19 times. He used the exact words as the **Power Formula**: "make a record" five times!

Mormon and Nephi Actually Made the Record by Fashioning Metal Plates

When Nephi and Mormon spoke of making a record, they meant it literally! These prophets had to first produce the metal plates before they could engrave their writings (see *2 Nephi* 5:39 and *3 Nephi* 5:10-11). So, they had to first **make the plates** before they could **make a record**.

The Book of Mormon is a Series of Power Formulas Between Prophets

The Book of Mormon appears to be the greatest example in the history of world literature of the practical application of the principles like those of the **Power** and the **Power Change Formulas**. Throughout the entire *Book of Mormon*, we can trace a succession of Record Keepers who would add to the Record, preserve it, and then pass it on to the next Record Keeper. Also, in many cases, we know that the predecessor would give a "charge" or instructions to their successor to do the same. These changes were actually **Power Formulas** for the next Record Keeper.

Are *The Book of Mormon* and Power Formula References to Making a Record Coincidental?

It is possible that a casual reader may look at Nephi's first verses of *The Book of Mormon*, and also these words of Mormon about making a record, and see only a coincidence in their similarity to L. Ron Hubbard's **Power Formulas**. However, as we look at *The Book of Mormon* in its entirety, we see a consistent pattern of actions by the authors of the Record to preserve and pass these writings on.

As one Record Keeper finished, he would prepare his successor. The way he prepared the next Record Keeper followed the pattern described in the **Power Formulas**.

Therefore, the entire *Book of Mormon* was made by men who would make a record for the Lord, and then get it into the hands of their successors. Because of this consistency, it becomes much more difficult to discount Nephi's and Mormon's references to making a record as being only coincidentally similar to the **Power Formula**.

The use of the term "make a record" in the **Power Formulas** and *The Book of Mormon* is not coincidental. The principles of the **Power Formulas** are true and *The Book of Mormon* is a true book and scriptural record. This is why we see "**make a record**" in both the **Power Formulas** and *The Book of Mormon*.

When his time as the Record Keeper came to an end, each Record Keeper would select a successor. He would then complete actions like those of the **Power Formula** for the next contributor to the Record. In this context, *The Book of Mormon* can be viewed as a series of **Power Formula**-like actions being carried out by the predecessor, and then followed by the successor using actions like those described in the **Power Change Formula**.

The Book of Mormon is a collective record of many inspired leaders all following these principles. The cumulative result of these inspired **Power Formulas** makes *The Book of Mormon* **a Power Formula from the Lord, for all of His children.**

Finding God's Power Formula Allows Us to Follow the Principle of Power Change with Him

As we come to know that the Record is true, we then know the Lord's **Power Formula** for our life on the earth. With this knowledge, we can follow the path, which leads us to our Father in Heaven's presence.

Because we have His Record and **Power Formula**, it is possible to follow the Savior. Nephi not only gave us a Record of the words of Christ, his Record also included the words of "The Father". Please note how the Father testified of the truthfulness of His Son's words and instructed us to follow His Son.

> **And I heard a voice from the Father, saying: Yea, the words of my Beloved are true and faithful. He that endureth to the end, the same shall be saved.**
>
> And now, my beloved brethren, I know by this **that unless a man shall endure to the end, in following the example of the Son of the living God, he cannot be saved** (*BofM:2 Nephi* 31: 15-16; emphasis added).

By now you will probably recognize that Nephi's instruction to "follow the example of Son of the Living God" teaches the same principle as the **Power Change Formula**. Nephi also explained what he meant by following the Savior. Although he was writing about 550 years prior to the birth of Christ, Nephi had seen the ministry of the Savior in a vision.

In this vision, Nephi saw that the Savior would be baptized, and that He would receive the Holy Ghost. Nephi asked us to consider the question: Why would the Savior be baptized? Baptism is for the remission of sins (see *NewT: Acts* 7:32-38). However, the Savior was without sin. What was the purpose in His being baptized? Nephi then answered this question.

> And now, if the Lamb of God, he being holy, should have need to be **baptized by water, to fulfill all righteousness**, O then, how much more need have we, being unholy, to be baptized, yea, even by water!
>
> **And now, I would ask of you, my beloved brethren, wherein the Lamb of God did fulfill all righteousness in being baptized by water?**
>
> Know ye not that he was holy? But not-withstanding he being holy, he showeth unto the children of men that, according to the flesh **he humbleth himself before the Father, and witnesseth unto the Father that he would be obedient unto him in keeping his commandments.**
>
> Wherefore, after he was baptized with water the Holy Ghost descended upon him in the form of a dove.
>
> And again, **it showeth unto the children of men the straightness of the path, and the narrowness of the gate, by which they should enter, he [Jesus Christ]** having set the example before them.
>
> And he said unto the children of men: **Follow thou me.** Wherefore, my beloved brethren, **can we follow Jesus save we shall be willing to keep the commandments of the Father [for that is what Jesus did]?**
>
> **And the Father said: Repent ye, repent ye, and be baptized in the name of my Beloved Son.**
>
> And also, the voice of the Son came unto me, saying: He that is baptized in my name, to him will the Father give the Holy Ghost, like unto me; wherefore, **follow me, and do the things which ye have seen me do** (*BofM: 2 Nephi* 31:5-12; emphasis added).

This last phrase: "...follow me, and do the things which ye have seen me do" is a perfect statement of the **Power Change Formula** from the Savior to each of us!

The Path

In these verses Nephi compares our lives to a journey. There is a path which leads back to our Father. The Savior has blazed the path. The path starts with faith in God the Father and in His Son, Jesus Christ. Next, repentance and baptism prepare us to receive a remission of our sins, and to receive the gift of the Holy Ghost. As the Holy Ghost changes our hearts or feelings, our old inclinations and dispositions to sin are removed as if "by fire". We thus become a new person and a child, or heir, of God.

The Gate to the Path: Repentance and Baptism

> Wherefore, **do the things which I have told you I have seen that your Lord and your Redeemer should do**; for, for this cause have they been shown unto me, that ye might know the gate by which ye should enter. **For the gate by which ye should enter is repentance and baptism by water; and then cometh a remission of your sins by fire and by the Holy Ghost** (*BofM: 2 Nephi* 31:17; emphasis added).

The Guide Along the Path: The Holy Ghost

> ...And also, the voice of the Son came unto me, saying: He that is baptized in my name to him will **the Father give the Holy Ghost, like unto me**...(*BofM: 2 Nephi* 31: 12; emphasis added).

The Direction to Take on the Path: Following The Savior's Example — Thereby Doing Power Change with Him

> **...follow me, and do the things, which ye have seen me do** (*BofM: 2 Nephi* 31:12; emphasis added).

The Destination of the Path: Eternal Life

> **...Wherefore, ye must press forward with a steadfastness in Christ, having a perfect brightness of hope, and a love of God and of all men. Wherefore, if ye shall press forward, feasting upon the word of Christ, and endure to the end, behold, thus saith the Father: Ye shall have eternal life** (*BofM: 2 Nephi* 31:20; emphasis added).

The Meaning of Eternal Life

The Father has specified the destination of the path of following His Son. That destination is eternal life. What does the Lord mean by this term, eternal life? Elder Bruce R. McConkie, who was one of the twelve apostles of the Church, defined eternal life in this way:

> As used in the scriptures **eternal life is the name given to the kind of life that our Eternal Father lives.** The word eternal as used in the name eternal life is a noun and not a adjective. It is one of the formal

names of Deity (*The Pearl of Great Price*: Moses 1:3; 7; 35; *The Doctrine and Covenants* 19:11) [these references are to revelations received by the prophet Joseph Smith,] and has been chosen by Him as the particular name to identify the kind of life that He lives... thus, God's life is Eternal Life; Eternal Life is God's life—the expressions are synonymous...

Immortality is to live forever in the resurrected state, and by the grace of God all men will gain this unending continuance of life. But only those who obey the fullness of the gospel law will inherit eternal life (D&C 29:43,44). It is "the greatest of all the gifts of God" (D&C 14:7), **for it is the kind, status, type, and quality of life that God himself enjoys. Thus those who gain eternal life receive exaltation; they are sons [and daughters] of God, joint heirs with Christ...they overcome all things, have all power, and receive the fullness of the Father. They are Gods**[35] (emphasis added).

God's Power Formula

With this understanding of the meaning of eternal life, we can see that following the Savior does more than take us to where He and the Father are. Following the path to Eternal Life will also mean that we will eventually be like the Father and the Son. **As we become like They are, we will also receive "all power."** This truly is **Power Change** on the highest order.

Nephi Finished His Record with an Address to His Future Readers

Nephi began his engraving by telling us that he was going to "**make a record**". His final message also dealt with the Record that he had made. This Record had been made over a lifetime of experience. As Nephi reflected on his life and his writings, he expressed six important thoughts about the Record, and about his contribution to it.

#1 Nephi was Humbled, and Felt Inadequate to 'Make a Record" for God

First, he expressed a humble concern about his ability to put into written words the wonderful and inspiring experiences of his life. Another Record Keeper, Moroni, was also felt humbled by the difficulty of putting his most deeply-felt convictions into engraved writings (see *BofM: Ether* 12:23-28).

In verse 33, Nephi expressed his understandable feelings of inadequacy in writing:

And now I, Nephi, cannot write all the things which were taught among my people; **neither am I mighty in writing, like unto speaking; for when a man speaketh by the power of the Holy Ghost the power of the Holy Ghost carrieth it unto the hearts of the children of men...And the words which I have written shall be made strong...** (*BofM:2 Nephi* 33:1, 4; emphasis added).

#2 The Record is of "Great Worth"

The second principle regarding his record was that Nephi knew that his writings were of "great worth." He realized that many people would not value his words, and would "cast many things away."

> But behold, there are many that harden their hearts against the Holy Spirit, that it hath no place in them; wherefore, they cast many things away which are written and esteem them as things of naught.
> But **I, Nephi, have written what I have written, and I esteem it as of great worth**, and especially unto my people. For I pray continually for them by day, and mine eyes water my pillow by night, because of them; and I cry unto my God in faith, and I know that he will hear my cry.
> And I know that the Lord God will consecrate my prayers for the gain of my people. And **the words which I have written in weakness will be made strong unto them; for it persuadeth them to do good; it maketh known unto them of their fathers; and it speaketh of Jesus, and persuadeth them to believe in him, and to endure to the end, which is life eternal** (*2 Nephi* 33:2-4; emphasis added).

Nephi trusted that the Lord would make up for his "weakness" in writing. His word would be made "strong" by the Lord. In preceding verses, Nephi gave us a key to help us understand how the Lord would make his words "strong" in their effect. This occurs as the Holy Ghost testifies to the reader that Nephi's words are true. Nephi put it this way: "...when a man speaketh by the power of the Holy Ghost [meaning, with the Lord's direction and inspiration] the power of the Holy Ghost carrieth it unto the hearts of the children of men" (*BofM: 2 Nephi* 33:1). This means that the Holy Spirit can produce an emotional impact in us as we read the words of truth. It is this emotional experience that actually changes our hearts—meaning our inner most desires and how we feel about God, ourselves and others.

The next question we might ask is, How does one receive this witness of the truthfulness of Nephi's words? Nephi answered this question in an earlier verse.

The key to receiving understanding from the Lord is prayer.

> Wherefore, now after I have spoken these words, **if ye cannot understand them it will be because ye ask not, neither do ye knock; wherefore, ye are not brought into the light,** but must perish in the dark.
> For behold, again I say unto you that if ye will enter in by the way, and receive the Holy Ghost, it will show unto you all things what ye should do.
> **But behold, I say unto you that ye must pray always**, and not faint; that **ye must not perform any thing unto the Lord save in the first place ye shall pray unto the Father in the name of Christ**, that he will consecrate thy performance unto thee, that thy performance may be for the welfare of thy soul (*BofM: 2 Nephi* 32:4-9).

As we pray, we can establish communication with God. He communicates back to us usually through the Holy Ghost, who is also known as the Holy Spirit. How does the Holy Spirit communicate with us? The prophet Joseph Smith answered that question in this way:

> ...A person may profit by noticing the first intimation of the spirit of revelation; for instance, when you feel pure intelligence flowing into you, it may give you sudden strokes of ideas...[33]

#3 Nephi's Record Came as a Result of the Love He and the Lord Feed for Us; and This Love is Tough Love

Nephi expressed his feelings of charity, meaning love, for those who would read his record. Because of his love, he refused to soft pedal the importance of the absolute necessity that we be "...reconciled unto Christ, and enter into the narrow gate, and walk in the straight path which leads to life...". Here is how Nephi, and the Lord, taught us, using tough love:

> And it [the record] speaketh harshly against sin, according to the plainness of the truth; wherefore, no man will be angry at the words which I have written save he shall be of the spirit of the devil.
> I glory in plainness; I glory in truth; I glory in my Jesus, for he hath redeemed my soul from hell.
> I have acharity for my people, and great faith in Christ that I shall meet many souls spotless at his judgment-seat.
> I have charity for the Jew—I say Jew, because I mean them from whence I came.

I also have charity for the Gentiles. But behold, for none of these can I hope except they shall be reconciled unto Christ, and enter into the narrow gate, and walk in the strait path which leads to life, and continue in the path until the end of the day of probation (*BofM, 2 Nephi* 33:5-9).

#4 Nephi Testified That His Words Were the "Words of Christ"

A fourth thought that Nephi expressed in this final chapter was that **his words and record were actually Christ's words. This means that Nephi's record is actually the Savior's record for us**.

> And now, my beloved brethren, and also Jew, and all ye ends of the earth, **hearken unto these words and believe in Christ**; and **if ye believe not in these words believe in Christ. And if ye shall believe in Christ ye will believe in these words, for they are the words of Christ, and he hath given them unto me; and they teach all men that they should do good.**
>
> And if they are not the words of Christ, judge ye—**for Christ will show unto you, with power and great glory, that they are his words**, at the last day; and you and I shall stand face to face before his bar; and **ye shall know that I have been commanded of him to write these things, notwithstanding my weakness** (*BofM: 2 Nephi* 33:10-11; emphasis added).

How could Nephi say with such conviction, "…if you believe in Christ, ye will believe in these words?" The reason is found in the above explanation of how the Lord would testify of the truth of his record through the power of the Holy Ghost.

Nephi Invited Us to Hearken to the Words of the Record and Believe in Christ

Nephi's invitation to the reader is worth considering again: "…hearken unto these words and believe in Christ." The word hearken is very appropriate for it means to listen and to obey.[34]

Nephi's prediction that the words, which he wrote in weakness would be made strong, is fulfilled as the Holy Spirit touches us and testifies that his words are the truth inspired by God. The influence of Nephi's Record on our lives is made strong by the confirming witness of the Holy Ghost.

If we do not resist His testimony, this same Spirit will also verify the truthfulness of the Record. This is why Nephi could say with such strength and power

"...if ye shall believe in Christ ye will believe in these words, for they are the words of Christ, and he hath given them unto me; and they teach all men that they should do good."

#5 Nephi Asked His Readers to Decide if He Spoke the Words of Christ or not

The fifth concept which Nephi taught about His record was a challenge. Those who read his words are to make a determination whether Nephi's words were the words of Christ, or not. In other words, the reader must consider this: "if these are not the words of Christ, judge ye." Here is the great challenge of *The Book of Mormon*.

The Book of Mormon is one of the few books on earth, which claims to contain God's words. Therefore, it is not to be read casually. Just reading *The Book of Mormon* isn't enough. We need to come to a conclusion regarding its truthfulness, for this decision with affect us for eternity.

#6 The Lord Will Hold Us Accountable for What We Do With His Record

The sixth concept that Nephi taught us about the Lord's record, is that we are accountable for our decision to believe or reject the words of Christ, which it contains. We are also responsible to hearken to the Savior's teachings, meaning we are also responsible for living by the Savior's teachings (see *BofM:2 Nephi* 33: 12-15).

A Summary of Nephi's Final Thoughts About the Record that God Had Inspired Him to Make for Us

In review then, Nephi concluded his writing by teaching truths about the Record of God—instructions for us that he, Nephi, had made. A summary of Nephi's inspired thoughts about the Record is found below.

1. How inadequate he felt to be tasked with the responsibility of making a Record from the Lord, for us, His children (*2 Nephi* 33:1, 4).

2. Despite his human feelings of inadequacy, Nephi knew that his record was of "great worth". Nephi also understood that many people would fail to realize this and would "cast away many things" [of great value in denying God's record that Nephi was writing] (*2 Nephi* 33:2).

3. The Lord's Record to us, given through Nephi, is a demonstration of God's love for us. Also, God's love is of necessity, tough love, for our benefit (*2 Nephi* 33:5-9).

4. That he, Nephi, was not the source of the Record. Rather, the Record he

engraved contained "...the Words of Christ..." (*2 Nephi* 33:10).

5. Nephi challenged his readers to decide if the above claim was true, or not: "...if these are not the words of Christ, judge ye..." (*2 Nephi* 33:11).

6. We are responsible for whether we receive and follow the Record or not, and our decision will have consequences in the life and in the eternities (*2 Nephi* 33:12-15).

Our individual answers to the question of whether *The Book of Mormon* is the word of Christ or not, will determine the path, and the bridge, which the rest of our lives will take. We must study, and pray to find the answer to this question. Then we must be courageous enough to follow the path that leads us back to our Father in Heaven.

In order for us to follow Christ and to do **Power Change** with Him we need to have a **Power Formula**. The Record of the **Power Formula** is found in His Scriptures, including *The Holy Bible* and most correctly in *The Book of Mormon*. The Lord inspired Nephi, Mormon and the other Record Keepers to "**make a record**." This is why *The Book of Mormon* is a gift from God, and His **Power Formula** for us.

Chapter 3

Jacob Followed Nephi's Instructions and Example, Thereby Accomplishing the Action Now Described as Power Change

When Nephi had finished his portion of the Record he gave his small set of plates to his brother, Jacob. Here is Jacob's account of that transfer, and of Nephi's instructions:

> For behold, it came to pass that fifty and five years had passed away from the time that Lehi left Jerusalem; wherefore, **Nephi gave me, Jacob, a commandment concerning the small plates, upon which these things are engraven.**
>
> And he gave me, Jacob, **a commandment that I should write upon these plates a few of the things which I considered to be most precious;** that I should not touch, save it were lightly, concerning the history of this people which are called the people of Nephi.
>
> For he said that the history of his people should be engraven upon his other plates, [the large plates of Nephi, which were handed down through the Nephite kings] and **that I should preserve these plates and hand them down unto my seed, from generation to generation.**
>
> And **if there were preaching which was sacred, or revelation which was great, or prophesying, that I should engraven the heads of them upon these plates,** and touch upon them as much as it were possible, for Christ's sake, and for the sake of our people.
>
> **I, Jacob, take it upon me to fulfill the commandment of my brother Nephi** (*BofM: Jacob* 1:1-4, 8; emphasis added).

Here we see the first of many examples of how *The Book of Mormon* Records were passed from one Record Keeper to the next. In addition to making a record and getting it into Jacob's hands, note how Nephi communicated with Jacob and instructed him in his responsibility as the next Record Keeper.

As evidenced by his communication with Jacob, **Nephi did not disconnect from his brother**. Also, as Nephi gave Jacob instructions regarding Record keeping, he did all he could to help Jacob become a successful Record Keeper. We will now compare Nephi's actions with the four steps of the **Power Formula**. Here are those four steps in brief:

1) Not disconnecting, by maintaining communication;
2) Making a record;
3) Getting the Record into the hands of the next person;
4) Doing all you can to help that person fulfill his "post" and responsibility.

We can see that Nephi's actions correspond perfectly with the actions of the **Power Formula**. We also see an example of records being received, and instructions followed by Jacob. Nephi instructed Jacob, and the future Record Keepers to continue recording, preserving, and passing the Record on. Jacob did exactly that. Jacob's actions corresponded perfectly to the **Power Change Formula**.

Jacob Made a Commitment to Keep the Record

From his writings, we learn that Jacob took the responsibility of his calling very seriously. Jacob acknowledged that he was willing to follow Nephi's example and instructions.

> ...I, Jacob, take it upon me to fulfill the commandment of my brother, Nephi (*BofM: Jacob* 1:8; emphasis added).

Jacob Also Received the "Hat" of Being the Spiritual Leader and Teacher of His People

Jacob actually received two assignments from Nephi. In addition to being the Record Keeper, Jacob along with his younger brother, Joseph, had been called by Nephi to be priests and teachers for their people. Perhaps no other teachers in either *The Holy Bible* or *The Book of Mormon* accepted their calling with a greater attitude of responsibility and determination. Jacob's and Joseph's commitment to fulfill his calling was evidenced by these words:

> For I, Jacob, and my brother Joseph had been consecrated priests and teachers of this people, by the hand of Nephi.
> And we did magnify our office unto the Lord, **taking upon us the responsibility, answering the sins of the people upon our own heads if we did not teach them the word of God with all diligence**...(*BofM: Jacob* 1:18-19; emphasis added).

During the period of Jacob's ministry, serious problems began to occur among the Nephites. Their group was probably relatively small at this time, and yet they were already troubled with pride, love of riches and adultery.

These problems created personal and family difficulties. These problems could have also lead to serious disunity and weakness in defending themselves against the Lamanites. Here is how Jacob responded to these troubling conditions:

> Yea, it grieveth my soul and causeth me to shrink with shame before the presence of my Maker that **I must testify unto you concerning the wickedness of your hearts.**
>
> And also **it grieveth me that I must use so much boldness of speech concerning you, before** your wives and your children, many of whose feelings are exceedingly tender and chaste and delicate before God, which thing is pleasing unto God.
>
> Behold, **ye have done greater iniquities than the Lamanites, our brethren. Ye have broken the hearts of your tender wives, and lost the confidence of your children, because of your bad examples before them**; and the sobbings of their hearts ascend up to God against you (*BofM: Jacob* 2:6, 7, 35; emphasis added).

Jacob did not shrink from testifying to this people about their need to repent. He vigorously encouraged them to make the needed corrections in their lives. In doing so, he fulfilled his responsibility to teach the people. Like Nephi, Jacob's actions are also an example of something we could call "tough love" today because of Jacob's warning voice. The people became fully accountable for their own behavior. They could not use the excuse of not knowing their duty.

Jacob Sorrowed for His Brethren

In addition to the problems among his own people, Jacob lived in a time of trouble, war and bloodshed among the Nephites and their brethren, the Lamanites. The rebellion of Laman and Lemuel and their families was a cause of great sorrow among the Nephites. In his final words, Jacob expressed this sorrow. We will review these words shortly.

Before we do so, we will first examine how Jacob felt some sadness as a result of the difficult circumstances of his childhood. He was born in the wilderness, and his family lived in a tent. Jacob was saddened in childhood by the rebellion and "the rudeness" of his older brothers, Laman and Lemuel.

You will recall that Laman and Lemuel rebelled against their father, Lehi, many times. These older brothers had plotted to kill Lehi. They had also tried to kill Jacob's brother Nephi. Evidently these experiences made a strong impression on Jacob's young mind.

Lehi was aware of the sorrows, which Jacob had suffered as a child. Shortly before his death Lehi gave Jacob a wonderful blessing in which he spoke of these negative experiences in Jacob's childhood. Here is part of that blessing:

> And now, Jacob, I speak unto you: Thou art my first-born in the days of my tribulation in the wilderness. And behold, in thy childhood **thou has suffered afflictions and much sorrow because of the rudeness of thy brethren.**
>
> Nevertheless, Jacob, my first-born in the wilderness, **thou knowest the greatness of God; and he shall consecrate thine afflictions for thy gain** (*BofM: 2 Nephi* 2:1-2; emphasis added).

Jacob's was a difficult life in many ways. However, perhaps Jacob's greatest sorrow was for his older brothers, and their families. He loved these brothers, but they felt hatred towards him and his people.

Jacob engraved these words describing the efforts to help his rebellious brothers and those who followed them. Jacob also wrote that their efforts were "in vain".

> And it came to pass that many means were devised to reclaim and restore the Lamanites to the knowledge of the truth but it was all in vain, for they delighted in wars and bloodshed, and **they had an eternal hatred against us, their brethren. And they sought by the power of their arms to destroy us** (*BofM: Jacob* 7:24; emphasis added).

To the end of his life, Jacob felt *sorrow because of his older brothers*' hatred and aggressive actions towards him and his people. Much of the sorrow Jacob experienced was **caused by Laman** and **Lemuel.** However, there was another type of sorrow which Jacob experienced. This was *sorrow for his brothers* because he loved them but he feared for their eternal well being.

Six Causes of Sorrow

There are at least six causes of sorrow in the world. These six are:

1) The sorrow we experience because of our own sins;
2) The sorrow we **cause** others because of our sins;
3) Sorrows we experience because of the harm caused to us by the sins or carelessness of others;
4) Sorrow related to a great loss, such as the death of a loved one, the loss of health through serious illness, or the loss of privilege, wealth or freedom;
5) Sorrow for someone we love, who has lost their way, or who is struggling with affliction. This type of sorrow, combined with love for those who are suffering, is also called compassion;
6) Sorrow caused by vicariously suffering for the sins of others. This is the suffering, combined with numbers two and five above, has been experi-

enced by Jesus Christ for us.

Almost everyone experiences, to some degree, the first five types of sorrow. However, only the Savior, Jesus Christ, has experienced the sixth type of sorrow listed above. Jesus Christ is also unique in another way: He is the only accountable person who has lived without sinning, therefore, He is the only one whose actions could have caused no sorrow for others.

The Great Messenger of Happiness

Indeed, the Savior's actions and interactions with others always had the opposite long-term effect than causing sorrow. If those He was speaking with would listen to Him, believe in Him, and then follow His council, they would be happier. His teachings, or Gospel, are "The Great Plan of Happiness" (*BofM, Alma* 42:8), Therefore, Jesus Christ is The Great Messenger of Happiness.

This does not mean that the Savior's followers are spared from experiencing sorrow. However, the sorrow felt by the Savior's followers can be overcome when they are "...swallowed up in the joy of Christ" (*BofM, Alma* 31:32-35:30).

In addition to having their relationship to the Savior, and their obedience to His commandments, the sorrow experienced by the followers of Jesus Christ, who turn to Him, can produce growth, and improvement.

An example of this was seen in the life of Jacob, which we considered earlier. Here, again, is the promise Jacob received from his prophet, and father, Lehi:

> ...and now, Jacob, I speak unto you: Thou art my first-born in the days of my tribulation in the wilderness. And behold, in thy childhood thou hast suffered afflictions and much sorrow, because of the rudeness of thy brethren.
>
> Nevertheless, Jacob, my first-born in the wilderness, thou knowest the greatness of God; and **he shall consecrate thine afflictions for thy gain** (*BofM, 2 Nephi* 2:1-2).

"All These Things Shall Give Thee Experience"

The prophet Joseph Smith learned a similar lesson while suffering great sorrow in horrible conditions while he was being held in a jail by his persecutors. Joseph prayed for help. Here is the Lord's comforting answer to his prayer:

> The ends of the earth shall inquire after thy name, and fools shall have thee in derision, and hell shall rage against thee;
>
> While the pure in heart, and the wise, and the noble, and the virtuous, shall seek counsel, and authority, and blessings constantly from under thy hand.

And thy people shall never be turned against thee by the testimony of traitors.

And although their influence shall cast thee into trouble, and into bars and walls, thou shalt be had in honor; and but for a small moment and thy voice shall be more terrible in the midst of thine enemies than the fierce lion, because of thy righteousness; and thy God shall stand by thee forever and ever.

And if thou shouldst be cast into the pit, or into the hands of murderers, and the sentence of death passed upon thee; if thou be cast into the deep; if the billowing surge conspire against thee; if fierce winds become thine enemy; if the heavens gather blackness, and all the elements combine to hedge up the way; and above all, if the very jaws of hell shall gape open the mouth wide after thee, **know thou, my son, that all these things shall give thee experience, and shall be for thy good.**

The Son of Man hath descended below them all. Art thou greater than he? (*D&C* 122:1-4, 7-8).

Jacob's Sorrow for, and Because of, His Brothers Caused Him to "Mourn Out" His Days

Jacob was an example of how a person's emotional tone level can sometimes be saddened by the behavior of someone they love. This is why Jacob tells us that he "mourned out" his days. See if you don't feel his emotional tone of sorrow as you read the conclusion of Jacob's record.

And it came to pass that many means were devised to reclaim and restore the Lamanites to the knowledge of the truth; but it all was vain, for they delighted in wars and bloodshed, and they had an eternal hatred against us, their brethren. And they sought by the power of their arms to destroy us continually...

And it came to pass that I, Jacob, began to be old; and the Record of this people being kept on the other plates of Nephi, wherefore, I conclude this record, declaring that I have written according to the best of my knowledge, by saying that the time passed away with us, and also our lives passed a way like as it were unto us a dream, we being wanderers, cast out from Jerusalem, born in tribulation, in a wilderness, and hatred of our brethren, which caused wars and contentions; wherefore, we did mourn out our days (*BofM: Jacob* 7:24, 26, emphasis added).

Jacob's Sorrow is an Internal Evidence of the Truthfulness of *The Book Of Mormon*

As Jacob engraved his final few verses, we can sense how he felt. These words could only have been written by someone who had personally known the sorrows, which Jacob had experienced. There is no way that Joseph Smith, or any modern writer, could have written with such feeling, without having actually experienced the tribulations of Jacob's life. **Therefore, the emotional impact of Jacob's life experience upon his writing is a strong internal evidence of the truthfulness of *The Book of Mormon*.**

As we review the lives and writings of other Record Keepers, we shall see many similar internal evidences that *The Book of Mormon* could not have been written by Joseph Smith, or by any other modern writer.

Jacob Completed His Record-Keeping Responsibilities by Doing a Power Formula for His Successor

Jacob eventually handed the Record over to his son, Enos. In doing so, Jacob gave Enos the same instructions, which he had received from Nephi. Enos promised that he would carry out these instructions.

> ...I said unto my son Enos: Take these plates.
> **And I told him the things, which my brother Nephi had commanded me, and he promised obedience unto the commands** (*BofM: Jacob* 7:27; emphasis added).

Jacob's First Farewell Was Written While His Emotional Tone Was Higher

Jacob actually made two endings to his record. The second, which we considered above, was in Jacob 7. This came "...after some years had passed away...", when he decided to add more to his account.

His first farewell is found at the end of Chapter 6. At this time, he was feeling more positive. His emotional tone was reflected in what he wrote. His remarks, while positive overall, also contain a warning to those who would later refuse to heed his teachings. This is a further internal evidence of the truthfulness of *The Book of Mormon*. Here is Jacob's first farewell:

> Wherefore, my beloved brethren, I beseech of you in words of soberness that ye would repent, and come with full purpose of heart, and cleave unto God as he cleaveth unto you. And while his arm of mercy is extended towards you in the light of the day, harden not your hearts...
> **O then, my beloved brethren, repent ye, and enter in at the strait**

gate, and continue in the way which is narrow, until ye shall obtain eternal life.

O be wise; what can I say more?

Finally, I bid you farewell, until I shall meet you before the pleasing bar of God, which bar striketh the wicked with awful dread and fear. Amen (*BofM, Jacob* 6:5, 11-13)

The instructions, or **Power Formula**, which Jacob had received from Nephi included directions that Jacob was to preserve the Record, and pass it to the next Record Keeper. Jacob made a promise to his brother, Nephi, to fulfill his commandments (see BofM: Jacob 1:8). He kept this promise. At the end of his life, Jacob could write:

...I conclude this record, **declaring that I have written according to the best of my knowledge** (*BofM: Jacob* 7:36; emphasis added).

Jacob completed actions like **Power Change** by following the example and instructions of his predecessor. Later, he also used the **Power Formula**-like actions of making a Record and giving it to his successor. What makes these actions even more amazing is that this was only the first of more than twenty times that actions like those of the **Power** and **Power Change Formulas** were used by *The Book of Mormon* Record Keepers!

In conclusion Jacob's record teaches many lessons. Among those are listed below.

1. The internal evidence of the truthfulness of the Record shown by the appropriateness of the Emotional Tone of Jacob's writing to his life experience.
2. An example of how the Lord can heal us, and turn sorrows and afflictions into gain in our lives.
3. Jacob's example of using **Power Formula** and **Power Change Formula**-like actions.
4. It was his hope that "...many of my brethren [and sisters, including each of us] may read my words".

It is my hope that each of you will read, believe and follow the Savior's teachings and **Power Formula** and Record: *The Book of Mormon*!

Chapter 4

Enos, the Third Record Keeper: an Example of Caring for Others and of the " Dynamics"

Enos, and the Dynamics

When Jacob finished his portion of the Record, he turned it over to his son, Enos. In Enos, we see a man who showed concern for his own well being, and for the well being of others. His concern seemed to parallel concepts taught by L. Ron Hubbard. These concepts are referred to as the Dynamics.

The Four Dynamics

L. Ron Hubbard originally defined a series of four urges or drives for survival, which he called **Dynamics**. Eventually, L. Ron Hubbard added four ore Dynamics. We will review these last four later in the chapter. Also, the subject of the Dynamics is considered in *Super Power*.

Each of us is more than an individual. We are also members of families, groups, and mankind. We desire survival for ourselves, for our families, groups and for mankind in general. Here is a partially paraphrased outline of these dynamics:

> **Dynamic One** is the urge for individual survival. for the individual and his symbiotes ("**symbiote**" means all entities and energies which aid survival).
> **Dynamic Two** is the urge of the individual toward survival through their family.
> **Dynamic Three** is the urge of the individual toward survival for the group or groups of which they are a part.
> **Dynamic Four** is the urge of the individual toward survival for mankind...
> The **absolute goal of survival is immortality or infinite survival.** This is sought by the individual in terms of himself as an organism, as a spirit or as a name or as his children, as a group of which he is member or as mankind and the progeny ... of others as well as his own[36] (emphasis added).

L. Ron Hubbard further explained the interdependence of these dynamics:
> The individuals who say, "I can live alone" is very interesting. He

can't live without lichen and moss [small plants that grow on trees, rocks and moist ground]. They create soil so that vegetables can grow. He can't live without a lot of odds and ends, like, for instance, trees to make firewood [and oxygen]. That is a life form. Most important, he is interdependent with the physical universe as he would sure play the devil (variation of have the devil's own time), [i.e., experience great difficulty] surviving as a human organism if he didn't have an earth to walk on.

The dynamics mean simply how many forms of survival are there. The number of dynamics add up to the number of fields or entities a man has to be in cooperation with to get along.[37]

Enos and The First Dynamic

L. Ron Hubbard taught that we first are concerned with our own survival. He also wrote that "the absolute goal of survival is immortality or infinite survival." This is the type of survival, or salvation, that Enos searched for. This is the first "dynamic".

Enos, wrote of "the wrestle, which I had before God, before I received a remission of my sins." It was the, "words, which I had often heard my father [Jacob] speak concerning eternal life and joy of the saints that sunk deep into my heart". His father, Jacob's, teachings prompted Enos to pray.

Enos prayed as no one in recorded scriptures, with the exception of the Savior, has ever prayed.

> Behold, it came to pass that I, Enos, knowing my father that he was a just man—for **he taught me in his language, and also in the nurture and admonition of the Lord**—and blessed be the name of my God for it—
> And I will tell you of the wrestle which I had before God, before I received a remission of my sins.
> Behold, I went to hunt beasts in the forests; and the words, which I had often heard my father speak concerning eternal life, and the joy of the saints, sunk deep into my heart.
> And my soul hungered; and I kneeled down before my Maker, and **I cried unto him in mighty prayer and supplication for mine own soul; and all the day long did I cry unto him; yea, and when the night came I did still raise my voice** high that it reached the heavens.
> And there came a **voice unto me, saying: Enos, thy sins are forgiven thee, and thou shalt be blessed** (*BofM: Enos* 1:1-5; emphasis added).

Enos and the Second and the Third Dynamics

When Enos was informed that his sins had been forgiven, and that he would be blessed, his guilt was swept away. This is an example of the Lord's healing power over sin and sorrow.

Enos also learned that this wonderful change came as a result of his faith in Jesus Christ.

> And I, Enos, knew that God could not lie; wherefore, **my guilt was swept away**. And I said: Lord, **how is it done?**
>
> And he said unto me: **Because of thy faith in Christ,** whom thou hast never before heard nor seen. And many years pass away before he shall manifest himself in the flesh; wherefore, go to, [carry on with your life] **thy faith hath made thee whole** (*BofM: Enos* 1:6-8; emphasis added).

Enos had obtained this answer to his prayer, which was a wonderful personal blessing, and thereby satisfied his concern about his own welfare. Next, his attention turned to the welfare of others.

His desire then turned to the welfare of his people, the Nephites. This was an expression of concern for his group. We can probably safely assume that Enos was unmarried at this time because he did not pray for his wife or his children. However, we know that Enos later married, for he had at least one child, a son named Jarom.

As Enos wrote of his nation, he referred to its members as his "brethren." In fact, he was closely related to every Nephite. Only two generations had passed since they had left Jerusalem. Therefore, his family (second dynamic) was also his nation or group (third dynamic).

Enos prayed for the Nephites in this way:

> ...I began to feel a desire for the welfare of my brethren, the Nephites; wherefore, I did pour out my whole soul unto God for them (*BofM: Enos* 9).

Again the Lord answered his prayer. In this case He told Enos that He would bless the Nephites "according to their diligence in keeping my commandments" (see *BofM: Enos* 10).

Enos and the Fourth Dynamic

Enos was still not through praying. After expressing his concern for his own eternal condition and for his own people, he then expressed his desire that the Lord would bless other members of mankind who were not a part of his group.

Enos prayed for the Lamanite people, even though these Lamanites had chosen to be the mortal enemies of the Nephites.

> And after I, Enos, had heard these words, my faith began to be unshaken in the Lord; and **I prayed unto him with many long strugglings for my brethren, the Lamanites**.
> And it came to pass that after I had prayed and labored with all diligence, **the Lord said unto me: I will grant unto thee according to thy desires, because of thy faith** (*BofM: Enos* 11-12; emphasis added)

Enos Prayed that the Record Would be Preserved in Order to Help Future Generations

Enos then specifically asked the Lord to preserve the Record that it might one day be used to bless the remnant of his grandfather Lehi's family. This remnant would include the descendants of Laman, Lemuel, and their families and followers.

> And now behold, **this was the desire which I desired of him**—that if it should so be, that my people, the Nephites, should fall into transgression, and by any means be destroyed, and the Lamanites should not be destroyed, **that the Lord God would preserve a record of my people, the Nephites; even if it so be by the power of his holy arm, that it might be brought forth at some future day unto the Lamanites**, that, perhaps, they might be brought unto salvation—
> For at the present our strugglings were vain in restoring them to the true faith. And they swore in their wrath that, if it were possible, they would destroy our records and us, and also all the traditions of our fathers.
> Wherefore, I knowing that the Lord God was able to preserve our records, I cried unto him continually, for he had said unto me:
> Whatsoever thing ye shall ask in faith, believing that ye shall receive in the name of Christ, ye shall receive it.
> And I had faith, and **I did cry unto God that he would preserve the Records; and he covenanted with me that he would bring them forth unto the Lamanites in his own due time** (*BofM: Enos* 13-16; emphasis added).

The Lord then confirmed that Enos' hope and prayer had also been the hope and prayer of those who had preceded him as keepers of the Record.

And **the Lord said unto me: Thy fathers have also required of me this thing; and it shall be done unto them according to their faith; for their faith was like unto thine** (*BofM: Enos* 1: 18; emphasis added).

Three Common Characteristics of the Record Keepers

1) Faith in God the Father, and in His Son, Jesus Christ

We can see at least three common characteristics in these Record Keepers. The first common characteristic was **faith** in God. The Lord told Enos that his "fathers" had asked the Lord for the same blessing upon their brethren. These fathers probably included his father Jacob, his grandfather Lehi, and his uncle Nephi. Also, Enos learned that these fathers had faith, which was like his own.

Nephi had prayed in faith that his words, meaning his record, would persuade others to "...do good..." to "...believe in Him [Jesus Christ]..." and to "...endure to the end, which is eternal life".

> But I, Nephi, have written what I have written, and I esteem it as of great worth, and especially unto my people. For I pray continually for them by day, and mine eyes water my pillow by night, because of them; and **I cry unto my God in faith, and I know that he will hear my cry. And I know that the Lord God will consecrate my prayers for the gain of my people.**
>
> And the **words which I have written in weakness will be made strong unto them; for it persuadeth them to do good**; it maketh known unto them of their fathers; and **it speaketh of Jesus, and persuadeth them to believe in him, and to endure to the end, which is life eternal** (*BofM: 2 Nephi* 33:3-4; emphasis added).

Jacob had also expressed that his faith in Jesus Christ was a motivating reason for his desire to "engraven...these plates."

> And if there were preaching which was sacred, or revelation which was great, or prophesying, that I should engraven the heads [essence or central points] of them upon these plates, and touch upon them as much as it were possible, for Christ's sake, and for the sake of our people.
>
> **For because of faith** and great anxiety, **it truly had been made manifest unto us concerning our people, what things should happen unto them.**

And we also had many revelations, and the spirit of much prophecy; wherefore, **we knew of Christ and his kingdom, which should come** (*BofM: Jacob* 1:4-6; emphasis added).

2) Obedience

The second characteristic shared by the Record Keepers was the virtue of obedience. When Nephi was asked by his father Lehi to return to Jerusalem to get the brass plates, Nephi told his father:

> **I will go and do the things which the Lord hath commanded, for I know that the Lord giveth no commandments unto the children of men, save he shall prepare a way for them that they may accomplish the thing which he commandeth them** (*BofM: l Nephi* 3:7; emphasis added).

Also, when Jacob was commanded by Nephi to keep, and to add to the Record, he replied:

> ...wherefore, I, Jacob, **take it upon me to fulfill the commandment of my brother Nephi** (*BofM: Jacob* 1:8; emphasis added).

When Jacob's time as the Record Keeper was finished, he asked Enos to take up this responsibility. Jacob recorded Enos' response this way:

> And I, Jacob, saw that I must soon go down to my grave; wherefore, **I said unto my son Enos: Take these plates. And I told him the things, which my brother Nephi had commanded me, and he promised obedience unto the commands** (*BofM: Jacob* 7:27; emphasis added).

Obedience and Power Change

If we think about it, **obedience to the example and instructions of a successful predecessor *is* the principle of Power Change.**

3) Love

The third common characteristic among the Record Keepers was their great concern, and love for others. Their love extended to the unborn people of future generations. This love was also extended to those outside their own group. Enos' love lead to a hope that the Lord would preserve the Records and "bring them forth unto the Lamanites in his own due time" (*BofM: Enos* 16).

Jacob also wrote of his motivating love as he recorded his words for the benefit of future readers:

> But whatsoever things we write upon anything save [except] it be upon plates must perish and vanish away; but **we can write a few words upon plates, which will give our children, and also our beloved brethren,** a small degree of knowledge concerning us, or concerning their fathers—
>
> **Now in this thing we do rejoice; and we labor diligently to engraven these words upon plates, hoping that our beloved brethren and our children will receive them with thankful hearts…**(*BofM: Jacob* 4:2-3; emphasis added).

The Conclusion of Enos's Work

Even among his own people, the work was difficult. Enos, like his father Jacob before him, had to vigorously teach his people to repent. Here is Enos' account of his difficulties in preventing the Nephites from self-destructing:

> And **there was nothing save it was exceeding harshness, preaching and prophesying of wars, and contentions, and destructions, and continually reminding them of death, and the duration of eternity**, and the judgments and the power of God, and all these things—stirring them up continually to keep them in the fear [… "reverence, awe, worship…"] of the Lord. I say there was nothing short of these things, and **exceedingly great plainness of speech, would keep them from going down speedily to destruction.** And after this manner do I write concerning them (*BofM: Enos* 23; emphasis added, see also **Fear** in the LDS *Bible Dictionary*).

From his record we learn that Enos was able to help the Nephites. Surely he would have wanted his people to do better than they apparently were doing. However, it was probably through his efforts, and the efforts of others like him, that the Nephites were kept from going down "speedily to destruction."

Enos' efforts to help the Lamanites did not meet with success during his lifetime. However, because of the Record, which he contributed to, many of the descendants of these people are receiving the blessings he prayed for. Enos was a wonderful example of someone who is concerned about others.

We shall see that Enos' concern for others was reflected in the life of his son Jarom. This is logical, for Jarom followed the example of his father as the next

Record Keeper. In following Enos' example, Jarom also used the action we now call **Power Change**. Enos and the other Record Keepers were concerned about others. Their efforts were examples of this concern for the survival, and for the eternal well being of others, as described in the Dynamics.

Four Additional Dynamics

As mentioned at the beginning of this chapter, L. Ron Hubbard first described four Dynamics.

These first four Dynamics are the ones dealing with **people**. L. Ron Hubbard later wrote of four additional Dynamics. These additional Dynamics are outlined below. These discuss the survival of:

5) the animal kingdom;
6) the physical universe;
7) the urge toward existence as or of spirits...the spiritual dynamic;
8) The Supreme Being, the God Dynamic.[38]

[Author's update. The topic of the Dynamics has been re-visited in the final book of this series: *Super Power*.]

How We Should Receive the Record

As we think about it, we are all included in the 4th Dynamic —mankind. Enos loved all of us, and they rejoiced in their efforts to help us. Enos's father, Jacob and the others whom the Lord called to "make a record" did "...labor diligently to engraven these words upon plates...". It was their hope the we "...will receive them with thankful hearts...". Each of us must examine our attitude towards our receiving the blessings of having God's Record and Power Formula. Do we receive it with joy? How do we *feel* about having access to such a treasure? Are we receiving it with thankful hearts? If now, we need to reconsider our *response* to the Record, and we need to consider our *responsibility* now that we have it.

You will recall that Nephi expressed that one reason why he made a record was his concern and love for his people (the 2nd Dynamic). In the verse quoted earlier Nephi wrote:

> But I, Nephi, have written what I have written, and I esteem it as of great worth, and especially unto my people. **For I pray continually for them by day, and mine eyes water my pillow by night**, because of them; and I cry unto my God in faith, and I know that he will hear my cry (*BofM: 2 Nephi* 33:3; emphasis added).

Nephi also expressed charity, which is pure Christ-like Love, for all people (3rd and 4th Dynamics). Here is how he expressed his feelings:

> **I have charity for the Jew**—I say Jew, because I mean them from whence I came.
> **I also have charity for the Gentiles**. But behold, for none of these can I hope except they shall be reconciled unto Christ, and enter into the narrow gate, and walk in the strait path which leads to life, and continue in the path until the end of the day of probation.
> And now, **my beloved brethren, and also Jew, and all ye ends of the earth,** hearken unto these words and believe in Christ...
> (*BofM: 2 Nephi* 33:8-9; emphasis added).

Now, returning to the third Record Keeper, Enos. In his prayer, Enos demonstrated a concern for his eternal welfare. He also showed concern for his people and other people who considered him an enemy. His desires to secure the blessings of the Lord for himself and others follows the pattern of the Dynamics.

Enos also reflected his love and concern for the welfare of his brethren, the Lamanites, in his actions. He lived out the remainder of his life trying to bring to pass the blessings which he had prayed for. Enos taught his son and his people (2nd and 3rd Dynamics). Also he "sought diligently to restore the Lamanites unto the "true faith of God" (4th Dynamic; see *Enos* 20).

There are other revelations given to Joseph Smith, which could possibly be correlated with the other Dynamics. This is a topic worthy of future research.

Chapter 5

Jarom, Omni, Amaron, Chemish, Abinadom and Amaleki: Men Who Preserved the Record in Very Difficult Times

Jarom

Enos' son, Jarom, carried on as the new Record Keeper. In doing so, he was following his father's instructions or commandments.

> Now behold, **I Jarom, write a few words according to the commandment of my father, Enos, that our genealogy may be kept.**
> And as these plates are small, and as **these things are written for the intent of the benefit of our brethren the Lamanites**, wherefore, it must needs be that I write a little; but I shall not write the things of my prophesying, nor of my revelations. For what could I write more than my fathers have written? **For have not they revealed the plan of salvation? I say unto you, Yea**; and this sufficeth me (*BofM: Jarom* 1-2; emphasis added).

God's Power Formula and the Plan of Salvation

In these verses, Jarom used the phrase "...the plan of salvation...". This is a wonderful descriptor or synonym for **God's Power Formula**. Another synonym would be the Gospel of Jesus Christ.

The Role of Record Keeper Changed

We might ask: Why weren't these Record Keepers writing for the benefit of their descendants, the Nephites? They seem to be writing more for the Lamanites. These prophets knew that eventually the Nephite nation would be destroyed, and that the surviving Nephites would be assimilated by the Lamanites (see *BofM: l Nephi* 12:20; *Jacob* 1:5-6; *Enos* 9-13; *Moroni* 1:1-2). They also knew that the Lamanites, and their descendants, would survive. This would be the remnant of their family who could benefit from the Records.

Jarom shared his father's concern, that "these things are written for the intent of the benefit of our brethren the Lamanites." However, he did not add a great deal to the Record himself.

This became the pattern for the next five Record Keepers. There were two reasons why these Record Keepers did not add a very much to the Record. First, these small plates were nearly full. The second reason is **that they were following a new set of instructions, or Power Formula**. You will recall that Jacob had been commanded by Nephi to:

> Write upon these plates **a few of the things which I consider to be most precious; that I should not touch, save it were lightly, concerning the history of this people which are called the people of Nephi.**
>
> And **if there were preaching which was sacred, or revelation which was great, or prophesying, that I should engraven the heads [dominant, important items] of them upon these plates**, and touch upon them as much as it were possible, for Christ's sake, and for the sake of our people (*BofM: Jacob* 1:2,4; emphasis added).

Please recall also that when Jacob passed the Record to Enos, he gave him the same instructions or the same **Power Formula**, which he had received from Nephi.

> And I, Jacob, saw that I must soon go down to my grave; wherefore, I said unto my son Enos: **Take these plates. And I told him the things, which my brother Nephi had commanded me, and he promised obedience unto the commands** (*BofM: Jacob* 7:27; emphasis added).

The Final Small Plates Record Keepers Became Record Preservers

When Enos passed the Record to Jarom, he did not give him these same instructions. Enos instructed Jarom to **preserve the Record, and keep a genealogy, and to then to pass the plates on**. The spiritual messages written by Nephi, Jacob and Enos had nearly fulfilled the purpose of these small plates. The important thing now was to preserve this Record.

If we look at these Record Keepers from this perspective, they did indeed follow the instructions or the **Power Formula, which they had received**. Although some of these men admitted that their lives needed mending, we should not judge the scarcity of their writings to be an indication of failure as Record Keepers. For, unlike their predecessors, their calling was to be mostly record preservers. Each of them fulfilled this assignment well.

Jarom Gave the Record to His Son Omni

The wars between the Nephites and the Lamanites continued. Omni's life was spent mainly in defense of his country. He was a humble man who did not feel worthy to add much to the Record. However, he and those who followed him: Ammaron, Chemish, Abinadom, and Amaleki, all performed a great service in preserving the Record during the times of danger.

It also appears from their writings that the **Spiritual Condition** of the Nephites had deteriorated. Here is Omni's short addition to the Record:

> Behold, it came to pass that **I, Omni, being commanded by my father, Jarom, that I should write somewhat upon these plates, to preserve our genealogy—**
> Wherefore, in my days, I would that ye should know that I fought much with the sword to preserve my people, the Nephites, from falling into the hands of their enemies, the Lamanites. But behold, I of myself am a wicked man, and I have not kept the statutes and the commandments of the Lord as I ought to have done.
> And it came to pass that two hundred and seventy and six years had passed away, and we had many seasons of peace; and we had many seasons of serious war and bloodshed. Yea, and in fine, two hundred and eighty and two years had passed a way, and **I had kept these plates according to the commandments of my fathers; and I conferred them upon my son Amaron.** And I make an end (*BofM: Omni* 1-3; emphasis added).

Please note that Omni did keep his genealogy in that he told us who his father was. Also, his father Jarom gave Omni the same instructions with regard to the Record. Both men "kept" or "preserved" the Record. Also Omni identified the next Record Keeper, his son, Amaron. This pattern was followed by these final Record Keepers, of the small set of Nephi's plates.

Omni Gave the Record to His Son Amaron

> **And now I, Amaron, write the things whatsoever I write, which are few, in the book of my father.**
> Behold, it came to pass that three hundred and twenty years had passed away, and the more wicked part of the Nephites were destroyed.
> For the Lord would not suffer, after he had led them out of the land of Jerusalem and kept and preserved them from falling into the hands of their enemies, yea, he would not suffer that the words

should not be verified, which he spake unto our fathers, saying that:

Inasmuch as ye will not keep my commandments ye shall not prosper in the land.

Wherefore the Lord did visit them in great judgment; nevertheless, he did spare the righteous that they should not perish, but did deliver them out of the hands of their enemies.

And it came to pass that I did deliver the plates unto my brother Chemish (*BofM: Omni* 4-8; emphasis added).

Amaron Turned the Record Over to His Brother, Chemish

Now I, Chemish, write what few things I write, in the same book with my brother; for behold, **I saw the last which he [Amaron) wrote, that he wrote it with his own hand; and he wrote it in the day that he delivered them unto me. And after this manner we keep the Records, for it is according to the commandments of our father.** And I make an end (*BofM: Omni* 9; emphasis added).

The Training or Power Formula Given to a New Record Keeper

Chemish gave us a valuable insight into the training he received from his brother Amaron, to be a Record Keeper. It is possible, and perhaps likely, that these same steps were followed with each transfer of the Record:

1) The new Record Keeper met with the previous Record Keeper;
2) The final engraving was observed by the new Record Keeper. In this way he could learn the physical skill of engraving the plates;
3) The Record was transferred on this same day;
4) The Record Keeper would gave his successor a set of instructions to keep and preserve the Record and pass it on to others. This was done "according to the commandments of our Father" (see *BofM: Omn*i: 1).

Thus, the training of a new Record Keeper included four steps. The present Record Keeper would meet with the one who was to take his place. During this meeting, the one who then had the Records would:

1) Communicate with his successor (i.e., not disconnect from his successor);
2) Make a record for him;
3) Give the successor the Record;
4) Do all you can to help the successor by giving instruction to the new Record Keeper about his duty.

These four steps also happen to be the four steps of the **Power Formula**!

Abinadom Received the Record from His Father, Chemish

> **Behold, I, Abinadom, am the son of Chemish.** Behold, it came to pass that I saw much war and contention between my people, the Nephites, and the Lamanites; and I, with my own sword, have taken the lives of many of the Lamanites in the defense of my brethren.
>
> And behold, **the Record [history] of this people is engraven upon plates which is had by the kings** [the large plates of Nephi], according to the generations; and I know of no revelation save that which has been written, neither prophecy; wherefore, that which is sufficient is written. And I make an end (*BofM: Omni* 10-11; emphasis added).

Abinadom's Son, Amaleki, was the Next Record Keeper

> Behold, I am Amaleki, the son of Abinadom. Behold, I will speak unto you somewhat...
>
> And it came to pass that I began to be old; and, having no seed, and knowing king Benjamin to be a just man before the Lord, wherefore, I shall deliver up these plates unto him, exhorting all men to come unto God, the Holy One of Israel, and believe in prophesying, and in revelations...(*BofM: Omni* 12, 25; emphasis added).

Amaleki Completed the Small Plate Records and Gave Them to King Benjamin

Did you note that each of these writers made a Record of his genealogy by telling us their relationship to the previous Record Keeper? They fulfilled the instructions of Enos and Jarom. In addition to recording his genealogy and preserving the plates, Amaleki added these words of testimony and exhortation:

> **...and believe... in the ministering of angels, and in the gift of speaking with tongues, and in the gift of interpreting languages, and in all things which are good; for there is nothing which is good save it comes from the Lord; and that which is evil cometh from the devil.**
>
> **And now, my beloved brethren, I would that ye should come unto Christ, who is the Holy One of Israel, and partake of his salvation, and the power of his redemption. Yea, come unto him, and offer your whole souls as an offering unto him, and continue in fasting and praying, and endure to the end; and as the Lord liveth**

ye will be saved (*BofM: Omni* 1:25-26; emphasis added).

Amaleki's words took up the last space on this small set of plates. This Record was now complete. His testimony was a fitting end to this wonderful set of Records. All that was now needed was to preserve and pass it on. As mentioned earlier, Nephi had also started another Record on a larger set of plates. Upon these large plates a historical, or secular Record was being kept by the Nephite kings.

Therefore, the current king, Benjamin, already had possession of the **large** plates of Nephi. Amaleki gave the **small** plates to king Benjamin. The completed or "full" smaller plates would be handed down from generation to generation, and used as scripture to teach the people.

About five hundred and fifteen years later, Mormon obtained the small plates. He added this unabridged small plate Record to his abridgment of Nephi's larger set of plates. Mormon's final Record included: his own first-person account, an abridged version of the large plates of Nephi, and the total small plate Record. His son Moroni completed the book. Moroni named the completed plates *The Book of Mormon* after his father. He then buried the plates for safekeeping, until the time was right for the Lord to reveal them to us through His modern prophet, Joseph Smith.

The prayers of the Record Keepers, Nephi, Jacob and Enos were answered. Their words were preserved, and the descendants of their brethren, the Lamanites, are receiving

their words and records. These records have gone forth to many, many others. Nephi predicted that *The Book of Mormon* will eventually be taken, to the "...ends of the earth" (*BofM: 2 Nephi* 33:10).

The Power of the Word, or Record, to Change Lives

Many have been brought to believe in and follow Jesus Christ as a result of reading the testimonies of Nephi, Jacob, Enos, Jarom and Amaleki. Also, we would not have received their testimonies had it not been for the efforts of Omni, Ammaron, Chemish and Abinadom to preserve the Record.

In this way, the Savior has shown forth his power—the power to change people's hearts, turning them from their iniquities, and turning them to their Father in Heaven (*BofM, 3 Nephi* 20:26). Through His Record, the Lord has made available His Power or the "...capability of...accomplishing" this mighty change in the hearts of men (see Definition of Power in the *Preface*).

We should be grateful to these Record Keepers who engraved and preserved these precious small plates of Nephi. We have been blessed by their faith, their obedience, their labors, and their love.

Through reading the testimonies of Jesus Christ written by these Record Keepers, our hearts are prepared to receive a personal testimony of the Savior.

This testimony comes by way of the Holy Spirit and usually in answer to our sincere prayers (see *BofM, Moroni* 10:45). Reading the Record prepares our hearts for this spiritual witness. Revelation from the Holy Spirit touches us, and changes our hearts. This is how *The Book of Mormon* has the power to change us, and this is how the *The Book of Mormon* is God's **Power Formula** for our lives.

We will now turn to another group of Record Keepers. These are the men, starting with king Benjamin, who engraved upon the larger set of plates that Nephi had constructed. Although they wrote upon a different set of metal plates, they continued to follow the **Power Formulas** they had received from the Lord, through His prophets and Record Keepers. Their testimonies and teachings are also a sacred record, and part of God's **Power Formula** for us.

THE POWER FORMULAS

Chapter 6

King Benjamin and The Power Formula

Benjamin was a Prophet, a Record Keeper, and a King

Approximately 270 years after Lehi left Jerusalem and took his family into the wilderness. After their ocean journey to the new world, Lehi's group soon divided into two groups. Those who followed the prophet Nephi had to flee from their aggressive brothers Laman and Lemuel.

Nephi's followers prevailed upon him to be their king or protector (see *BofM: 2 Nephi* 5:18 and 6:2). Nephi's descendants reigned for many generations. We are going to concentrate on the final two Nephite kings, Benjamin and Mosiah.

King Benjamin was perhaps the greatest king in history. In addition to being a great king, Benjamin was a record keeper and a prophet. What makes his life even more amazing is that he raised a son to be at least his equal as both a king and as a spiritual leader.

Although he was their king, Benjamin did not put himself above his people. He maintained a close relationship with them. He even worked among them to provide for his own needs. Here is his description of his relationship with his people:

> And even **I, myself, have labored with mine own hands that I might serve you, and that ye should not be laden with taxes,** and that there should nothing come upon you, which was grievous to be borne...(*BofM: Mosiah* 2:14; emphasis added).

If king Benjamin had thought of himself as being better than his people, this could have eventually led to a severance of communication with them. This would have been a "disconnection" from the people. Disconnection would have made it impossible for Benjamin to have had such a profound influence for good on his people.

Avoidance of this disconnection is the first step of the **Power Formula**. Benjamin fulfilled this step and all of the other steps of the **Power Formula**. Here, again, are these steps:

1) The first law of the **Condition of Power** is, **don't disconnect**. You can't just

deny your connections, what you have got to do is take ownership and responsibility for your connections...;
2) The first thing you've got to do is **make a record** of all its lines, and that is the only way you'll ever be able to disconnect. So on a **Condition of Power**, the first thing you have to do, is write up your whole post. You have made it possible for the next fellow in to assume the state of **Power Change**. If you don't **write up the whole post,** you're going to be stuck with a piece of that post, since time immemorial, and a year or so later somebody will still be coming to you and asking you about the post which you occupied;
3) The responsibility is to **write the thing up, and get it into the hands of the guy who is going to take care of it;**
4) Do all you can to make the post occupiable (emphasis added).[39]

When one has achieved a **Condition of Power**, he or she is obligated to help others achieve that same **Condition**. The process of teaching others the principles of success, and then helping them to succeed, is called the **Power Formula**.

According to the fourth step of the **Power Formula**, a leader should try to facilitate the transfer of Power to those who follow him. This is exactly what king Benjamin did for his son, Mosiah.

Before we see how Benjamin transferred Power to Mosiah, we need to establish that a **Condition of Power** existed among the Nephites during this time. Mormon commented on Benjamin's reign in this way:

> And now there was no more contention in all the land of Zarahemla, among all the people who belonged to king Benjamin, so that **king Benjamin had continual peace all the remainder of his days** (*BofM: Mosiah* 1:1; emphasis added).

This state of continued peace and the absence of contention showed that the condition of the Nephite government during king Benjamin's reign was one of Power. Not only did the Nephites enjoy peace while Benjamin ruled they also enjoyed:

1) Prosperity (see *BofM: Mosiah* 2:30);
2) Protection from their enemies (see *Mosiah* 2:30);
3) A low tax or possibly no tax burden (see Mosiah 2:12 and 14);
4) Freedom from unfair imprisonment (see *Mosiah* 2:13);
5) Proper enforcement of good laws (see *Mosiah* 2:13);
6) Freedom from slavery (see *Mosiah* 2:13);
7) Correct teaching of true principles (see *Mosiah* 2:13);
8) An excellent example of service with a challenge for the Nephites to be "...in the service of your God," by being "...in the service of your fellow beings" (see *Mosiah* 2:15-19).

BENJAMIN'S RECORD

Benjamin was determined to not disconnect from the people. Also, he would not disconnect from the Lord who was the true source of his **Power**. He maintained communication with his people, and with his Father in Heaven.

Examples Showing How King Benjamin Did Not Disconnect From Others

There are a number of verses in Mormon's abridgment of Mosiah's record, which show that **Benjamin was a man who was determined not to disconnect.** These verses are from Benjamin's final address to his people. He was reviewing his reign, and giving an account of his stewardship as their king.

> Behold, I say unto you that because **I said unto you that I had spent my days in your service, I do not desire to boast, for I have only been in the service of God**.
> And behold, I tell you these things that ye may learn wisdom; that ye may learn that **when ye are in the service of your fellow beings ye are only in the service of your God.**
> **Behold, ye have called me your king; and if I, whom ye call your king, do labor to serve you, then ought not ye to labor to serve one another?** And behold also, if I, whom ye call your king, who has spent his days in your service, and yet has been in the service of God, do merit any thanks from you, O how you ought to thank your heavenly King!
> ...**And I, even I, whom ye call your king, am no better than ye yourselves are;** for I am also of the dust. And ye behold that I am old, and am about to yield up this mortal frame to its mother earth (*BofM: Mosiah* 2:16-19, 26; emphasis added).

Benjamin would not allow himself be distant, superior or disconnected from the people. During the farewell message, Benjamin also taught:

> **I have not commanded you to come up hither that ye should fear me, or that ye should think that I of myself am more than a mortal man.**
> **But I am like as yourselves, subject to all manner of infirmities in body and mind;** yet I have been chosen by this people, and consecrated by my father, and was suffered [allowed] by the hand of the Lord that I should be a ruler and a king over this people; and have been kept and preserved by his matchless power, **to serve you with all the might, mind and strength, which the Lord hath granted unto me** (*BofM: Mosiah* 2:10-11; emphasis added).

With the exception of the Savior, we cannot find a better example than Benjamin of maintaining ties with others, and of not disconnecting from the people he led. As mentioned earlier, Benjamin even worked among the people for his own support.

> And even **I, myself, have labored with mine own hands that I might serve you, and that ye should not be laden with taxes**, and that there should nothing come upon you which was grievous to be borne—and of all these things which I have spoken, ye yourselves are witnesses this day (*BofM: Mosiah* 2:14).

Working with the people allowed Benjamin to teach by example service, to keep their tax burden down, and perhaps most importantly, to maintain the love of his people.

King Benjamin's Three Power Formulas

As we look closely at Mosiah's record, we can see that there were actually three examples of actions like the **Power Formula** and **Power Change** that occurred in the first six chapters of Mosiah. Below is a brief outline of these three **Power Formulas**.

1) Benjamin's Power Formula for the Next Spiritual Leader and Record Keeper of His People

The first **Power Formula**-like actions employed by Benjamin was the spiritual preparation of his son, Mosiah. In the first eleven verses of Mosiah, Benjamin taught his sons the importance of the Records (see *BofM: Mosiah* 1:6-7). This lesson was probably a culmination of a lifetime of preparation of Mosiah to become the next spiritual leader and Record Keeper of these people.

2) Benjamin's Power Formula for the Next King

The second **Power** and **Power Change Formulas** involved the governmental **Power Change**. This occurred when king Benjamin passed the reins of government to his son, Mosiah. Benjamin declared to the people that Mosiah was to be their king as well as their spiritual leader. This was the second **Power Formula**. Benjamin passed **two hats** to Mosiah. These were:

1) Spiritual Leader/Record Keeper; and
2) The position of King.

3) Benjamin's Spiritual Power Formula for His People

The third **Power Formula** had to do with the **Spiritual Condition** of each person in the kingdom. Benjamin wanted the people to be brought to a **Spiritual Condition** like his own. Benjamin spoke to his people about the Savior and a making a covenant to keep His commandments. The contents of this address were delivered to Benjamin by an angel. These wonderful teachings constituted a **Spiritual Non Existence** through **Power Formulas** for his people.

Next, we will review these three **Power Formulas** in greater detail.

The First Power Formula: Benjamin Passed the Role of Record Keeper and of Spiritual Leader to Mosiah

As Benjamin was getting ready to pass Power to Mosiah, he called his sons together. Benjamin taught his sons the principles that we now recognize as the **Power Formula**. Benjamin emphasized the importance of the sacred Records.

Benjamin studied the scriptural Records like the previous authors of scripture. Benjamin became a **Record Keeper** because he was first a **record reader and follower**!

In terms of the **Conditions Formulas**, we could say Benjamin achieved **Spiritual Power** by following the **Power Formulas** of others. This is the **Power Change Formula**. He correctly ascribed his success to following the counsel of others. In addition, he realized that these same leaders had themselves learned from the Greatest Leader of all — The Lord!

Mormon, as he abridged the small plates, commented on how Benjamin taught his sons the value of the Records.

> **And he also taught them concerning the Records, which were engraven on the plates of brass** [the plates of brass included many Old Testament scriptures, and they were brought from Jerusalem by Nephi and Lehi] saying:
> My sons, I would that ye should remember that **were it not for these plates, which contain these records and these commandments, we must have suffered in ignorance, even at this present time, not knowing the mysteries of God.**
> For it were not possible that our father, Lehi, could have remembered all these things, to have taught them to his children, except it were for the help of these plates...(*BofM: Mosiah* 1:3-4; emphasis added).

Reading this verse brought to mind a statement by L. Ron Hubbard, to the effect that, "if it isn't written, it isn't true"[40]. In other words, instructions and directions should be recorded if they are meant to be authoritative and, to have a lasting effect. It is the responsibility of the one giving the instruction to **make a record** of his instructions. A verbal record would not have been able to stand the test of time, and be transferred accurately from one generation to the next.

Also, people should not be held responsible for following verbal instruction. Because memory is fallible, in the future neither the person giving the instruction nor those receiving it can be certain what these prior instructions were. With a written record, the reader becomes responsible for his or her actions regarding the counsel received in that record.

Until the Record is made, the responsibility for getting the instructions accomplished remains with the one giving the instructions. **An exception to this statement would occur when the responsibility for writing the instruction down has been delegated to the receiver. This is the pattern followed in nearly all of God's revealed instructions to His prophets.** To my knowledge, there are two or three times when God actually wrote something down for us. The first was when the finger of the Lord engraved the Ten Commandments upon the stone tablets. Second, the Lord, or one of His angelic messengers wrote a message to King Belshazzer. This is the source of the saying: "The writing is on the wall" (see *Exodus* 31:18, *Deuteronomy* 9:11, and *David* chapter 5).

Chapter 8 of John's gospel in The New Testament also records a time when the Savior wrote something. This occurred while He was being confronted by those who opposed Him. They had brought "...a woman taken in adultery...". They demanded that He tell them what judgment He would make in her case. John reported:

> This they said, tempting Him, that they might have to accuse Him. But Jesus stooped down, and with His finger wrote on the ground, as though He heard them not...
>
> So when they continued asking him, he lifted up himself, and said unto them, He that is without sin among you, let him first cast a stone at her.
>
> And again he stooped down, and wrote on the ground.
>
> And they which heard it, being convicted by their own conscience, went out one by one, beginning at the eldest, even unto the last: and Jesus was left alone, and the woman standing in the midst.
>
> When Jesus had lifted up himself, and saw none but the woman, he said unto her, Woman, where are those thine accusers? hath no man condemned thee?
>
> She said, No man, Lord. And Jesus said unto her, Neither do I condemn thee: go, and sin no more (see *New Test. John* 8:1-11).

John did not include the context of the Savior's writing in his gospel. However, one possible explanation of His writing is given in the section in John chapter eight in *The Power Formulas, Part Two*.

To my understanding, the work of writing and other scriptures was delegated by the Lord to His prophets and Record Keepers.

Next, Benjamin stressed the importance of being able to understand the language of the Record. He also taught his sons how the Record had benefited their people:

> ...for he [Lehi] having been taught in the language of the Egyptians therefore he could read these engravings [the plates were written in a reformed Egyptian] therefore **he could read these engravings, and teach them to his children, that thereby they could teach them to their children,** and so fulfilling the commandments of God, even down to this present time.
>
> I say unto you, my sons, **were it not for these things [the Records upon the plates]**, which have been kept and preserved by the hand of God, that we might read and understand of his mysteries, and have his commandments always before our eyes, that **even our fathers would have dwindled in unbelief, and we should have been like unto our brethren, the Lamanites,** who know nothing concerning these things, or even do not believe them when they are taught them, because of the traditions of their fathers, which are not correct (*BofM: Mosiah* 1:4-5; emphasis added).

It is interesting that Benjamin taught these truths to his "sons" rather than just to his chosen successor, Mosiah. Benjamin showed love for all his sons, and also prepared them to assume leadership if something were to happen to Mosiah.

Benjamin Taught That Without the Scriptural Record the People Would Have "Dwindled" in Their Spiritual Condition

In this verse above, Benjamin used the term "dwindled in unbelief." This term, "dwindled in unbelief," as used in *The Book of Mormon*, means to:

1) To diminish; to become less; to shrink; to waste or consume away;
2) To degenerate; to sink; to fall away.[41]

We can also define the term "dwindle in unbelief" as it relates to the subject of the **Conditions Formulas**. **To dwindle in unbelief means to go down in Spiritual Condition**. Benjamin's prediction of what would have happened to the Nephite nation if they had no Scriptural records was based upon a historical precedent. The Nephites had located another group of people from the Holy

Land during the time of Benjamin's father, king Mosiah[1] [this Mosiah was the father of king Benjamin and the grandfather of king Mosiah[2]].

These people had crossed the ocean shortly after Lehi and his family. For nearly two hundred years they had lived upon this continent separately. They were not known to the Nephites. This group was led by a man named Mulek.

One difference between Lehi's and Mulek's groups is that the people of Lehi's group had access to the holy scriptures. The Mulekites did not bring a scriptural record with them.

Mormon described what happened when the descendants of Lehi met the descendants of Mulek for the first time. At this time the descendants of the Mulekite people were led by a man named Zarahemla. Please note the example of "dwindling" that resulted from not having a scriptural record. Here is Mormon's account of these events:

> And they [the Nephites] discovered a people, who were called the people of Zarahemla. Now, there was great rejoicing among **the people of Zarahemla; and also Zarahemla [the king of these Mulekites] did rejoice exceedingly, because the Lord had sent the people of Mosiah with the plates of brass, which contained the Record of the Jews...**
>
> And at the time that Mosiah discovered them, they had become exceedingly numerous. Nevertheless, **they had many wars and serious contentions, and had fallen by the sword from time to time; and their language had become corrupted; and they had brought no records with them; and they denied the being of their Creator;** and Mosiah, nor the people of Mosiah, could understand them (*BofM: Omni* 1:14, 17; emphasis added).

Fortunately, the Nephites and the people of Zarahemla, merged into one nation under king Mosiah[1]. The Records were then made available to all. Also, these people were instructed in the language of the Nephites.

> But it came to pass that Mosiah caused that they should be taught in his language...
>
> And it came to pass that the people of Zarahemla, and of Mosiah, did unite together; and Mosiah was appointed to be their king (*BofM: Omni* 1:18-19).

Benjamin valued the brass plate records, and he included these plates as part of the Record he gave to his son, Mosiah. In speaking of the value of the sacred Records, Benjamin taught his sons the following:

> O my sons, I would that ye should remember that these sayings [Benjamin's teachings] are true, and **also that these records [the Brass Plates] are true.** And behold, also the **plates of Nephi, which contain the Records and the sayings of our fathers from the time they left Jerusalem until now, and they are true;** and we can know of their surety because we have them before our eyes [these records had been passed on to Benjamin from the previous Record Keepers].
>
> And now, my sons, I would that ye should remember to search them diligently, that ye may profit thereby; and I would that ye should **keep the commandments of God, that ye may prosper in the land according to the promises which the Lord made unto our fathers** (*BofM: Mosiah* 1:6-7; emphasis added).

Benjamin maintained contact with his sons, including Mosiah. He kept the Record and added to it. These two actions are equivalent to the first two steps of the **Power Formula**. Benjamin's actions included one that we now recognize as the third step of the **Power Formula**, which is to get the Record "…into the hands of the guy who is going to take care of it…" (*BofM: Mosiah* 1:16).

As the Record Keepers and the people followed God's commandments, they were successful. Their prophets made a Record of how obedience to the commandments of God had worked for them. The Record Keepers passed the Record on. In this way, they helped future generations also learn to "prosper in the land".

A Cycle of Power Formulas and Power Change

Each Record Keeper completed actions like a Power Formula. The next Record Keeper would then learn the truths contained on previous Records, and try to follow these teachings. He would also teach the people from the Record. In this way **the successor Record Keepers carried out the actions, which were like those in the Power Change Formula.** Then to complete the cycle, this new Record Keeper would preserve the Record, add to it, and pass it to the next Record Keeper. As they passed the Record to the next Record Keeper they would teach them their duty.

In this way they repeated the **Power Formula**-like actions they had observed from their predecessors. Benjamin was a great example of this cycle because he followed the previous teachings, added his portion to the Records, and then gave all the plates to his son, Mosiah[2].

The Second Power Formula: Benjamin Passed the Kingdom to Mosiah

In addition to passing the Records to Mosiah, Benjamin also passed to him the responsibility and the authority of being the next king. We can be confident that

THE POWER FORMULAS

Benjamin spent his life teaching and preparing Mosiah to receive the office of king. Benjamin's teachings and preparation of Mosiah are an example of "doing all you can do" to help someone assume a new position. This, of course, is the fourth and final step of the **Power Formula**! Mormon commented on this change of power in this way:

> And it came to pass that after king Benjamin had made an end of teaching his sons, that he waxed old, and he saw that he must very soon go the way of all the earth; therefore, **he thought it expedient that he should confer the kingdom upon one of his sons.**
>
> **Therefore, he had Mosiah^2 brought before him;** and these are the words which he spake unto him, saying: My son, I would that ye should make a proclamation throughout all this land among all this people, or the people of Zarahemla, and the people of Mosiah [king Mosiah^1] who dwell in the land, that thereby they may be gathered together; for **on the morrow I shall proclaim unto this my people out of mine own mouth that thou art a king and a ruler over this people,** whom the Lord our God hath given us.
>
> And moreover, **I shall give this people a name,** that thereby they may be distinguished above all the people which the Lord God hath brought out of the land of Jerusalem; and this I do because they have been a diligent people in keeping the commandments of the Lord (*BofM: Mosiah* 1:9-11; emphasis added).

In verses 9 and 10, Benjamin declared his intention to transfer power by proclaiming to the people that Mosiah would be their new king. This is a great example of Step 4 in the **Power Formula**, which is to "Do all you can to make the post occupiable."

In verse 11, Benjamin explained a second purpose of this gathering. He was going to teach the people and to give them a name that thereby his people may be distinguished. He was going to teach the people about Jesus Christ. This is the name through which spiritual power can be obtained.

Benjamin's teachings to the people, found in the second through sixth chapters of Mosiah, constituted a **Spiritual Power Formula** for the people. Benjamin was able to do this for his people because they had prepared themselves by "...being a diligent people in keeping the commandments of the Lord". First, however, Benjamin transferred the power of the kingdom and the Record to his son, Mosiah:

> And it came to pass that after king Benjamin had made an end of these sayings to his son, that he **gave him charge concerning all the affairs of the kingdom;**

And moreover, **he also gave him charge concerning the Records, which were engraven on the plates of brass and also the plates of Nephi...**(*BofM: Mosiah* 1:15-16; emphasis added).

Among the definitions Noah Webster ascribed to the verb form of the word **charge** are these:

> 5) to lay on or impose as a task;
> 8) to entrust;
> 13) to lay on, give, communicate, as an order, command or earnest request...to exhort;
> 14) to give directions to; to instruct authoritatively.

Webster's definitions of the noun **charge** include:

> 6) the person and thing committed to another's custody, care or management; a trust.[42]

Probably all of these definitions are related to the meaning of *charge* as used by Benjamin above.

As Benjamin gave the Records to Mosiah, his actions fulfilled exactly what L. Ron Hubbard would later call the third step in the **Power Formula**: "...get it [the Record] into the hands of the guy who is going to take care of it...". (see The Steps of The Power Formula noted at the beginning of this book).

We know that these records contained the scriptural account of the plates of brass, and the small plates of Nephi. The large plates had been kept by the Nephite kings, and they contained an account of "...the reigns..." of these kings. In these large plates of Nephi, Mosiah would have a Record, or **Power Formula** for his position as king. In contrast the small plates of Nephi, and the plates of brass would be a Record or **Power Formula** for spiritual leadership, and for being the scriptural record keeper.

When king Benjamin called the people together near the end of his life, he wanted the people to hear his final address as king. The people responded in great numbers. In fact, so many came that Benjamin had a tower built so that he could be seen and heard by as many of them as possible.

Next, Benjamin fulfilled the fourth step of the **Power Formula** for Mosiah. Benjamin did all he could to help Mosiah succeed, by declaring openly the transfer of authority to him. Benjamin also admonished his people to support Mosiah. These people were promised national prosperity and security, if they "...keep the commandments of my son..."

> And moreover, I say unto you [all the people there gathered] that I have caused that ye should assemble yourselves together, that I might declare unto you **that I can no longer be your teacher, nor your king;**
>
> For even at this time, my whole frame doth trembleexceedingly while attempting to speak unto you; but the **Lord God** doth support me, and hath suffered [or allowed] me that I should speak unto you, and **hath commanded me that I should declare unto you this day, that my son Mosiah is a king and a ruler over you.**
>
> And now, my brethren, **I would that ye should do as ye have hitherto done. As ye have kept my commandments, and also the commandments of my father, and have prospered, and have been kept from falling into the hands of your enemies, even so if ye shall keep the commandments of my son, or the commandments of God which shall be delivered unto you by him, ye shall prosper in the land, and your enemies shall have no power over you** (*BofM: Mosiah* 2:29-31; emphasis added).

Benjamin did something, which was very unusual for a king. He actually gave up Power before his death! His concern was for the welfare of his people. When Benjamin realized that he was no longer physically able to handle the responsibility of being the king, he willingly transferred Power. Please note also how he was following the Lord's direction in doing so (see verse 30).

Benjamin Did All He Could to Make the Post of King Occupiable for Mosiah

Benjamin left no doubt in anyone's mind about who was to be the next king and spiritual leader. In addition, Benjamin let his people know that it was the "...Lord God...'who commanded Benjamin to name'...Mosiah a king, and a ruler over you." He also explained to the people that if they would follow Mosiah, that they would continue in a state of prosperity and security, which is the **Condition of National Power**.

His promise was that if the people would "...keep the commandments of my son, or the commandments of God which shall be delivered unto you by him, ye shall prosper in the land, and your enemies shall have no power over you." Thus the Nephites could maintain **their condition of security and prosperity by following the correct principles that they would receive from Mosiah[2]. In this way they would enjoy a continuation of the success that their nation had experienced by following the inspired leadership of Benjamin.**

Please also note that Benjamin reminded the people of how they had prospered by following his father, Mosiah[1]. **Benjamin, was in fact, showing his people that they had already witnessed a successful Power Change, from**

king Mosiah to himself. Also, if they would support the new king, another successful Power Change, with its blessings of prosperity and survival, would occur.

> ...As ye have kept my commandments, **and also the commandments of my father, and have prospered,** and have been **kept from falling into the hands of your enemies, even so if ye shall keep the commandments of my son,** or the commandments of God which shall be delivered unto you by him, ye shall prosper in the land, and your enemies shall have no power over you (*BofM: Mosiah* 2:31; emphasis added).

King Benjamin took care of the **Power Transfer** of the government by telling his people that his son, Mosiah, was going to be the new king, and thereby fulfilling the last step in the **Power Formula** completely in terms of the governmental status. As mentioned earlier, Benjamin had also given his son "charge" of the Records. **Benjamin now had completed two separate Power Formulas for his son Mosiah^2!**

How Did King Benjamin Know How to Use Perfectly the Principles of the Power Formula?

Please consider this question: If someone had handed Benjamin a list of the steps of the **Power Formula**, and asked him to use it to transfer power to his successor, could he have done it any better than this? L. Ron Hubbard did not discover and write these steps of the **Power** and **Power Change Formulas** until the mid 1900s. How was Benjamin so wise as to be able to do this so well, and do it nearly 2000 years before L. Ron Hubbard wrote of these **Formulas**?

The answer to this question is that his knowledge came by revelation, and from the teachings and example (**Power Formula**) of his earthly father. Benjamin was inspired, and so is *The Book of Mormon* Record, which tells his story.
Survival and Salvation

Before we review Benjamin's third **Power Formula**, which was to give **Spiritual Power** to his people, we will first consider **survival** and **salvation**. L. Ron Hubbard wrote about **survival** and how important **survival** is as a motivation in our lives. He wrote:

> The goal of life can be considered to be infinite survival. Man as a life form can be demonstrated to obey in all his actions and purposes the one command "Survive!"[43].

Did you note that Mr. Hubbard used the term "infinite survival" in this quotation? Please compare survival to salvation. **Salvation is much like survival**. Salvation is sometimes thought to refer to success in the life hereafter. However, salvation also refers to success in this life. Therefore, **salvation is survival in the highest form, or infinite survival.**

In 1843, the prophet, Joseph Smith, said this about salvation:

> **Salvation means a man's being placed beyond the power of all his enemies.**[44]

Here, the prophet considered salvation in terms of obtaining sufficient power to insure that all enemies who intend to cause harm, would be unable to do so. Survival can also be thought of in this light. The enemies, which the prophet was referring to here, are those who would do harm to our **Spiritual Condition**, as well as those who seek to harm our bodies.

Joseph Smith also taught that none of God's laws or commandments deal **only** with temporal or physical matters. Everything the Lord teaches or commands us has an effect upon our spiritual well being. Even those commandments, which may seem to be dealing with physical matters affect our **Spiritual Condition**.

This means that those **actions, which would promote spiritual salvation will also promote physical survival.** The prophet Joseph Smith taught:

> ...All things, whatsoever God in his infinite wisdom has seen fit and proper to reveal to us while we are dwelling in mortality in regard to our mortal bodies are revealed to us in the abstract and independent...of this mortal tabernacle or our body, **but are revealed to our spirits precisely as though we had no bodies at all. And those revelations, which will save our spirits, will save our bodies.** God reveals them to us in view of no eternal disillusion of the body of the tabernacle.
>
> ...When his commandments teach us, it is a view of eternity; for **we are looked upon by God as though we were in eternity.** God dwells in eternity, and does not view things as we do.[45]

In teaching these ideas, the Prophet Joseph Smith was probably drawing upon revealed information which he had received from "...the voice of Jesus Christ, your Redeemer...". The following revelation is part of a compilation of revelations received by Joseph Smith and other prophets of the Church. This compilation is called the ***The Doctrine and Covenants of the Church of Jesus Christ of Latter-day Saints***. In one of these revelations, the Savior taught:

> Wherefore, verily I say unto you that **all things unto me are spiritual, and not at any time have I given unto you a law which was**

temporal; neither any man, nor the children of men; neither Adam, your father, whom I created.

Behold, I gave unto him that he should be an agent unto himself; and I gave unto him commandment, but no temporal commandment gave I unto him, for **my commandments are spiritual; they are not natural nor temporal,** neither carnal nor sensual (*D&C* 29:34-35; emphasis added).

Salvation is More Important Than Survival

Every one of the Lord's teachings, laws or commandments is concerned with our physical survival as well as spiritual salvation. However, the Lord's main concern is with our **Spiritual Condition**. Our **temporal condition**, or the condition of our bodies, is **temporary**. Our **Spiritual Condition** will be the determining factor in our **eternal** lives. In nearly every case, if we make choices that will better our **Spiritual Condition** (**salvation**), we will better our physical **survival** as well.

A few individuals may be forced to make "either/or" choices between salvation (**Spiritual Condition** or **Ethics**) and the survival of their bodies. Joseph Smith commented on the relative importance of our physical survival as compared to our **Spiritual Condition**. This quote comes from a letter Joseph wrote while being unjustly imprisoned. In this letter, he made it clear that the survival of the body was of much less importance than the salvation of the soul:

> Dear brethren, do not think that our hearts faint, as though some strange thing had happened unto us, for we have seen and been assured of all these things beforehand, and have an assurance of a better hope than that of our persecutors. Therefore, God hath made broad our shoulders for the burden. We glory in our tribulation, because **we know that God is with us, that He is our friend, and that He will save our souls. We do not care for [worry about] them that can kill the body; they cannot harm our souls. We ask no favors at the hands of mobs, nor of the world, nor of the devil,** nor his emissaries, the dissenters and those who lie and make falsehoods to take away our lives. **We have never dissembled, nor will we for the sake of our lives.**[46]

During this same period, the saints, or members of the Church in Missouri, were being persecuted and killed. Later in this letter, Joseph Smith, referring to the Savior's teachings, encouraged these people to:

> **...hold on even until death: for "he that seeks to save his life**

THE POWER FORMULAS

shall lose it; and he that loses his life for my sake and the Gospel's shall find it," saith Jesus Christ (see *NewT: Matthew* 10:39; 16:24; *Luke* 17:33; emphasis added).

As noted in this citation from the New Testament, Jesus Christ also taught that salvation was more important than survival.

The Source of Salvation and Survival

Next, we shall look at Benjamin's teachings, which were in effect a **Power Formula** to his people. In a part of these instructions, Benjamin gave this unambiguous declaration of the source of our salvation.

> And moreover, I say unto you, that **there shall be no other name given nor any other way nor means whereby salvation can come unto the children of men, only in and through the name of Christ, the Lord Omnipotent** (*BofM: Mosiah* 3:17; emphasis added).

Benjamin also taught that their Source of our salvation is also the Source of our survival.

> Yea, and moreover I say unto you, that **if this highly favored people of the Lord should fall into transgression, and become a wicked and an adulterous people**, that the Lord will deliver them up, that thereby they become weak like unto their brethren; and **he will no more preserve them by his matchless and marvelous power, as he has hitherto preserved our fathers.**
> For I say unto you, that **if he had not extended his arm in the preservation of our fathers they must have fallen into the hands of the Lamanites, and become victims** to their hatred (*BofM: Mosiah* 1:13-14; emphasis added).

Benjamin's Third Power Formula, the Spiritual Preparation of His People, Step 1

The remainder of Benjamin's final address, was directed to his people. These teachings, found in Mosiah Chapters 2 through 5 combined with his instructions to his sons, constitute Benjamin's contribution to the Record. Benjamin wanted each person to find salvation, and he wanted their nation to survive. Through teaching them, Benjamin maintained contact with his people to the very end of his life. This fulfilled the action described in **Power Formula**, Step 1: "don't disconnect..."[48].

Benjamin Completed the Actions, Like Those of the Power Formula Steps 2 and 3, for His People

When the people gathered to hear king Benjamin's last sermon, he took actions, which also correspond to all of the other steps of the **Power Formula**, for them. As previously mentioned, the king had a tower built so that he could be seen and heard by the multitude.

Even though Benjamin spoke from a tower, many people could not hear his address. So what did Benjamin do? You guessed it! **He had his words written down and distributed to the people.** In having his words written and passed to the people, he carried out the same actions later described by L. Ron Hubbard in the **Power Formula**, steps 2 and 3. In review, the 2nd and 3rd steps of the **Power Formula** are to:

> [2]**...make a record,** write the thing up and [3] get it into the hands of the guy who is going to take care of it...[49].

Here is Mormon's account of how Benjamin had a record of his speech made and distributed to his people:

> For the multitude being so great that king Benjamin could not teach them all within the walls of the temple, therefore he caused a tower to be erected that thereby the people might hear the words which he should speak unto them.
>
> And it came to pass that he began to speak to his people from the tower; and they could not all hear his words because of the greatness of the multitude; therefore **he caused that his words which he spake should be written and sent forth among those that were not under the sound of his voice, that they may also receive his words** (*BofM: Mosiah* 2:7-8; emphasis added).

Here we see that Benjamin is doing the second and the third steps of the **Power Formula** for his people. He did so by **making a record**, and getting it into their hands. We have already reviewed how Benjamin was dedicated to maintaining contact with his people. In doing so, Benjamin also fulfilled what we now know as Step 1 of the **Power Formula**, by not "disconnecting".

The key to Benjamin's teachings was a great prophesy of the Savior's birth. This prophecy came hundreds of years before Jesus Christ was born. Like the Old Testament Prophets, such as Moses and Isaiah, Benjamin knew of Jesus Christ, and prophesied of his ministry. Benjamin's message was that Christ would be the source of man's salvation.

Benjamin Also Taught the People About Spiritual Rebirth, Which is Equivalent to a Spiritual Non Existence Formula

Among the wonderful truths Benjamin taught from the tower was a description of the changes that occur in us as we experience spiritual rebirth. This is perhaps the finest definition anywhere of what it means to be spiritually reborn:

> For the natural man is an enemy to God, and has been from the fall of Adam, and will be, forever and ever, unless he **yields to the enticings of the Holy Spirit, and putteth off the natural man and becometh a saint through the atonement of Christ the Lord, and becometh as a child, submissive, meek, humble, patient, full of love,** willing to submit to all things which the Lord seeth fit to inflict upon him, **even as a child doth submit to his father** (*BofM: Mosiah* 3:19; emphasis added).

"No More Disposition to Do Evil." The Power of Jesus Christ to Turn Us From Our Iniquities and to Cure Addiction

As we read Benjamin's parting address, we can see that the **Spiritual Condition** of these people was elevated by this experience of listening to their great leader. They were determined to live righteously. At the conclusion of his address, king Benjamin used another technique that L. Ron Hubbard advocated. Benjamin surveyed this people to see if his words had produced the desired effect. We will consider these things later.

Those who had heard king Benjamin, reported that they had experienced a mighty change in their hearts. As a result of this change, they could say: "**we have no more disposition to do evil, but to do good continually.**"

> And now, it came to pass that when king Benjamin had thus spoken to his people, he sent among them, desiring to know of his people if they believed the words, which he had spoken unto them.
> And they all cried with one voice, saying:
> Yea, we believe all the words which thou hast spoken unto us; and also, we know of their surety and truth, because of **the Spirit of the Lord Omnipotent, which has wrought a mighty change in us, or in our hearts, that we have no more disposition to do evil, but to do good continually** (*BofM: Mosiah* 5:1-2; emphasis added).

This verse contains a description of how the Lord can cure us of our addictions. This occurs as the Spirit of the Lord produces a "mighty change in us, or in our hearts." The result of this process is a change of **disposition**, from being inclined to seek for, and to do, evil to being inclined to seek for and to do good.

It is important that we understand the meaning of the word *heart* as used in the scriptures. Regarding the meaning of *heart,* Elder Dallin H. Oaks of the Council of the Twelve Apostles of the The Church of Jesus Christ of Latter-day Saints has written:

> *Heart* is often used to identify the extent to which one is receptive to the message of the gospel. Nephi said, "The Lord...did visit me and did soften my heart that I did believe" (*BofM: 1 Nephi 2:16*)... *Heart* can also refer to motive, desires, and attitudes...[50]

Among the definitions given by Noah Webster for the word "heart" are these:

> 4) the seat of the affections and passions, as of love, joy, grief, enmity, courage, pleasure...
> 6) the seat of the understanding; as an understanding *heart*...
> 7) the seat of the will; hence, secret purposes, intentions or designs...
> 11) disposition of mind...[51]

When the scriptures speak of this change of heart, they mean much more than just changing our thinking. As the Lord's spirit changes a person who has repented and exercised faith in Jesus Christ, it is truly "...a mighty change...". This change affects our motives, desires, and attitudes. It also changes our affection, understanding, will, courage, disposition, conscience, strength and our power to produce. In short, **a change of heart is a change in our emotional make up, and the main or most important change which occurs, is in our ability to feel and express love to others**.

This change of heart is mighty, for it helps us in every important area of our lives. Perhaps this is why the apostle Paul, and the prophet Alma, described those who have received this change as being "...a new creature" (*NewT: 2 Corinthians 5: 17; BofM: Mosiah* 27:26).

This change is so profound that is like a new birth. Those who receive this change of heart are "...born again" (*NewT: John* 3:3). Alma taught that this change of heart is essential, if we are to "...inherit the kingdom of God."

> And the Lord said unto me: Marvel not that **all mankind, yea, men and women**, all nations, kindreds, tongues and people, **must be born again**; yea, born of God, changed from their carnal and fallen state, **to a state of righteousness, being redeemed of God, becoming His sons and daughters;**
>
> **And thus they become new creatures; and unless they do this, they can in no wise inherit the kingdom of God** (*BofM: Mosiah* 27:25-26).

THE POWER FORMULAS

Benjamin Demonstrated and Taught His People the Principle of Not Disconnecting From Others

King Benjamin had already shown his people an example of not disconnecting as he worked among them. He also warned his people to avoid pride and greed. He knew that if the people began to view themselves as being better than their fellowmen, this would lead to a separation from those whom they considered to be below them. This disconnection would be a violation of the first principle of the **Power Formula**.

Benjamin was actually teaching his people the first principle of what we now call the Power Formula. These verses also have a great application to our lives and to the conditions we face in the world today.

> And also, ye yourselves will succor [give sustenance helper aid to] those that stand in need of your succor; **ye will administer of your substance unto him that standeth in need; and ye will not suffer [allow] that the beggar putteth up his petition to you in vain, and turn him out to perish.**
>
> **Perhaps thou shalt say: The man has brought upon himself his misery; therefore I will stay my hand, and will not give unto him of my food, nor import unto him of my substance that he may not suffer, for his punishments are just.** But I say unto you, O man, **whosoever doeth this the same hath great cause to repent;** and except he repenteth of that which he hath done he perisheth forever, and hath no interest in the kingdom of God.
>
> **For behold, are we not all beggars? Do we not all depend upon the same Being, even God, for all the substance which we have...**(*BofM: Mosiah* 4:16-19; emphasis added).

Benjamin Surveyed His People

As noted above, when Benjamin had finished his speaking, he took a **survey** of the people (see *BofM: Mosiah* 5:1). It is interesting to note that L. Ron Hubbard emphasized the importance of surveys. He wrote this regarding the importance of surveying as a help to an organization:

> ...You have to inspect and survey and gather data and set operating and primary targets before you can set production targets...[52]

In the verse below, please note how Benjamin gathered data and surveyed his people.

BENJAMIN'S RECORD

And now, it came to pass that **when king Benjamin had thus spoken to his people, he sent among them, desiring to know of his people if they believed the words which he had spoken unto them. And they all cried with one voice, saying; Yea, we believe all the words, which thou hast spoken unto us...**(*BofM: Mosiah* 5:1; emphasis added).

When he had finished taking this survey, Benjamin **followed up** by getting the names of those who accepted his teachings. Also, he officially handed over the reigns of the government to Mosiah.

And now, king Benjamin thought it was expedient, **after having finished speaking to the people, that he should take the names of all those who had entered into a covenant with God to keep his commandments.**
And it came to pass that there was not one soul, except it were little children, but who had entered into the covenant and had taken upon them the name of Christ.
And again, it came to pass that w**hen king Benjamin had made an end of all these things, and had consecrated his son Mosiah to be a ruler and a king over his people, and had given him all the charges concerning the kingdom, and also had appointed priests to teach the people, that thereby they might hear and know the commandments of God, and to stir them up in remembrance of the oath which they had made**, he dismissed the multitude, and they returned, everyone, according to their families, to their own houses (*BofM: Mosiah* 6:1-3; emphasis added).

King Benjamin Used Actions Like Step 4 of the Power Formula, to Help His People

Here Benjamin **continued a successful action he had instituted years before.** He appointed teachers to help the people. He instituted this action back when his nation was in danger (see BofM: Words of Mormon 12-18). Benjamin wanted the people to be reminded by those teachers of the changes in their lives, and of the promises, which they had made.

In this way, he could help the people to achieve the highest possible **Spiritual Condition**, even after he was gone! This is the spirit of the **Power Formula**, Step 4, which is:

Do all you can to make the post occupiable.[53]

THE POWER FORMULAS

The Connection Between Individual Integrity and National Security

The Book of Mormon also teaches that the condition and security of a nation is directly tied to the **Spiritual Condition** of that nation's people. **The survival potential of a government parallels the survival potential of the people it represents.** Near the end of the book of Mosiah, Benjamin's son and successor, king Mosiah recorded:

> Now it is not common that the voice of the people desireth anything contrary to that which is right; but is **common for the lesser part of the people to desire that which is not right;** therefore this shall ye observe and make it your law — **to do your business by the voice of the people.**
>
> **And if the time comes that the voice of the people doth choose iniquity, then is the time that the judgments of God will come upon you; yea, then is the time he will visit you with great destruction even as he has hitherto visited this land** (*BofM: Mosiah* 29:26-27; emphasis added).

Here we see an association between the condition of the people and their government. If the moral and **Spiritual Condition** of the majority of the people is low, then their nation is in danger of destruction. This is a common theme of warning in *The Book of Mormon*.

The Book of Mormon record tells of two separate nations, which did not survive because of the moral and spiritual decline of their people. These nations were the Nephites, and an earlier nation known as the Jaredites. We will review the stories of the decline of these nations later.

Benjamin was wise enough to realize that in order for his nation to survive and prosper, the nation would need to have leaders, **and** followers, who would make the right choices. **Therefore, Benjamin did the Power Formula with both his successor king, and with the people.**

A Summary of King Benjamin's Power Formula-Like Actions

Again, let's ask ourselves, could anyone have done the **Power Formula** better? Benjamin, not only used actions like the **Power Formula** perfectly, **he did it on three different levels!** In review, Benjamin's three **Power Formulas** were:

1) A **Power Formula** for Mosiah^2, to prepare him to be the next Record Keeper, and spiritual leader of these people;
2) A **Power Formula** for Mosiah^2 to become the next king;

3) A **Power Formula** for all people of his kingdom, and for we who would later read his record, showing the path to eternal life.

As we conclude our consideration of king Benjamin, perhaps you will agree with me that he was one of the greatest mortal kings to ever rule. Benjamin finished his instructions, his **Power Formula**, by organizing the people so that they could succeed as well without him as they had with him. This is the true spirit of the **Power Formula**.

The Book of Mormon is the finest example of the application of the principles taught in the **Power Formulas**. It contains the inspired examples, teachings and record of Benjamin, and many others like him. This is why ***The Book of Mormon*** **is the Lord's Power Formula for our lives!**

THE POWER FORMULAS

Chapter 7

King Mosiah² And Power Change

King Mosiah² and the Power Change Formula

With the exception of the relationship between Jesus Christ and God the Father, the story of Benjamin is, without comparison, an example of the use of principles like those of the **Power** and **Power Change Formulas. Just as Benjamin gave us the perfect example of using principles like those of the Power Formula, his son and successor, Mosiah, gave us the perfect example of using the principles like those found in the Power Change Formula.** These verses demonstrate how Mosiah exactly followed his father Benjamin's successful actions:

> And Mosiah began to reign in his father's stead. And he began to reign in the thirtieth year of his age, making in the whole, about four hundred and seventy-six years from the time that Lehi left Jerusalem.
> And king Benjamin lived three years and he died.
> And it came to pass that **king Mosiah did walk in the ways of the Lord, and did observe his judgments and his statutes, and did keep his commandments in all things whatsoever he commanded him** [Power Change as the spiritual leader accomplished].
> **And king Mosiah did cause his people that they should till the earth.**
> **And he also, himself, did till the earth, that thereby he might not become burdensome to his people, that he might do according to that which his father had done in all things** [Power Change as king accomplished]. And there was no contention among all his people for the space of three years (*BofM: Mosiah* 6:4-7; emphasis added).

King Mosiah² and The Power Change Formula

Anyone who is familiar with L. Ron Hubbard's **Conditions Formulas** will recognize in these verses that king Mosiah carried out the actions of the **Power Change Formula** perfectly. This is L. Ron Hubbard's **Power Change Formula:**

What a song it is to inherit a successful pair of boots. There is nothing to it, just step in the boots and don't bother to walk. If it was in a normal state of operation, which it normally would have been for anybody to have been promoted out of it, you just **don't change anything.** So, anybody wants anything signed that your predecessor wouldn't sign, don't sign it. Keep your eyes open, learn the ropes, and depending on how big the organization is, after a certain time, see how it is running and run it as a normal operating condition if it is not in anything but its normal operating condition. If you **go through the exact same routine that your predecessor went through,** sign nothing that he wouldn't sign, **don't change a single order, look through the papers that have all been issued at that period of time, these are the orders that are extent,** and get as busy as a devil just enforcing those orders, **and your operation will increase and increase** (emphasis added).[54]

Although this description of the **Power Change Formula** is directed toward the transfer of power within a business, the principle can be applied to all types of leadership. The essence of the **Power Change Formula** is found in the phrases: "... don't change anything" and "go through the exact same routine that your predecessor went through."

Mosiah by "... doing according to that which his father had done in all things," picked right up where his father, Benjamin, had left off. From the beginning, he maintained the governmental **Condition of Power**, which his father had achieved. In fact, Mosiah started **Power Formula** for his people by not disconnecting from them. He used his father's example on how to not disconnect:

> **He also did till the earth, that thereby he might not become burdensome to his people, that he might do according to that which his father had done in all things** (*BofM: Mosiah* 6:7; emphasis added).

This is the action that Benjamin had taught Mosiah by example. You will recall that Benjamin said:

> **And even I, myself, have labored with mine own hands that I might serve you, and that ye should not be laden with taxes, and that there should nothing come upon you which was grievous to be borne—and of all these things which I have spoken, ye yourselves are witnesses this day** (*BofM: Mosiah* 2:14; emphasis added).

RECORD OF MOSIAH²

Mosiah² Followed Benjamin's Example of Leadership

As we might predict, Mosiah's reign was also very successful. This was because he led the people in the same way as Benjamin had led them. Near the end of his reign, Mosiah spoke about his father Benjamin's success as king. He explained that the success of his own leadership was due to following the laws, which, he had learned from Benjamin and "our fathers".

> Therefore, if it were possible that you could have just men to be your kings, who would establish the laws of God, and judge this people according to his commandments, yea, if ye could have men for your kings who would do even as my father **Benjamin** did for this people— I say unto you, if this could always be the case then it would be expedient that ye should always have kings to rule over you.
> **And even I myself have labored with all the power and faculties which I have possessed, to teach you the commandments of God, and to establish peace throughout the land, that there should be no wars nor contentions, no stealing, nor plundering, nor murdering, nor any manner of iniquity;**
> And whosoever has committed iniquity, him have I punished according to the crime which he has committed, **according to the law which has been given to us by our fathers** (*BofM: Mosiah* 29:13-15; emphasis added).

Mosiah continued the successful actions of his father Benjamin. This included teaching his people the commandments of the God. In doing so, he was successful in "establishing peace throughout the land." He also enforced the law, as his father had done (see *BofM: Mosiah* 2:13). This is also another example of the principle of the **Power Change Formula**: "...don't change anything...".

Mosiah Warned of Tyranny by Unrighteous Kings

Mosiah was also wise enough to know that some kings would not lead according to true principles. The resultant poor leadership would cause great suffering and catastrophe. Some of the people in his kingdom had learned this lesson the hard way.

These people had lived in a Nephite colony. One of their kings was a man named Noah. He was an unrighteous and tyrannical leader. Because of his "leadership", his people ended up in subjugation to their aggressive Lamanite neighbors.

Eventually, these people escaped their captors, with the help of the Lord, and of a new and inspired leader named Alma. This group of people joined Mosiah's people

THE POWER FORMULAS

and Alma later became the leader of the Church (see *BofM: Mosiah* 9 and 10).

The experience of these people may have helped Mosiah decide to change the type of government among the Nephites. Mosiah made these observations about the risks of being united by kings:

> Now I say unto you, that **because all men are not just, it is not expedient that ye should have a king or kings to rule over you.**
>
> For behold, **how much iniquity doth one wicked king cause to be committed, yea, and what great destruction!**
>
> And behold, now I say unto you, **ye cannot dethrone an iniquitous king save it be through much contention, and the shedding of much blood.**
>
> **For behold, he has his friends in iniquity, and he keepeth his guards about him; and he teareth up the laws of those who have reigned in righteousness before him; and he trampleth under his feet the commandments of God;**
>
> **And he enacteth laws,** and sendeth them forth among his people, yea, laws **after the manner of his own wickedness;** and whosoever doth not obey his laws he causeth to be destroyed; and **whosoever doth rebel against him he will send his armies against them to war, and if he can he will destroy them;** and thus an unrighteous king doth pervert the ways of all righteousness.
>
> And now behold I say unto you, it is not expedient that such abominations should come upon you (*BofM: Mosiah* 29:16-17, 21-24; emphasis added).

How Wicked Kings, Tyrants and Despots Violate the Principles of The Power Formula

We can see many evidences, throughout history and in our own time, of the results of tyrannies, as described by Mosiah. Each of these autocratic and suppressive examples of tyrannical leadership is also an example of violation of the principles of the **Power Formula**. This is because these leaders have definitely 'disconnected' from their people, thus using actions opposite to the 1st step of the Power Formula, which is: "...don't disconnect...".

Mosiah Passed the Responsibility of Spiritual Leadership to Alma, Thereby Producing a Separation Between Church and State

The size of the Nephite nation was increasing as a result of probable national population growth and the addition of Alma's people. Mosiah must had realized that he would no longer be able to both lead their government and administer to the spiritual needs of all the people. Therefore, he gave Alma authority to organize

RECORD OF MOSIAH²

churches or local congregations among the people.

And it came to pass that king **Mosiah granted unto Alma that he might establish churches** throughout all the land of Zarahemla; and **gave him power to ordain priests and teachers over every church.**
  Now this was done because there were so many people that they could not all be governed by one teacher; neither could they all hear the word of God in one assembly;
  Therefore they did assemble themselves together in different bodies, being called churches; every church having their priests and their teachers, and **every priest preaching the word according as it was delivered to him by the mouth of Alma** [thus following the principle of **Power Change** in their position as spiritual teachers and also leaders of these people].
  And they were called the people of God. And the Lord did pour out his Spirit upon them, and they were blessed, and prospered in the land (*BofM: Mosiah* 25: 19-21, 24).

King Mosiah Made a Separation Between Church and State Law

Mosiah also made a separation between the laws of the land the Church law. This is demonstrated by an incident when Alma was required to administer Church discipline to members who had committed serious sins. Please note how Mosiah declined judgment in these cases. He directed Alma to assume his role as spiritual leader, and judge in the Church.

...and it became expedient that those who committed sin, that were in the Church, should be admonished by the Church.
  And it came to pass that they were brought before the priests, and delivered up unto the priests by the teachers; and the priests brought them before Alma, who was the high priest.
  Now king Mosiah had given Alma the authority over the Church. And it came to pass that Alma did not know concerning them; but there were many witnesses against them; yea, the people stood and testified of their iniquity in abundance.
  Now there had not any such thing happened before in the Church; therefore Alma was troubled in his spirit, and he caused that they should be brought before the king.
  And he said unto the king: Behold, here are many whom we have brought before thee, who are accused of their brethren; yea, and they have been taken in divers iniquities. **And they do not repent of their iniquities;** therefore we have brought them before thee, that thou

mayest judge them according to their crimes.

But king Mosiah said unto Alma: Behold, I judge them not; therefore I deliver them into thy hands to be judged (*BofM: Mosiah* 26:6-12; emphasis added).

Note also that Alma did not try to discipline those who were not members of the Church. Mormon commented that "...it became expedient that those who committed sin **who were in the Church, should be admonished by the Church**" (*BofM: Mosiah* 26:6; emphasis added).

Later, when those who had disassociated themselves from the Church began to persecute Church members, this became a civil matter. At this point Mosiah, acting in his role as the authority of the state, intervened.

> And now it came to pass that the persecutions, which, were inflicted on the Church by the unbelievers became so great that the Church began to murmur, and complain to their leaders concerning the matter; and they **did complain to Alma. And Alma laid the case before their king, Mosiah.** And Mosiah consulted with his priests.
>
> And it came to pass that king Mosiah sent a proclamation throughout the land round about that there should not any unbeliever persecute any of those who belonged to the Church of God.
>
> And **there was a strict command throughout all the Churches that there should be no persecutions among them, that there should be an equality among all men** (*BofM: Mosiah* 27:1, 3; emphasis added).

We can see that this law applied to both those inside and outside the Church, for there was "equality among all men." This is a remarkable example of separation between Church and state. Also, Mosiah taught the principle of "equality among all". This principle was also recognized by the writer of our Declaration of Independence when he wrote that "...all men are created equal".

Mosiah Turned the Power of Government Over to His People

Mosiah proposed a solution to the problems presented by iniquitous kings. **He decided to pass the "hat" of government to the people instead of another king.**

> And now I desire that this inequality should be no more in this land, especially among this my people; **but I desire that this land be a land of liberty, and every man may enjoy his rights and privileges alike**, so long as the Lord sees fit that we may live and inherit the land, yea, even as long as any of our posterity remains upon the face of the land.
>
> And now it came to pass, after king Mosiah had sent these things

forth among the people they were convinced of the truth of his words.

Therefore **they relinquished their desires for a king**, and became exceedingly anxious that every man should have an equal chance throughout all the land; yea, and e**very man expressed a willingness to answer for his own sins.**

Therefore, it came to pass that they assembled themselves together in bodies throughout the land, to **cast in their voices concerning who should be their judges, to judge them according to the law** which had been given them; and **they were exceedingly rejoiced because of the liberty which had been granted unto them** (*BofM: Mosiah* 29:32, 37-39; emphasis added).

Because of the inspired leadership of three righteous kings, Mosiah[1], Benjamin and Mosiah[2], these people were prepared to accept the burdens, responsibilities, and the opportunities of self-government. Also, note the feeling of joy, which they experienced with their increased liberty.

The people elected judges who led the people, "according to the law which had been given." Mosiah was the last Nephite king. In effect, this was a **Power Formula** for governmental leadership, from king Mosiah to his people. He communicated, and thereby did not disconnect with them. This was **Power Formula Step 1**.

Mosiah must have also made a record and gotten it into the hands of the people, because it was written: "...after king Mosiah had sent these things among the people, they were convinced of the truth of his words" (see *Mosiah* 29:37). These are **Power Formula Steps 2** and **3**. Then, Mosiah did all he could to empower the people of his nation. The actions described above can be described by this phrase: **The Power Formula Step 4** Now you can see why Mosiah, equaled or perhaps exceeded, the accomplishments of his father, king Benjamin.

Important Events in the Life of Mosiah

Mosiah's life was not without severe trial and difficulty. Probably chief among his trials was the rebellion of his own sons. We will recount their story later. Also, we will review their eventual conversion and the great missionary work of these sons of Mosiah.

Another highlight in Mosiah[2]'s life was the translation of the book of Ether from 24 ancient plates. His people found the records of a previous nation, and Mosiah translated the plates. This group had crossed the ocean shortly after the time of the Tower of Babel. We will examine an abridgment of these plates later.

Mosiah also preserved his people from the Lamanite aggression. Benjamin's prophecy proved to be true. For in following Mosiah's inspired and righteous leadership, the people found that their enemies had "no power" over them (see *BofM: Mosiah* 2:21).

Mosiah Maintained Peace, Increased Freedom and Became Beloved by His People

We might ask, how did his people feel about Mosiah who was their king, their teacher and their Record Keeper? Mormon, as he abridged or edited the plates containing Mosiah's Record, gave us this insight into how the people felt about Mosiah and his reign as their king.

> **And they did wax [grow] strong in love towards Mosiah; yea, they did esteem him more than any other man**; for they did not look upon him as a tyrant who was seeking for gain, yea, for that lucre which doth corrupt the soul; for **he had not exacted riches of them, neither had he delighted in the shedding of blood; but he had established peace in the land, and he had granted unto his people that they should be delivered from all manner of bondage; therefore they did esteem him, yea, exceedingly, beyond measure** (*BofM: Mosiah* 29:40; emphasis added).

This verse shows that, like Benjamin, Mosiah refused to become disconnected from his people. Also, this verse gives testimony that throughout his life, Mosiah followed the teachings of both his earthly father Benjamin and his Father in Heaven. In doing so, Mosiah accomplished what we would now recognize as the **Power Change Formula** for both of his areas of responsibility.

Mosiah Used Principles Like the Power and Power Change Formulas, on Three Levels

Just as his father, Benjamin, passed two hats to his son: 1) King, and 2) Record Keeper/Spiritual Leader, so Mosiah followed both **Power Formulas**, thereby accomplishing **Power Change** on two levels.

> And it came to pass that **king Mosiah did walk in the ways of the Lord, and did observe his judgments and his statutes, and did keep his commandments in all things whatsoever he commanded him** [**Power Change** as spiritual leader].
> And king Mosiah did cause his people that they should till the earth. **And he also, himself, did till the earth, that thereby he might not become burdensome to his people, that he might do according to that which his father had done in all things.** And there was no con-

tention among all his people for the space of three years [**Power Change** as king] (*BofM: Mosiah* 6:6-7 emphasis added).

We know that Mosiah also did **Power Change** as Record Keeper. This is evidenced by the fact that we have Mormon's abridgement of his record, The Book of Mosiah.

When his reign was over, Mosiah used actions like the **Power Formula** on three levels. These three levels were:

1) With Alma[1] as spiritual leader of the Church (see *BofM: Mosiah* 25:19, 26:6);
2) With the people to transfer the power to govern (see *Mosiah* 29:32-39);
3) With Alma's son, Alma[2] as the next Record Keeper (see *Mosiah* 28:20).

It seems obvious, that *The Book of Mormon* must be an inspired work. If Joseph Smith, in the 1820s, made up *The Book of Mormon,* how could he have incorporated in it the same management principles that L. Ron Hubbard taught over a century later?

Because it claims to be the word of God, it is extremely important to approach *The Book of Mormon* seriously. This is especially true for those who already accept the validity of the **Power Formulas**.

Very few of the world's books claim to contain the words of God. It is unlikely that any other book claiming to be scripture, demonstrates examples of the **Power Formulas** principles as well as *The Book of Mormon*. For this reason, and many others, *The Book of Mormon* merits your thoughtful and prayerful consideration.

A Challenge

Here is a challenge to those who understand and accept these **Conditions Formulas**: Please read *The Book of Mormon* from cover to cover. You will be able to follow the conditions of the people of *The Book of Mormon,* and you will see the principles like the **Conditions Formulas** being applied by these people.

Please look for yourself, because there are still more of these correlations to be found. When you have done so, ask yourself this question: Could a man in his mid twenties, and with only the equivalent of a fifth grade school education, fabricate *The Book of Mormon*? You might also ask yourself, could you or could anyone fabricate such a book and yet include so many true principles? If you answer these questions "no" then you are obliged, as a searcher after truth, to accept this challenge and read *The Book of Mormon* with an open heart.

Mosiah[2] and Benjamin Were Probably the Greatest Kings Who Have Yet Ruled on the Earth

In Mosiah, we see perhaps the only other king in history who ruled as well as Benjamin. What other example do we have of a king who protected his people, taught them the truth, worked along side them, made a separation between church and state and even led his people gently into a representative form of government?

The reasons for Mosiah's success were his devotion to following the ways of his wonderful earthly father, Benjamin, and to keeping the commandments of his Heavenly Father. How pleased both of his fathers must be with Mosiah! May our lives also give our Father in Heaven reason to rejoice, as we follow His Son, Jesus Christ, who is the "King of Kings" (*NewT: l Timothy* 6:15).

Chapter 8

Alma² and the Sons of Mosiah: From the Spiritual Conditions of Confusion and Treason, to Conditions of Spiritual Power

Following a very successful reign, which included a change in type of government from a kingdom to a representative style government: Mosiah² passed the Records on to Alma². Regarding this transfer of the Record, Mormon wrote:

> And now, as I said unto you, that after king Mosiah had done these things, **he took the plates of brass, and all the things which he had kept, and conferred them upon Alma,** who was the son of Alma; yea, **all the Records,** and also the interpreters, and **conferred them upon him, and commanded him that he should keep and preserve them, and also keep a record of the people, handing them down from one generation to another, even as they had been handed down from the time that Lehi left Jerusalem** (*BofM: Mosiah* 28:20; emphasis added).

This is beginning to sound very familiar, isn't it?

When the Record Keeper, transferred custody of the Record to the new Record Keeper, he trained his successor by using principles exactly like those of the **Power** and **Power Change Formulas**.

Please take a minute to look at the above quotation to see how many principles like those of these formulas you can identify in this *one verse* of *The Book of Mormon*. Here are the similar principles:

1) **Power Formula, Step 1, "don't' disconnect...**"[55] Mosiah maintained communication with his people, and with Alma. Otherwise, Mosiah would not have been able to communicate with his successor, nor complete the transfer of the Records;

2) **Power Formula, Step 2, "...make a record..."**[56] Mosiah took all of the previous Records, and added his own teachings. He also made a translation of the twenty-four Jaredite plates to make a Record for his successors, and for his people;

3) **Power Formula, Step 3, "... get it [the Record) into the hands of the

guy who is going to take care of it..."[57] Mosiah conferred "all the Records..." upon Alma^2;

4) **Power Formula, Step 4,** "do all you can to make the post occupiable..."[58] Mosiah gave instructions to Alma^2 about what he should do with the Record. Alma was to preserve the old Records, add new writings to it, and hand it "...down from one generation to another."

5) **Power Change Formula, "...don't change anything..."**[59] In giving the above instructions, Mosiah taught Alma to do the things which the Record Keepers had been doing "...from the time Lehi left Jerusalem." Alma was to follow a series of Record Keepers who each followed their predecessor. This is the principle of **Power Change** perfected.

Where else in world literature do we have such an example of the extensive and **recurring** use of principles like those of the **Power Formula** and **Power Change Formulas**? Could we find a better example of these principles being used in any other book? It is doubtful that these principles could be better illustrated.

Because *The Book of Mormon* preceded L. Ron Hubbard, and his **Power Formulas** by over 100 years, there can be only one explanation of how these truths are contained in *The Book of Mormon*—**it must be the word of God**! Joseph Smith wrote this about *The Book of Mormon*:

> Concerning this **record** the Prophet Joseph Smith said: **"I told the brethren that *The Book of Mormon* was the most correct of any book on earth**, and the keystone of our religion, and a **man could get nearer to God by abiding it precepts, than by any other book"** (*BofM: Introduction page*; emphasis added).

The Book of Mormon is also **"the most correct of any book on earth," when it comes to the illustration of the principles of the Power and Power Change Formulas!**

Alma^2 Assumed Three "Hats" of Responsibility

The Alma who was given the Records was not the same Alma whom Mosiah had earlier made the head of the Church. The first Alma (or Alma^1) died at nearly the same time as Mosiah. It was Alma's son, Alma^2, who was given the plates along with the instructions above, by Mosiah.

Alma^2 added much to the Record. In fact, nearly one fifth of *The Book of Mormon* comes from Mormon's abridgment of Alma's writings.

Being the Record Keeper was not Alma's^2 only responsibility. He was also the first elected leader, or chief judge, of their new government. In addition, he became the leader of the Church.

> Therefore, it came to pass that they assembled themselves together in bodies throughout the land, **to cast in their voices concerning who should be their judges**, to judge them according to the law which had been given them; and they were exceedingly rejoiced because of the liberty which had been granted unto them.
> And it came to pass that they did appoint judges to rule over them, or to judge them according to the law; and this they did throughout all the land.
> And it came to pass that **Alma was appointed to be the first chief judge, he being also the high priest**, his father having conferred the office upon him, and having **given him the charge concerning all the affairs of the Church** (*BofM: Mosiah* 29:39-42; emphasis added).

Alma² was given:

1) The power of the government, by the vote of the people;
2) The power of Church leadership by the Lord, and through His prophet, Alma¹
3) The responsibility of keeping the sacred Record, by the Lord, through Mosiah.

Alma² did **Power Change** with both king Mosiah, and with his father Alma¹, **who was the high priest** over the church. How did Alma respond to these great challenges? He responded in the same way Mosiah and the others before him had responded. According to Mormon:

> **And now it came to pass that Alma did walk in the ways of the Lord, and he did keep his commandments, and he did judge righteous judgments; and there was continual peace through the land.**
> And thus commenced the reign of the judges throughout all the land of Zarahemla, among all the people who were called the Nephites; and **Alma was the first and chief judge** (*BofM: Mosiah* 29:43-44; emphasis added)

Like Mosiah, Alma² did **Power Change** on three levels. First, as noted previously, he became the new Record Keeper. In doing so, he preserved the Record and added to it. Second, as leader of the Church, he "did walk in the ways of the Lord and he did keep his commandments..." Third, as leader of the government, or chief judge, "he did judge righteous judgments."

In making these "righteous judgments" Alma relied upon the laws, which he had received from Mosiah.

> Now it came to pass that in the first year of the reign of the judges over the people of Nephi, from this time forward, **king Mosiah** having gone the way of all the earth, having warred a good warfare, walking uprightly before God, leaving none to reign in his stead; nevertheless he **had established laws**, and they were acknowledged by the people; therefore they were obliged to abide by the laws which he [Mosiah] had made (*BofM: Alma* 1:1; emphasis added).

Alma^2 followed the policies or laws of his predecessor, Mosiah. Thereby, he gave another example of using the action now called **Power Change**! Mosiah had followed the policies and leadership style of his father, Benjamin (see Mosiah 6:4-7). Benjamin had been following the example of his father as well (see Mosiah 2:31).

Thus, we see four successive applications of actions like the **Power** and **Power Change Formulas** among these government leaders and Record Keepers.

Power Formula, Power Change Cycles of Action

These Record Keepers used a cycle of action. First they would follow their predecessor's example and instructions, which is equivalent to doing **Power Change**. Next, they would prepare and help their successor, and give him the Record, which is equivalent to doing a **Power Formula** for them.

These cycles of **Power** and **Power Change Formula-** like actions are in addition to the cycles discussed previously for the Small Plate Record Keepers. From Nephi through Amaleki these cycles were repeated by nine Record Keepers. Therefore, we have already received thirteen examples of these cycles in *The Book of Mormon*. Also, this cycle would be repeated ten more times!

In the Appendix, all of these record transfers and **Power Formula**-like actions are compiled for easy review.

Alma's Life was an Example of the Savior's Power to Improve Our Condition

Prior to the time that Alma^2 accepted these heavy responsibilities, a great change had occurred in his life. Alma wasn't always an example of one who followed the Lord and His prophets. At one time, Alma^2 was in a very low **Spiritual Condition**. L. Ron Hubbard identified a number of conditions below the constructive starting point of **Non Existence**. He called these conditions: **Liability,**

Doubt, Enemy, Treason and **Confusion**.⁶⁰

We can find evidence in Mosiah and Alma's records of how Alma was once in these low conditions. We can also see how he was raised from these depths eventually to a condition of spiritual power. In doing so, Alma² used actions like those of these lower **Conditions Formulas**.

Alma² and his companions, the sons of king Mosiah, had, at one time, secretly tried to destroy the Church. This action was evidence of their **Condition of Treason** to their fathers, to their Church, and to their God. These young men then experienced a miraculous conversion similar to the conversion of Paul in *The New Testament*. We shall pick up their story at the point of Alma's² spiritual rebirth, which is the **Spiritual Non Existence Formula**.

Being Born of God Equals Doing a Non Existence Formula for Our Spiritual Condition

Being born of God is coming out of a **Non Existence Condition in our relationship to our Father in Heaven**. The **Non Existence Formula** is a set of actions to be taken by a person just beginning in a new position. These actions also apply to our spiritual growth. Without following these steps, we cannot achieve our full spiritual growth potential. **Spiritual growth is any change in awareness, emotion and action, which makes someone more like God.**

In fact, completing the **Spiritual Non-Existence Formula**, or being "born of God" is the make/break point of our eternal progression! This means that starting with this "rebirth" condition, and in all conditions above it, our correct actions will produce true spiritual growth. **Also, as our spiritual condition improves, so will our emotional tone level.**

If we are below this **Spiritual Non Existence** level in our relationship to our Heavenly Father, we are headed in the direction of decreased spirituality and decreased emotional tone, until we take corrective action..

As we fall in Condition, our survival potential is decreased. If we decide to not take corrective action, we will eventually become permanently separated from our Heavenly Father. This separation is called spiritual death. However, our spirits cannot actually cease to exist.

Spiritual rebirth is so crucial to our eternal development, that we will consider this formula in detail. Here is L. Ron Hubbard's definition for the **Non Existence Formula**:

1) Find a comm [communication] line;
2) Make yourself known;
3) Discover what is needed and/or wanted;
4) Do produce and/or present it.⁶¹

Spiritual Non Existence Formula, Step 1, Finding a Communication Line to God and to His Representatives

"Find a comm [communication] line" means to find a way to establish communication. Who is it that we are to be in communication with? In our occupations, we need to communicate with our supervisors, and fellow workers. This is so that we can learn what is expected of us.

In order for us to do the **Non Existence Formula** as a Child of God, we need to establish communication with our Father in Heaven. This can be done through personal prayer, and through communicating with someone who has communication with Him. A key word in Step 1 of the **Non Existence Formula** is **"find"**. **This word implies desire and action on our part.**

"No Man is an Island No Man Stands Alone"

Some people think that they have no need of help and guidance from other people, or from a church. They say something like this, "I can pray to God myself and don't need a church." This statement is half true. We can and should pray to God. However, the scriptures indicate that Jesus Christ organized His followers into a Church for their mutual benefit.

God works through His children to help each of us. By leading us to His Church, He leads us to the channel through which we can receive His guidance through receiving the gift of the Holy Ghost.

The Power and Authority of God, Which is His Priesthood, is Found in His Church

The power to bestow the gift of the Holy Ghost is called the Priesthood. This authority was given by the Savior Jesus Christ to his apostles. The Savior has called new apostles in modern times. These men have also been given His priesthood power and authority.

These apostles, under inspiration, call and ordain others to hold this power. Those holding this power can bestow the gift of the Holy Ghost by a blessing given by the laying on of hands upon those who have exercised their faith in Jesus Christ by repenting and being baptized. This is also how the Gift of the Holy Ghost was bestowed in the New Testament (see *Acts* 19:1-6).

The gift of the Holy Ghost is the right to have the guidance of this member of the Godhead with us always. This is the comm [communication] line with God that we are looking for.

It is also through His Church, which contains His priesthood authority, that the ordinances of salvation and exaltation are available to God's children. These include ordinances which are available only in God's temples.

THE RECORD OF ALMA²

How the Lord Teaches Us

Each member of the Church of Jesus Christ is given the gift of the Holy Ghost. This gift means that, if they live worthily, they can **"always have His Spirit (the Holy Ghost) to be with them"** (see *BofM: Moroni* 3:4; emphasis added). This gift entitles one to more consistent and deeper communication with God through His messenger, the Holy Ghost.

Initial and Preliminary Inspiration From the Holy Ghost Leads People to The Savior and His Church Where They Can Receive the Gift of The Holy Ghost

The influence of His Spirit leads us to His representatives, and His Church on the earth. Those who follow these promptings will eventually receive the gift of the Holy Ghost. This was the case with Paul in *The New Testament*.

Paul, or Saul, as he was called prior to his conversion, had been persecuting the members of the Lord's Church. Paul was visited by the resurrected Savior as he walked along the road to Damascus. This was a dramatic and powerful vision. During His communication with Paul, the Lord directed him to go to Damascus. The Savior also told Paul that "…it shall be told thee what thou must do" (*NewT: Acts* 9:6).

When he arrived in Damascus, Paul was met by a member of the Lord's Church, named Ananias. The Lord could have taught Paul Himself, yet He did not do so. He blessed Ananias's life by inspiring him to teach Paul. When we have established personal communication with the Lord, through receiving the gift of the Holy Ghost, what is He going to teach us? Will the Lord reveal His entire plan and all truth to each of us individually? Probably not. The Lord uses His children to teach one another. One reason He operates this way is to give us opportunities for growth and service.

One last question before we move on: Which church should we look for, as we try to find communication with the Lord's spirit? As the apostle Paul was later speaking to new members of the Church he gave us the insight into how Christ had organized His Church. Please note how Paul characterized the foundation and cornerstone of the Lord's Church.

> Now therefore **ye are no more strangers and foreigners, but fellow citizens with the saints, and of the household of God**;
> And are built upon the **foundation of the apostles and prophets, Jesus Christ himself being the chief corner stone**;
> In whom all the building fitly framed together groweth unto an holy temple in the Lord (*NewT: Ephesians* 2:19-21; emphasis added).

The Church of Jesus Christ will be a Church which has Jesus Christ as its chief cornerstone, and living apostles and prophets as its foundation. There is such a Church on earth today. This Church also publishes the Lord's **Power Formula**: *The Book of Mormon*.

Jesus Christ has established this Church upon the earth in these "latter" or last days prior to His return to the earth. He has named His Church **The Church of Jesus Christ of Latter-day Saints** (see *D&C* 115:1-5). The word "saints" means members of the Church of Jesus Christ (see *NewT: Ephesians* 2:19-21).

The Spiritual Non Existence Formula, Step 2: Making Ourselves Known to God

The second step is to **"make yourself known..."**[62]. The verb "make" indicates that we must first have a desire to learn, and we must **act** by establishing communication. It is impossible to do **Spiritual Existence** in a passive way. We cannot just sit and wait for someone to come by and teach us what we need to know. Indeed, the very word communication means to:

> ...**interchange thoughts or knowledge**; good understanding between men...**to impart reciprocally**.[63]

Communication requires the exchange of information between, two or more, intelligent beings. We make ourselves known to the Lord and His servants, as we communicate with them.

Spiritual Non Existence Formula, Step 3: Discovering What God Wants Us to Do

This brings us to Step 3 of the **Non Existence Formula**: "discover what is needed and/or wanted..."[64] For our **Spiritual Condition**, this question is, "what does God want me to do and be?" In order to find the answer to this questions, we must ask. Also, if we want a correct answer, **we must ask someone who knows**.

Scriptural Examples of Finding Out What the Lord Wants Us to Do

How should one ask this most important question? Here are some examples of how this question has been asked in the scriptures:

1) **"Lord what wilt thou have me do...?"** (Paul asking Jesus on the road to Damascus; *NewT: Acts* 9:1-6; emphasis added);
2) **"Good master, what shall I do that I may inherit eternal life?"** ("A cer-

tain ruler" who was "very rich" asking Jesus; *NewT: Luke* 18:18-22; emphasis added);

3) **"...what shall these my brethren do...?** They had cast us out because of our exceeding poverty; and **we have no place to worship our God; and behold, what shall we do?"** (The "foremost" or spokesman for a large group of Nephites; *BofM: Alma* 32:1-6; emphasis added);

4) **"Now, when they heard this [Peter's testimony of Christ] they were pricked in their hearts and said unto Peter and the rest of the apostles, men and brethren, what shall we do?"** (This question was asked by "Jews, devout men, and of all nations under heaven," who had gathered to Jerusalem for the Feast of Pentecost; *NewT: Acts* 2:5, 37-38; emphasis added).

5) **"...the king said: what shall I do that I may have this eternal life of which thou hast spoken. Yea, what shall I do that I may be born of God?"** (A Lamanite king asked this question of a missionary named Aaron; *BofM: Alma* 22:15; emphasis added).

These are five examples from the scriptures of people trying to discover what is needed and/or wanted of them by their Father in Heaven.

What the Lord Wants Us to Do

Now we will look at the answer to this question of "what shall we do"? In Acts, Chapter 2 the apostle Peter had been teaching "the multitude" of "devout men...of all nations" which "came together and were amazed, because every man heard the disciples speaking to them in their own language" (see *NewT: Acts* 2:5).

This event occurred after Christ's crucifixion and resurrection. Peter's address to these people was preceded by a great miracle. The Holy Spirit had been given to Christ's followers, and these disciples were able to teach those who had come to Jerusalem from many foreign lands for the Feast of Pentecost.

The disciples were able to speak in "other tongues," **so that** "every man heard them speak in his own language". Thus, we see that the gift of tongues was given for the **purpose** of teaching the Gospel to those who spoke another language or "tongue".

Peter gave his personal witness of the Savior:

> Therefore let all the house of Israel know assuredly, that God hath made that same Jesus, whom ye have crucified, both Lord and Christ (*NewT: Acts* 2:36).

THE POWER FORMULAS

The next verse is a perfect example of someone using principles like those taught in the **Non Existence Formula**. These people first established "...a comm line..." by speaking to Peter. Next, they wanted to find out what was needed and wanted, so they asked, "what shall we do?" Here is their question, and Peter's answer:

> Now when they heard this, they were pricked in their heart, and said unto Peter and to the rest of the apostles, **Men and brethren, what shall we do?**
>
> Then Peter said unto them, **Repent, and be baptized everyone of you in the name of Jesus Christ for the remission of sins, and ye shall receive the gift of the Holy Ghost** (*NewT: Acts* 2:37-38; emphasis added).

The First Thing God Wants Us to Do: Have Faith in Him, and in His Son, Jesus Christ

Above, Peter answered the question of what is needed and wanted of us by our Father. Peter could sense that the Holy Spirit had inspired these people or "pricked" their hearts. These men were beginning to have faith in Jesus Christ. **Peter also knew that they were developing faith because of their communication to him.** They established a communication line, made themselves known, and asked, "What shall we do?"

Peter answered: "Repent and be baptized everyone of you in the name of Jesus Christ, for the remission of sins, and ye shall receive the gift of the Holy Ghost."

Spiritual Non Existence Formula, Step 4: Doing What God Wants Us to Do

We will now review the response of these "devout men," to Peter's instructions:

> **Then they that gladly received his word were baptized:** and the same day there were added unto them about three thousand souls.
>
> **And they continued steadfastly in the apostles' doctrine and fellowship, and in breaking of bread [regularly worshipping with other members of the Church and receiving the sacrament of the Lord's supper], and in prayers** (*NewT: Acts* 2:41-42; emphasis added).

THE RECORD OF ALMA²

How The Father, The Son and The Holy Ghost Help Us

This help He offers us has a name. It is called **Grace**. Also, His help or Grace in our lives is how He completes the final step of the **Power Formula** for us. The Father, Son and Holy Spirit work in perfect unity to "...do all [They] can to help [us] occupy the post", of becoming like They are.

The Father helps us through giving life to our spirits, putting His great plan of happiness and progression into effect, and by calling and training Jesus Christ to be our Savior.

Jesus Christ, the Son of God the Father, gives us His Gospel, which contains God's **Power Formulas** for us. He has caused His prophets to prepare Records of His teachings or **Power Formula**, and He taught us how to live by His words and His example. He has also made it possible for us to overcome the obstacles of sin and death through His atoning sacrifice for us, and through the universal resurrection He has put into effect.

The Holy Spirit helps us by testifying to us of the reality of the Father and the Son, and of the truth of Their teachings, and prompting us to repent when we sin. The Holy Ghost also changes our hearts so we can eventually think, do, and be as They are. He also serves as our guide along the path back to the presence of the Savior and our Heavenly Parents.

Paul had asked a similar question: "Lord, what will thou have me do?" After exercising faith in Jesus Christ, and repenting, Paul received a similar answer: "...be baptised, and wash away thy sins..."(*NewT, Acts* 9:16; 22:16).

The Second Thing God Wants Us to Do: "...Repent..."
Repentance and Remission of Sin, a Cycle of Action

L. Ron Hubbard taught us an interesting concept called the **Cycle of Action**. He felt that any action is made up of three parts. Here is the definition he gave for a **Cycle of Action**:

...start, change and stop compromise a cycle of action.[66]

The action of repentance can be considered from this viewpoint. True repentance **starts** with **recognition** that we have sinned, and a feeling of **responsibility and remorse for our sins.** Next, repentance involves **change** as we confess our sins, forsake them, and when possible, make restitution for the damage we have caused.

Unfortunately, many people consider this to be the end point of this cycle. However, the **change** part of repentance is not complete without baptism and receiving the Gift of Holy Ghost. The final step in the repentance **Cycle of Action** is to **stop committing sin and replace sinful behaviors with doing things that are good, and thus helpful**, to ourselves and to others. Without stopping harmful thoughts words and behaviors, *and* replacing these with helpful thoughts, words, and behaviors, the cycle of remission of sins is incomplete.

The "R"s of Repentance (How to Repent) or The Lord's 12-Step Program

1. **Recognize** that you have sinned, and your **Spiritual Condition** is in **Ruin.** Accept **Responsibility** for your sins, see the need for change, and demand improvement in your life. With the addition of **Faith** in Jesus Christ as our Savior, your sins can be forgiven and the burden of sin can be removed. This awareness then moves us to **Hope**.

2. Feel **Remorse** for the harm that your sins have caused to others, and to yourself. Also feel sorrow for the suffering and sadness your sins have caused the Father and the Son to feel.

3. **Release** negative feelings towards others who have sinned against you, by forgiving them, even if they have not repented and sought your forgiveness. **Replace** feelings of hatred with feelings of love for these people.

4. **Request** forgiveness through confessing your sins to God, and to those you have harmed.

5. Make **Restitution** whenever possible.

6. **Resist** the circumstances that led up to your sins, so these temptations can be avoided in the future. Also, pray for God's help to do so. **Refuse** to again place yourself in the path of temptation. I other words, don't "...enter into temptation" (*BofM 3 Nephi* 18:8).

7. **Refrain** from committing those sins again, and pray for God to help you do so.

8. **Rebirth** through being baptised and receiving the Gift of the Holy Ghost, which changes your disposition to commit sins.

9. **Remission** (forgiveness of sins), occurs as a result of Faith in Jesus Christ, and the steps above.

10. **Release** the guilt and remorse because of your sins, by also forgiving yourself. This includes replacing self hatred with love of self.

11. **Replace** harmful thoughts and actions with helpful and good thoughts and actions, such as reading the scriptures, praying, attending church and loving and serving others.

12. **Rejoice** in gratitude to the Father, and to His Son Jesus Christ, that your sins are forgiven (see *BofM Alma* 36:1-22).

"No Unclean Thing Can Dwell With God"

The Lord places great importance upon our becoming clean, meaning free from sin. You may want to refer to a few of these Biblical and Book of Mormon references on this topic (see *OldT: Leviticus* 16:30, *Job* 15:3, 17:4, *Psalms* 24:4; *NewT: Luke* 11:49, *John* 13:16).

For some, it is difficult to understand why the Lord requires us to be clean. Often, it is even difficult for us to acknowledge that we are not clean. An Old Testament Proverb speaks of this tendency.

> All the ways of a man are clean in his own eyes; but the LORD weigheth the spirits. (*OldT: Proverbs* 16:2).

The Book of Mormon prophet Nephi commented on why we need to become clean.

> Wherefore, if ye have sought to do wickedly in the days of your probation, then ye are found unclean before the judgment-seat of God; and **no unclean thing can dwell with God;** wherefore, ye must be cast off forever.
> And the Holy Ghost giveth authority that I should speak these things, and deny them not (*BofM: 1 Nephi* 10:21-22; emphasis added).

Repentance without remission of sin through baptism and being sanctified by the reception of the **Holy Ghost cannot fulfill these purposes of repentance. In order to be complete, the cycle of repentance and remission of sin requires: faith in Jesus Christ, repentance, baptism by immersion for the remission of sin and receiving the Gift of the Holy Ghost.**

Also, repentance is a principle, and Cycle of Action that we need to use every day of our lives. It is the process of personal quality control, and "course correction" on the straight and narrow path that leads us back to our Heavenly Parents.

The Third Thing God Wants Us to Do: "...Be Baptized..."

After **faith in Jesus Christ** has started to grow in our hearts, and we have repented, the third thing He wants us to do is to be **baptized**.

The Purpose and Symbolism of Baptism

Peter taught in the verse above that the purpose of baptism was "...for the remission of sins...".

The mode of baptism was also very significant. Paul taught that baptism is symbolic of the death and burial of our natural man, followed by a spiritual rebirth. Only baptism by **immersion** fits the symbolic meaning of baptism. Here is Paul's analogy:

> Know ye not, that so many of us as were baptized into Jesus Christ were baptized into his death?
>
> **Therefore we are buried with him by baptism into death: that like as Christ was raised up** from the dead by the glory of the Father, even so **we also should walk in newness of life**.
>
> For **if we have been planted together in the likeness of his death, we shall be also in the likeness of his resurrection:**
>
> Knowing this, that our **old man [the natural man] is crucified with him**, that the body of sin might be destroyed, that henceforth we should not serve sin (*NewT: Romans* 6:3-6; emphasis added).

Being Born of God Means Starting to Become Like God

In the verses cited earlier, Peter taught the purpose of baptism is "...for the remission of sins...".

When a person is cleansed of their sins, it is through the power of Jesus Christ. How did Jesus obtain such **power**? He obtained this power through His lineage as God's son, through His intelligence, through His obedience, and through His perfect love for the Father and for every person. He really was, and is, the very best of our Father's spirit children.

These qualities prepared and led Him to make His atoning sacrifice. During this sacrifice He suffered the consequences of our sins. In this way, He obtained the right, and the ability, to forgive or provided "...remission of..." our sins.

Jesus Christ was obedient to His Father because of His perfect love for Him. He was willing to suffer the spiritual and physical agony of the Atonement and death because of His perfect love for us.

We Need to be Born of God, or Born Again, Because We All Have Experienced "Spiritual Death"

The effects of sin are separation from our Father in Heaven, unhappiness, and eventually, physical death. As mentioned previously, when we are separated from our Father in Heaven, this is defined as "spiritual death". Each of us was separated from Him when we left His presence by coming to this earth.

Also, each of us have committed sins. As we sin, we disconnect ourselves from God's influence in our lives. This is a spiritual separation from God.

We have all experienced "spiritual death", and this is why we need to re-establish our physical and spiritual proximity and relationship to our Heavenly Father.

THE RECORD OF ALMA²

How Jesus Christ Overcame Physical Death for Everyone

Jesus Christ has overcome death for all of us. We shall all be resurrected because of Him (see *NewT: 1 Corinthians* 15:21-22). The resurrection is a free gift from the Savior to all of God's children. Through His Book of Mormon prophet, Alma², God has taught that this resurrection will be complete and perfect:

> The soul shall be restored to the body, and the body to the soul; yea, and every limb and joint shall be restored to its body; yea, even a hair of the head shall not be lost; but all things shall be restored to their proper and perfect frame (*BofM, Alma* 40:23).

This resurrection will occur for all who have lived upon the earth, and we don't have to nor can we do anything to merit it.

Jesus Christ Has Made it Possible for Us to Overcome Spiritual Death, and be Reunited With Our Father in Heaven

In addition to overcoming physical death for us, Jesus Christ also has the power to free us from the effects of our sins through remitting or forgiving these sins, thus restoring our connection to the Father.

However, **His power to free us from the effects of our sins cannot operate in our lives until we: exercise faith in Him by repenting of our sins, being baptized, and receiving the gift of the Holy Ghost**. As we do these things, the Holy Ghost changes our very nature by producing a mighty change of our hearts, so that we have "...no more disposition to evil, but to do good continually..." (see *BofM, Mosiah* 5:1-2). This is what it means to be born again, or born of God.

The Savior Set Our Goal

Receiving the gift of the Holy Ghost allows us to consistently have the inspiration of this member of the Godhead to guide us on our great journey through life. The Savior set the goal of our journey in His Sermon On The Mount. Here is the goal that the Jesus Christ set for us:

> **Be ye therefore perfect, even as your Father which is in Heaven is perfect** (*NewT: Matthew* 5:48; emphasis added).

With the help of the Holy Ghost, we can follow the Savior's example until we are eventually "made perfect" by the power of Jesus Christ (see *BofM: Moroni* 10:32-33).

In terms of the **Conditions Formulas**, this process of becoming like our Father in Heaven is a process of doing Spiritual **Super Power Change** by following the example of Jesus Christ. This topic is the major theme of **Super Power**. We are far from this goal at present, but we at least know how the process starts. Becoming like our Father in Heaven and Jesus Christ can only occur with Their help.

We need to understand that this process of becoming perfect, like our Father in Heaven, starts with **faith in Jesus Christ, repentance, baptism and receiving the gift of the Holy Ghost.** These four actions represent the answer to the question of finding out "...what is needed and wanted..." of us by the Lord (see reference below).

These men took the same action as described in the last step of the **Non Existence Formula**. **After discovering what is needed and wanted, they did indeed "do, produce and/or present it".**[65]

Those who accepted Peter's message completed the process of choosing to have faith in Jesus Christ, and repenting, which had started, as they were touched in their hearts while listening to Peter. **The way that their repentance was completed was through baptism "...for the remission of sins... [and through receiving]... the gift of the Holy Ghost".** After baptism, these men endured, or persisted on the course they had started on as, **"...they continued steadfastly in the apostles' doctrine and fellowship"** (see *New T. Acts* 2:37-39).

Thus, having **faith in Jesus Christ, repenting, being baptized for the remission of sins and receiving the gift of the Holy Ghost is the Spiritual Non Existence Formula.** This is how we can be born again, or born of God. **This is how, and when, we start to become like God.**

Alma, an Example of Coming Out of Spiritual Non Existence

Now, we will return to the account of Alma. In his youth Alma[2] sought to destroy the Church, which his father, Alma[1] led. His life was changed after he was made aware of his true condition by an angel.

Years later, as Alma[2] prepared to turn over the Records to his son Helaman, he recounted his experience with the angel. He taught Helaman how he, Alma[2], had been "born of the Spirit." Here is his account of what led up to this rebirth:

> And now, O my son Helaman, behold, thou art in thy youth, and therefore, I beseech of thee that thou wilt hear my words and learn of me; for I do know that whosoever shall put their trust in God shall be supported in their trials, and their troubles, and their afflictions, and shall be lifted up at the last day.
>
> And I would not that ye think that I know of myself—not of the temporal but of the spiritual, not of the carnal mind but of God.
>
> **Now, behold, I say unto you, if I had not been born of God I should not have known these things; but God has, by the mouth**

of his holy angel, made these things known unto me, not of any worthiness of myself;

For I went about with the sons of Mosiah, seeking to destroy the Church of God; but behold, God sent his holy angel to stop us by the way.

And behold, he spake unto us, as it were the voice of thunder, and the whole earth did tremble beneath our feet; and we all fell to the earth, for the fear of the Lord came upon us.

But behold, the voice said unto me: Arise. And I arose and stood up, and beheld the angel.

And he said unto me: If thou wilt **of thyself** be destroyed, seek no more to destroy the Church of God.

And it came to pass that I fell to the earth; and it was for the space of three days and three nights that I could not open my mouth, neither had I the use of my limbs.

And the angel spake more things unto me, which were heard by my brethren, but I did not hear them; for when I heard the words if thou wilt be destroyed of thyself, seek no more to destroy the Church of God—**I was struck with such great fear and amazement lest perhaps I should be destroyed,** that I fell to the earth and I did hear no more.

But I was racked with eternal torment, for **my soul was harrowed up to the greatest degree and racked with all my sins.**

Yea, I did remember all my sins and iniquities, for which I was tormented with the pains of hell; yea, I saw that I had rebelled against my God, and that I had not kept his holy commandments.

Yea, and I had murdered many of his children, or rather led them away unto destruction; yea, and in fine so great had been my iniquities, that the very thought of coming into the presence of my God did rack my soul with inexpressible horror.

Oh, thought I, that I could be banished and become extinct both soul and body, that I might not be brought to stand in the presence of my God, to be judged of my deeds.

And now, for three days and for three nights **was I racked, even with the pains of a damned soul** (*BofM: Alma* 36:3-16; emphasis added).

Although Alma "...Experienced the Pains of Hell..." Prior to His Spiritual Rebirth, the Outcome was Positive, Because He was Now Aware That His Life Was in Power

Alma gave us a great insight into his painful feelings of regret, sorrow, and of the fear that came upon him as he recognized sins. He also became aware of his precarious situation. Alma now understood that his life was in **Ruin**. Even though Alma was feeling horrible, this was actually an improvement in his **Spiritual Condition**, because he was now aware of how low he had allowed to fall.

In the final book of this series, *Super Power*, we will review another of L. Ron Hubbard's important conditions: **The Awareness Side**. There, we will see that learning that we are in **Ruin** allows us to take the next steps up this scale to **Need of Change**, **Demand for Improvement**, and **Hope** (see also *What is Scientology?* Bridge Publications, Los Angeles, 1993 and 1998, pages 170, 172 and 180).

Also, increasing awareness is related to progression in other ways. These include becoming aware of our **Spiritual Condition**, so we can improve, with God's help. Also, a key to improved **Spiritual Condition** is becoming aware of our sins, recognizing our sins, and understanding the harm we have caused to ourselves and to others—first step in repentance.

After recognizing that we have sinned comes the feelings of remorse and regret. Alma described the remorse he felt as being like a lake of "fire and brimstone." Our Father **does not** send us to an actual lake of fire and brimstone, however, this simile gives a very strong mental picture of how we will feel at the time of judgment if we have chosen not to avail ourselves of the blessings of repentance and forgiveness.

Earlier, King Benjamin had taught how we can avoid this sad state if we will yield

> ... to the enticing of the Holy Spirit, and putteth off the natural man and becometh a saint through the atonement of Christ... (*BofM: Mosiah* 3:19).

King Benjamin also taught about the eventual condition of those who **knowingly** choose to not repent:

> And now I have spoken the words which the Lord God hath commanded me.
>
> And thus saith the Lord: They shall stand as a bright testimony against this people, at the judgment day; whereof they shall be judged, every man according to his works, whether they be good, or whether they be evil.
>
> And if they be evil they are consigned to an awful view of their own guilt and abominations, which doth cause them to shrink from the presence of the Lord into a state of misery and endless torment, from whence they can no more return; therefore they have drunk damnation to their own souls.
>
> *And their torment* is as a lake of fire and brimstone, whose flames are unquenchable, and whose smoke ascendeth up forever and ever. Thus hath the Lord commanded me. Amen (*BofM: Mosiah* 3:23, 24, 25, 27; emphasis added).

THE RECORD OF ALMA²

Alma's Feelings of Fear, Despair and Joy are Internal Evidences of the Truthfulness of *The Book of Mormon*

Alma's description was very graphic. Many of us can confirm, from our own experience how one feels when we are totally aware of our low condition. We are never more alone than when we are cut off from our Father. When this happens, we lose the guidance, reassurance and comfort He provides for us through the Holy Spirit.

Even on the earth we can feel a portion of the despair which **"...cometh because of iniquity...,"** and which comes when we feel that we **"...have no hope..."** (*BofM: Moroni* 10:22; emphasis added).

This is what hell feels like, or as Alma stated it, these are the "... pains of hell." To those who have experienced even a portion of this torment, you know from Alma's words that he was telling the truth. This is an internal testimony of the truthfulness of *The Book of Mormon*. These feelings expressed by Alma could have only been described by a man who had actually experienced them!

These feelings cannot be mistaken or forgotten once experienced. Nor will we ever forget the wonderful and contrasting feeling of joy that fills our hearts as we begin to believe in Jesus Christ, repent and are forgiven and have regained hope. Listen as Alma gives his account of the great change of emotional tone that he experienced as his heart was changed by faith, repentance, forgiveness, and by receiving the Holy Ghost.

> And it came to pass that as I was thus racked with torment, while I was harrowed up by the memory of my many sins, behold, **I remembered also to have heard my father prophesy unto the people concerning the coming of one Jesus Christ, a Son of God, to atone for the sins of the world.**
>
> Now, as my mind caught hold upon this thought, I cried within my heart: **O Jesus, thou Son of God, have mercy on me**, who am in the gall of bitterness, and am encircled about by the everlasting chains of death.
>
> And now, behold, when I thought this, **I could remember my pains no more**; yea, I was harrowed up by the memory of my sins no more.
>
> **And oh, what joy, and what marvelous light I did behold;** yea, my soul was filled with joy as exceeding as was my pain!
>
> Yea, I say unto you, my son, that there could be nothing be nothing so exquisite ["...to the highest degree; extreme..."][67] and so bitter as were my pains. Yea, and again I say unto you, my son, that on the other hand, **there can be nothing so exquisite and sweet as was my joy.**
>
> Yea, me thought I saw, even as our father Lehi saw, God sitting upon his throne, surrounded with numberless concourses of angels, in the attitude of singing and praising their God; yea, and **my soul did long to be there.**

But behold, my limbs did receive their strength again, and **I stood upon my feet, and did manifest unto the people that I had been born of God** (*BofM: Alma* 36:17-23; emphasis added).

Isn't it amazing how Alma's emotional tone changed so profoundly, and so quickly!

Alma's Remarkable Change in Emotional Tone

L. Ron Hubbard wrote of a series of emotional tones that people go through. Here is a portion of what he wrote about the Tone Scale:

> A person in apathy rises through various tones. These tones are quite uniform; one follows the next and people always come up through these tones, one after the other. These are the tones of affinity, and the tone scale of Dn and Scn [Dianetics and Scientology] is probably the best possible way of predicting what is going to happen next or what a person actually will do. The tone scale starts well below apathy. In other words, a person is feeling no emotion about a subject at all. On many subjects and problems people are actually well below apathy. There the tone scale starts, on utter, dead null far below death itself. Going up into improved tones one encounters the level of body death, apathy, grief, fear, anger, antagonism, boredom, enthusiasm and serenity, in that order. There are many stops between these tones. A person in grief, when his tone improves feels fear. A person in fear, when his tone improves feels anger.[68]

The Tone Scale

This is a short and incomplete version of L. Ron Hubbard's Tone Scale. The numbers assigned are for comparison within the scale only:

4.0	Eagerness, Exhilaration	1.1	Covert Hostility
3.5	Strong Interest	1.0	Fear
3.0	Conservation	0.5	Grief
2.5	Boredom	0.2	Apathy
2.0	Antagonism	0.0	Death [69]
1.5	Anger		

As Alma realized that he had been in a **Condition of Treason** to both his earthly and Heavenly Fathers, his Emotional Tone went down to the depths of Fear and Grief, and to the point that he even wished for death. Alma wrote:

THE RECORD OF ALMA[2]

> **...the very thought of coming into the presence of my God did rack my soul with inexpressible horror [fear].**
>
> **Oh, thought I, that I could be banished and become extinct both soul and body,** that I might not be brought to stand in the presence of my God, to be judged of my deeds (*BofM: Alma* 36: 14-15; emphasis added).

Although Alma's condition and emotional tone became temporarily lower, Alma was progressing because his tone was now based on an awareness of his true Condition.

> And he said unto me: If thou wilt of thyself be destroyed, seek no more to destroy the Church of God.
>
> **And it came to pass that I fell to the earth; and it was for the space of three days and three nights that I could not open my mouth, neither had I the use of my limbs** (*BofM: Alma* 36:0; emphasis added).

Alma's Tones and Conditions

It appears from these comments that Alma's **Condition** actually fell, for a period, from **Treason** to **Confusion**. The **Condition of Confusion** is the lowest condition mentioned by L. Ron Hubbard. Alma's inability to function is an indication of his confused state. He did not hear, speak or respond for three days.

Here is L. Ron Hubbard's definition of the **Condition of Confusion**, and of the **Confusion Formula**:

> There is a **Condition** below **Treason**. It is a **Condition of Confusion**. In a **Condition of Confusion** the being, or area, will be in a state of random motion. There will be no real production, only disorder or confusion.
>
> In order to get out of **Confusion** one has to find out where he is. It will be seen that the progress upward would be, **in Confusion, find out where you are; in Treason, find out that you are; and for Enemy, find out who you are.**
>
> **The formula for Confusion is: find out where you are.** Note: It is important that the person who is in **Confusion** be cleared up on the definition of **Confusion** as given here:
>
> **Confusion can be defined as any set of factors or circumstances which do not seem to have any immediate solution.** More broadly, a confusion in this universe is random motion or an uncontrolled randomness. A confusion is only a confusion so long as no factor is clearly de-

fined or understood. Confusions, no matter how big and formidable they may seem, are composed of data or factors or particles. They have pieces. **Grasp one piece and locate it thoroughly. Then see how the others function in relation to it and you have steadied the confusion and, relating other things to what you have grasped, you will soon have mastered the confusion in its entirety.** This is done before the formula itself is started (emphasis added).

The additional formula for the **Condition of Confusion** is:

1) Location [Locational: a process to help a person locate things and themselves in the environment] on the area in which one is;
2) Comparing where one is to other areas where one was;
3) Repeat Step 1.[70]

We shall see shortly what data Alma grasped onto to bring him out of this **Condition**. Alma was able to locate where he was. As noted above, Alma was actually in hell. He was also able to compare with he was with where he could and should have been.

In this **Condition**, Alma's mind "caught hold upon this thought", and he was able to come out of his confused **Condition**. Please notice the thought that Alma grasped onto:

> And now, for three days and for three nights was I racked, even with the pains of a damned soul.
>
> And it came to pass that as I was thus racked with torment, while I was harrowed up by the memory of my many sins, behold, **I remembered also to have heard my father prophesy unto the people concerning the coming of one Jesus Christ, a Son of God, to atone for the sins of the world.**
>
> Now **as my mind caught hold upon this thought, I cried within my heart, O Jesus, thou son of God, have mercy on me**, who am in the gall of bitterness, and am encircled about by the everlasting chains of death (*BofM: Alma* 36:16-18; emphasis added).

Please note the similarity of the wording of the **Confusion Formula** and Alma's report of his experience. First, in the **Confusion Formula,** we are taught that we should **"...grasp one piece..."** of data or information to help get out of a **Condition of Confusion**. Alma stated that he was being tormented by the memory of his many sins. Thus, his mind must have been "...in random motion...", shifting from one regretful memory to another.

Certainly no constructive ideas could come out of such an experience, and it could only be regarded as a period of great confusion and groping for something or someone to relieve the great burden he was feeling. Again, this is how L. Ron Hubbard defined **Confusion**: "...circumstances which do not seem to have any immediate solution" (see reference above). We know from reading Alma's account that he was looking for a solution to his confusing and painful condition.

Then, something else entered Alma's mind. This was something his father had taught him about Jesus Christ, who would atone for the sins of the world. Here was a thought to grasp onto. So Alma's mind **"caught hold"** of this idea, for Jesus Christ and His atonement provided the escape route of forgiveness of Alma's tremendous burden of sin.

Jesus Christ: Our Stable Datum

The concept that Alma "grasped" and "caught hold upon" was faith in Jesus Christ and his atonement for our sins. Faith in Jesus Christ and His atonement is the central truth for progression in our universe. Mr. Hubbard called a central idea of a body of knowledge its **stable datum**. He defined stable datum in this way:

> Any body of knowledge more particularly and exactly, is built from one datum. That is its stable datum. Invalidate it and the entire body of knowledge falls apart. A stable datum does not have to be the correct one. It is simply the one that keeps things from being in a confusion and on which others are aligned....[71]

Alma's Experience was an Example of the Savior's Power to Raise our Emotional Tone Level

What happened to Alma next is perhaps the single most profound example of the **Power of Jesus Christ to heal and change the lives of people.**

> And now, behold, when I thought this, **I could remember my pains no more; yea, I was harrowed up by the memory of my sins no more.**
> **And oh, what joy, and what marvelous light I did behold; yea, my soul was filled with joy as exceeding as was my pain!**
> Yea, I say unto you, my son, that there could be nothing so exquisite and so bitter as were my pains. Yea, and again I say unto you, my son, that on the other hand, there can be nothing so exquisite and sweet as was my joy (*BofM: Alma* 36:19-21; emphasis added).

As Alma took the action of exercising his newly-acquired faith in Jesus Christ and repenting, his Emotional Tone was converted to Exhilaration, which the scriptures describe as Joy.

THE POWER FORMULAS

Five Things Which Can Raise a Person's Emotional Tone Level

L. Ron Hubbard identified and wrote about four things, which could raise a person's Tone Level. He wrote:

> **There are four valid therapies,** if we wish to use the term loosely. **First there is dianetic processing.** This rids the individual of the pain and painful emotion which aberrates his reason. **Second there is education.** This indoctrinates the individual with the culture in which he lives and gives him the skills of survival, better enabling him to survive. **The third is changing his environment** into one, which is less restimulative, is happier for him and in which he can better survive. This would include nutrition, medical care, and recreation. **The fourth is regulating the amount of MEST [Matter, Energy, Space and Time], which the individual should control.** He can be given less if he has too much [regulatory responsibility, which can cause stress]...
>
> ...All four of these therapies do the same thing: they enhance the survival of the individual by giving him better tools of survival, better conditions in which to survive, better reasons for survival. **Any of these do one basic thing: they raise the individual on the tone scale** (emphasis and explanatory opinion added).[72]

From Alma's experience, we learn that there is a fifth, and far more efficient method of raising Tone Level. This greatly accelerated change comes through the power of Jesus Christ. **Also, it is only through His power that we can reach the highest Condition and highest Emotional Tone.**

The Sons of Mosiah Were Additional Examples of the Savior's Power to Raise Tone and Condition

You will recall that four sons of Mosiah, the Nephite king, accompanied Alma, as he sought to destroy the Church. Mormon did not write in as great of detail about the change in the **Spiritual Condition** of the sons of Mosiah, as he did about Alma's experience. However, he did write enough to allow us to see that their experiences, and their changes in **Emotional Tone** and **Spiritual Condition** mirrored those of Alma.

> And now it came to pass that **Alma began from this time forward to teach the people, and those who were with Alma at the time the angel appeared unto them, [the sons of Mosiah]** traveling round about through all the land, publishing to all the people the things which **they** had heard and seen, and preaching the word of God in much tribu-

lation, being greatly persecuted by those who were unbelievers, being smitten by many of them.

But notwithstanding all this, **they** did impart much consolation to the Church, confirming their faith, and exhorting them with long-suffering and much travail to keep the commandments of God.

And four of them were the **sons of Mosiah; and their names were Ammon, and Aaron, and Omner, and Himni;** these were the names of the sons of Mosiah (*BofM: Mosiah* 27:32-34; emphasis added).

Alma², Ammon, Aaron, Omner and Himni first taught their own people, the Nephites. Later, Alma became the leader of the Church, and he dedicated his life to teaching the gospel. The sons of Mosiah turned their attention to helping improve the **Spiritual Condition** of "...their brethren, the Lamanites." They became great missionaries.

Alma² and Mosiah's sons were motivated by compassion, for they did not want anyone to suffer as they had suffered. Mormon described their suffering. In this description, he taught that Mosiah's sons had also experienced "much anguish of soul because of their iniquities". This verse is an indication that these brothers went through a process of repentance and forgiveness as Alma had done.

And thus did the Spirit of the Lord work upon them, for they were the very vilest of sinners. And the Lord saw fit in his infinite mercy to spare them; nevertheless they suffered much anguish of soul because of their iniquities, suffering much and fearing that they should be cast off forever (*BofM: Mosiah* 28:4; emphasis added).

The Relationship Between Our Awareness, Our Conditions, and Our Emotional Tone Levels

From the recorded experiences of Alma², the sons of king Mosiah, and Paul, we can we can also see how Awareness, Condition and Emotional Tone are interrelated. It seems obvious that the first change that had to occur in the lives of these men was that they needed to become aware of their own state.

Before any of these men, or us, can improve our **Conditions**, and our long-term **Emotional Tone Levels**, we must first become aware of how we are doing *as determined by the Lord's standards*. Alma and his friends, as well as Saul, who later was know as the apostle Paul, must have all thought that they were doing well, by the world's standards.

Saul was a learned Pharisee. Mosiah's sons were the children, and potential heirs of a king, and Alma²'s father was the prophet and leader of the Church. All of these men were in positions of high esteem in *their* estimations. It is very probable that they *perceived* themselves to be in a high **Condition** when, in the Lord's view, they were all in very low and precarious **Conditions**. Probably no one on earth could have made these men realize that they were, in fact, living lives of spectacular failure. It took heavenly messengers, an angel's visit, in the case of Alma and Mosiah's sons, and the Savior Himself to realize that their lives were in **Ruin**.

As noted above, Alma learned that his **Condition** was descending through **Treason** into **Confusion**. Also, his **Emotion Tone Level** was very low (**Fear**) and falling towards **Death**.

No doubt, similar awarenesses also occurred to Mosiah's sons and to Saul. What brought these men **Up** in **Awareness**, **Condition** and in **Emotional Tone**? They all latched onto the **Stable Datum of Faith in the Lord Jesus Christ as the Source they could look to for forgiveness of their sins!**

Also, faith in Jesus Christ and the forgiveness He has made available, increased their awareness to need for **Change and Demand for Improvement and Hope**.

Through faith in Jesus Christ, repentance, baptism and receiving the gift of the Holy Ghost, these men were all spiritually reborn.

With spiritual rebirth came tremendous increases in **Awareness, Condition**, and **Emotional Tone Level**. In fact, we could even say that this is one definition of Spiritual Rebirth:

> The wonderful and ultimate increase in one's **Awareness**, our **Spiritual Condition**, and our **Emotional Tone Level** that occurs in our lives, only as we learn of our Savior Jesus Christ, choose to have faith in Him, and keep His commandments by repenting, being baptized, and receiving the life-renewing and changing gift of the Holy Ghost.

The Sons of Mosiah Spoke of the Great Change in Their Emotional Tone Level, after Spiritual Rebirth

To see the great contrast in the feeling or Emotional Tone Level of these sons of Mosiah after their spiritual rebirth, we will turn to Ammon's report of their later missionary experiences. Ammon stated:

> Therefore, let us glory, yea, we will glory in the Lord; yea, **we will rejoice, for our joy is full**; yea, we will praise our God forever. Behold, who can glory too much in the Lord? Yea, who can say too much of his great power, and of his mercy, and of his long-suffering towards the children of men? **Behold, I say unto you, I cannot say the smallest part which I feel.**
>
> Who could have supposed that our God would have been so merciful as to have snatched us from our awful, sinful, and polluted state?
>
> Behold, we went forth even in wrath, with mighty threatenings to destroy his Church (*BofM: Alma* 26:16-18; emphasis added).

THE RECORD OF ALMA²

Alma and the Sons Of Mosiah Received Assurance of Gaining the Highest Condition of All—Eternal Life, Which is Super Power

Like Alma, the sons of Mosiah were so determined to continue following their Savior that they received an assurance from Him that they would be given eternal life. Receiving eternal life is the goal of our existence. In terms of the **Spiritual Conditions**, obtaining eternal life represents eventually obtaining the **Condition of spiritual Power** and **Super Power.**

Eternal Life, or **Super Power**, means more that just immortality. It means living in Their presence, and eventually becoming like our Jesus Christ and our Heavenly Parents. The word *eternal* in this phrase refers to the **quality** or type of life we can enjoy as well as the **quantity** of life. More information about Eternal Life, or **Super Power**, is contained in the final book of this series: *Super Power*.

In Chapter 1, we considered the meaning of eternal life. Here is a review of a portion of what Elder Bruce R. McConkie, a modern apostle, wrote perceptively of the meaning of eternal life.

> **God's life is Eternal Life, Eternal Life is God's life**—the expressions are synonymous.
>
> **Accordingly, eternal life is not a name that has reference only to the unending duration of a future life; immortality is to live forever in the resurrected state, and by the grace of God all men will gain this unending continuance of life. But only those who obey the fullness of the gospel law will inherit eternal life** (D&C 29:43-44). It is "the greatest of all gifts of God" (D&C 14:7), for **it is the [Condition], kind, status, type and quality of life that God Himself enjoys.** Thus those who gain eternal life receive exaltation; they are sons [and daughters] of God, joint heirs with Christ,...**they overcome all things, have all power** and receive the fullness of the Father[73] (emphasis added).

The assurance of Eternal Life for his sons, came to king Mosiah as he prayed to know whether he should allow his sons to go on a dangerous mission to their enemies, the Lamanites. The Lord revealed to him that his sons should go on this mission, and that they would receive the greatest of all rewards: eternal life.

> And king **Mosiah went and inquired of the Lord** if he should let his sons go up among the Lamanites to preach the word.
> And the Lord said unto Mosiah: Let them go up, for many shall believe on their words, and **they shall have eternal life**; and I will deliver thy sons out of the hands of the Lamanites (*BofM: Mosiah* 28:6-7; emphasis added).

Although it is not recorded in this verse, **Mosiah must have felt a marvelous joy at this wonderful announcement!** We can imagine Mosiah's great concern, and grief as his sons had rebelled and fought against him and the Lord earlier. Now, in great contrast, Mosiah received a revealed message unparalleled in all scriptural history: **that four of his sons would receive Eternal Life!**

Alma[2] had done similar work, as the sons of Mosiah. He devoted his life to teaching the gospel, and he received a similar assurance of eternal life. Alma recounted his conversion experience and this assurance of eternal life to his son, Helaman, about 25 years after his conversion.

> **But behold, my limbs did receive their strength again, and I stood upon my feet, and did manifest unto the people that I had been born of God.**
>
> Yea, and **from that time even until now, I have labored without ceasing, that I might bring souls unto repentance; that I might bring them to taste of the exceeding joy of which I did taste; that they might also be born of God, and be filled with the Holy Ghost. [Here Alma defined the purposes of missionary work: to raise the emotional tone and spiritual condition of those that are taught the Gospel of Jesus Christ].**

Alma continued:

> And **I have been supported under trials and troubles of every kind, yea, and in all manner of afflictions;** yea, God has delivered me from prison, and from bonds, and from death; yea, and I do put my trust in him, and **he will still deliver me.**
>
> **And I know that he will raise me up at the last day, to dwell with him in glory...**(*BofM: Alma* 36:23, 24, 27, 28; emphasis added).

This declaration by Alma that "...I know that he will raise me up at the last day, to dwell with him in glory ... " shows that the Lord had accepted Alma's sacrifices just as He had accepted those of the sons of Mosiah. These men had changed from a **Condition of Treason** to a **Condition of Spiritual Power**. Also, the Lord had revealed to them that this change was going to be **permanent** and that their rewards were **sure**. They would have eternal life "...with Him...", which is **Super Power**.

Paul of *The New Testament* wrote of a similar assurance he received. Like Alma and the sons of Mosiah after his conversion, Paul dedicated the rest of his life to teaching the gospel. He, like Alma, Ammon, Aaron, Omner and Himni, spent his life "...zealously striving to repair all the injuries which they [and he] had done to the Church" (*BofM Mosiah* 27:35).

THE RECORD OF ALMA[2]

As a result of this devotion, Paul was able to say:

> I have fought a good fight, I have finished my course, I have kept the faith:
> **Henceforth there is laid up for me a crown of righteousness, which the Lord, the righteous judge, shall give me at that day: and not to me only, but unto all them also that love his appearing** (*NewT: 2 Timothy* 4:7-8; emphasis added).

This is the great goal of life, and very few people ever achieve it **during this lifetime**. When this occurs, it is called making our calling and election sure. Everyone who achieves this goal, whether in this life, or the life to come, will do so **because of their faith in Jesus Christ, and their obedience to His plan, and because of His power of atonement**.

Many, many more will receive this reward in the next life, than will receive it during this life. Why is it that only a comparative few receive such assurances while **in this life**? Probably because very few people receive sufficient trials to demonstrate to the Lord, during this short earth life, that they will serve Him at all costs.

The Power Formulas, Part Two and Part Three contain information about **The Honor That Comes Only from God**. These sections describe the qualifications that the Savior listed for how we can obtain Eternal Life.

In his final blessing to his son Jacob, the prophet Lehi also foresaw and prophesied that "Jacob would be "redeemed." This is equivalent to the promise Mosiah received that his sons inherit eternal life. What is particularly interesting about Lehi's words is what he said before and **after** he told Jacob that he was redeemed. As you read these verses please note how Jacob's trials or afflictions were related to this ultimate blessing. Also, please note why Jacob was redeemed.

> And now, Jacob, I speak unto you: Thou art my first-born in the days of my tribulation in the wilderness. And behold, in thy childhood thou hast suffered afflictions and much sorrow, because of the rudeness of thy brethren.
> Nevertheless, Jacob, my first born in the wilderness, thou knowest the greatness of God; and **he shall consecrate thine afflictions for thy gain.**
> **Wherefore, thy soul shall be blessed, and thou shalt dwell safely with thy brother, Nephi; and thy days shall be spent in the service of thy God. Wherefore, I know that thou art redeemed, because of the righteousness of thy Redeemer...** (*BofM: 2 Nephi* 2:1-3; emphasis added).

Although Jacob responded well to his afflictions, and although he would spend the rest of his days in the service of God, this would not be sufficient for him to be given Eternal Life. The reason he was redeemed was because of **"...the righteousness of thy Redeemer"**. Jacob relied upon the Savior's power of atonement.

It is through the power of Jesus Christ that we are ultimately able to reach the end goal of the straight and narrow path. This goal is to be with, and to be like, our Savior and our Heavenly Parents. This is the meaning of Eternal Life.

The Stories of Alma and the Sons of Mosiah and Paul Give Us Hope

All of us have done things in our lives which have hurt others, and ourselves. Most of us feel some degree of remorse or even anguish because of the harm, and pain we have caused. However, very few of us will ever sink to the depths of anguish experienced by Alma, Paul and the sons of Mosiah. That they could be brought out of their extremely low **Conditions** and unhappy **Emotional Tone Levels** by the power of the Savior, should give us hope.

Perhaps we may feel that it was the angel who brought about this great change in their lives. Although the angel did make them aware that their lives were in **Ruin**, he did not bring them out of their **Conditions of Treason**.

You will recall that it took three days before Alma could stand and declare that he had been born of God. You will also recall that it was Alma's faith in Jesus Christ, and his repentance, which allowed the Lord to change his heart. It was this spiritual rebirth, and the change wrought in his heart by the Holy Ghost, which brought about Alma's wonderful improvement in **Awareness**, **Emotional Tone Level** and **Spiritual Condition**.

Even though most of us will never see an angel in this life, all of us can gain faith in Jesus Christ, repent of our sins, be baptized for the remission of our sins and receive the gift of the Holy Ghost. Through this process, our sins can be forgiven, and we can be healed spiritually. We can be brought to rejoice with Alma, the sons of Mosiah and those to whom they taught the gospel. We will be able to say with Ammon, who was one of king Mosiah's sons:

> **... We will rejoice, for our joy is full; yea, we will praise our God forever. Behold, who can glory too much in the Lord? Yea, who can say too much of his great power, and of his mercy, and of his long-suffering towards the children of men? Behold, I say unto you, I cannot say the smallest part, which I feel** (*BofM: Alma* 26:16; emphasis added).

Alma, the sons of Mosiah, and many others, are examples of the wonderful power of the Savior to heal us spiritually. He has the power to raise our **Awareness**, our **Emotional Tone Level** and to change our **Conditions** from the lowest to the highest possible levels.

This means that the Savior can even bring us from **Confusion** and **Treason** through **Spiritual Non Existence** and eventually to Eternal Life, which is **the Condition of Spiritual Super Power**. Jesus Christ has the power to do this wonderful work. However, the power of Jesus Christ to forgive our sins can only operate in our lives if we allow it to do so. We have the right, and the responsibility, to choose.

Choosing Faith

Elder Neil Anderson, who is a living apostle of Jesus Christ has taught:

> A friend of mine had a young daughter die in a tragic accident. Hopes and dreams were shattered. My friend felt unbearable sorrow. He began to question what he believed. The mother of my friend wrote me a letter and asked if I would give him a blessing.
>
> As I laid my hands upon his hear, the impression that came to me was: "Faith is not only a feeling, it is a decision." He would need to choose faith. My friend did not know everything, but he knew enough. He chose the road of faith and obedience. He got on his knees. His spiritual balance returned.
>
> It has been several years since that event. A short time ago, I received a letter from his son who was now serving a mission. It was full of conviction and testimony. As I read his beautiful letter, I saw how a father's choice of faith in a very difficult time had deeply blessed the next generation.
>
> Challenges, difficulties, questions, doubt — these are part of mortality, but we are not alone. As disciples [followers] of the Lord Jesus Christ, we have enormous spiritual reservoirs of light and truth available to us. Fear and faith cannot coexist in our heart at the same time. Jesus said: "Be not afraid, only believe..." [as we continue to choose to have faith in Jesus Christ] our questions and doubts are resolved or become less concerning to us. Our faith becomes simple and pure...Jesus said: "Except ye become as little children, ye shall not enter into the kingdom of heaven.
>
> Hadley Peay is now seven years old. Hadley was born with a very serious hearing impairment requiring extensive surgery to bring even limited hearing. Her parents followed with tireless training to help her learn to speak. Hadley and her family have cheerfully adapted to the challenge of her deafness.
>
> Once, when Hadley was four, she was standing in the checkout line at the grocery store with her mother. She looked behind her and saw a little boy sitting in a wheelchair. She noticed that the boy did not have

legs.

Although Hadley had learned to speak, she had difficulty controlling the volume of her voice. In her louder voice, she asked her mother why the little boy did not have legs.

Her mother quietly and simply explained to Hadley that "Heavenly Father makes all of His children different." "OK," Hadley replied.

Then, unexpectedly, Hadley turned to the little boy and said, "Did you know that when Heavenly Father made me, my ears did not work? That makes me special. He made you with no legs, and that makes you special. When Jesus comes, I will be able to hear and you will get your legs. Jesus will make everything all right."

"Except ye … become as little children, ye shall not enter into the kingdom of heaven."[79]

Our **Eternal Condition** and our **Eternal Emotional Tone** will be determined by our decisions. We can choose Eternal Life by choosing to have faith in and to love and follow our Father in Heaven and His Son, Jesus Christ. Their record, *The Book of Mormon* contains examples of those who have chosen to have faith in Jesus Christ. It also teaches us how we can do the same.

Chapter 9

Bridges

We are going to divert our attention briefly from the succession of *The Book of Mormon* Record Keepers. In doing so, we will review a fictional story, which teaches an important lesson. We will then return to correlate this lesson to *The Book of Mormon*.

World literature contains many epic stories, which compare **life to a journey** or a **quest**. Perhaps one of the best of these stories is found in a fantasy trilogy titled, *The Lord of the Rings*. The author of this trilogy was J.R.R. Tolkien.

Tolkien used fantasy, and folklore to weave a remarkable story of a **heroic quest**. In his tale, we see examples of friendship and betrayal; bravery and fear; love and hate; peace and war; self-sacrifice and selfishness, and the eventual triumph of good over evil. Book One of this trilogy is called *The Fellowship of the Ring*. This book contains two chapters which teach marvelous lessons.

The main heroes of *The Lord of the Rings* are small, peace loving people called Hobbits. One of these Hobbits, Frodo, had been given the great responsibility of keeping and destroying a ring of power. This ring was being sought by an evil being, who already had great power. If this ring were to fall into the hands of this evil tyrant, then his power would be so great that he would have had dominion over everyone.

The Hobbits were guided in their quest by a great wizard named Gandalf. These Hobbits, Gandalf and a few friends started on a journey to try to penetrate into the very heart of the enemy's territory. There they would try to help Frodo finish his mission. These friends and companions on this quest were Gimli, Pippin, Merry, Legolas, Boromir, Aragon and Gandalf.

Frodo's goal was to throw the ring back into a molten pool of lava and fire from which it was originally smelted. According to the story, this was the only way to keep their evil enemy from eventually obtaining this ring, and the power he sought.

Throughout their journey, they were threatened and attacked by the servants of this enemy. Their lives were nearly always in danger. At one point, they had to enter a path, or tunnel, which went under and through a great mountain, called Moria. The chapter titled *Journey in the Dark* tells of their travels through these underground tunnels.

Only one in the group, Gandalf, knew the way through this great maze of tunnels. Therefore, Gandalf served as the guide for the group. Upon reaching this mountain, and while being pursued by their enemies, Gandalf first had to find and open the entrance to this path under the mountain. Once they had all entered the mountain the rock door closed behind them. This meant that they had but one choice, to finish their journey through the mountain.

> Well, well!" said the wizard. "The passage is blocked behind us now, and there is only one way out—on the other side of the mountains.
> "Who will lead us now in this deadly dark?"
> "I will," said Gandalf, "and Gimli shall walk with me. Follow my staff!"
> As the wizard passed on ahead up the great steps, he held his staff aloft, and from its tip there came a faint radiance. The wide stairway was sound and undamaged. Two hundred steps they counted, broad and shallow; and at the top they found an arched passage with a level floor leading on into the dark.[74]

They pressed on in the dark tunnels for two days, and then found a great cavern. This cavern contained evidence of previous inhabitants. These were dwarfs who had once mined the mountain. However, all of them had been destroyed in a great battle against evil forces.

On the last "morning" of this subterranean trek, Gandalf and his company heard the drum beat of an approaching army coming to destroy them, also. They were nearly trapped in a great cavern, but with Gandalf's help they were able to escape through a tunnel, which led toward the exit from the mountain. As they were escaping, they were led by Gandalf to a bridge over a great chasm.

When they reached the other side of the bridge they noticed that the pursuing army stopped at the other side of the bridge. Next, the enemy soldiers stopped and parted in fear. Then a great cave monster, or "Balrog," stepped forward to destroy these heroes.

Upon seeing this beast, Gandalf knew how the previous dwellers in the mountain had been destroyed. He also realized that the only hope for those of his company was for him to stand and defeat this monster. The battle was joined on the bridge.

This story has great symbolism, and is similar to two great stories in scripture. The first is the battle of David and Goliath. Like David, Gandalf was acting as a champion for his group. This means that **he represented them in the battle, and their fates were tied to whether he was victorious or not.** If he failed to conquer, then all of those who were enlisted with him would also be defeated. Only he, in the group, had the power to overcome such an enemy.

Another way in which David's struggle was similar to Gandalf's was in the source of their power to overcome their evil enemies. Both David and Gandalf, from all external appearances, should not have been able to conquer. However, each of them had received power through aligning themselves with truth and right. Also, each of them had received power through preparing themselves.

BRIDGES

As mentioned, this fictional story does have some resemblance to the story of David. However, there is another scriptural account which it more fully resembles. This is especially true in the outcome of the battle. Here is how Tolkien told the story of the battle. See if you can recall a similar story in the scriptures.

"Look ahead!" called Gandalf. "The Bridge is near. It is dangerous and narrow."

Suddenly Frodo saw before him a black chasm. At the end of the hall the floor vanished and fell to an unknown depth. The outer door could only be reached by a slender bridge of stone, without curb or rail that spanned the chasm with one curving spring of fifty feet. It was an ancient defense of the Dwarves against any enemy that might capture the First Hall and the outer passages. They could only pass across it in single file. At the brink Gandalf halted and the others came up in a pack behind.

"Lead the way, Gimli!" he said. "Pippin and Merry next. Straight on, and up the stair beyond the door!"

Arrows fell among them. One struck Frodo and sprang back. Another pierced Gandalf's hat and stuck there like a black feather. Frodo looked behind. Beyond the fire he saw swarming black figures: there seemed to be hundreds of orcs. They brandished spears and scimitars, which shone red as blood in the firelight. **Doom, doom** rolled the drumbeats, growing louder and louder, **doom, doom**.

Legolas turned and set an arrow to the string, though it was a long shot for his small bow. He drew, but his hand fell, and the arrow slipped to the ground. He gave a cry of dismay and fear. Two great trolls appeared; they bore great slabs of stone, and flung them down to serve as gangways over the fire. But it was not the trolls that had filled the Elf with terror. The ranks of the orcs had opened, and they crowded away, as if they themselves were afraid. Something was coming up behind them. What it was could not be seen: it was like a great shadow, in the middle of which was a dark form, of a man-shape maybe, yet greater; and a power and terror seemed to be in it and to go before it.

It came to the edge of the fire and the light faded as if a cloud had bent over it. Then with a rush it leaped across the fissure. The flames roared up to greet it, and wreathed about it; and a black smoke swirled in the air. Its streaming mane kindled, and blazed behind it. In its right hand was a blade like a stabbing tongue of fire; in its left it held a whip of many thongs.

"Ai! ai!" wailed Legolas. "A Balrog! A Balrog is come!"

Gimli stared with wide eyes. "Durin's Bane!" he cried, and letting

THE POWER FORMULAS

his axe fall he covered his face.

"A Balrog," muttered Gandalf. "Now I understand." He faltered and leaned heavily on his staff. "What an evil fortune! And I am already weary."

The dark figure streaming with fire raced towards them. The orcs yelled and poured over the stone gangways. Then Boromir raised his horn and blew. Loud the challenge rang and bellowed, like the shout of many throats under the cavernous roof. For a moment the orcs quailed and the fiery shadow halted. Then the echoes died as suddenly as a flame blown out by a dark wind, and the enemy advanced again.

"Over the bridge!" cried Gandalf, recalling his strength. **"Fly! This is a foe beyond any of you. I must hold the narrow way.** Fly!" Aragorn and Boromir did not heed the command, but still held their ground, side by side, behind Gandalf at the far end of the bridge. The others halted just within the doorway at the hall's end, and turned, unable to leave their leader to face the enemy alone.

The Balrog reached the bridge. Gandalf stood in the middle of the span, leaning on the staff in his left hand, but in his other hand Glamdring [his sword] gleamed, cold and white. His enemy halted again, facing him, and the shadow about it reached out like two vast wings. It raised the whip, and the thongs whined and cracked. Fire came from its nostrils. But Gandalf stood firm.

"You cannot pass!" he said. The orcs stood still, and a dead silence fell. "I am a servant of the Secret Fire, wielder of the flame of Anor. You cannot pass. The dark fire will not avail you, flame of Udun. Go back to the Shadow! You cannot pass!"

 The Balrog made no answer. The fire in it seemed to die, but the darkness grew. It stepped forward slowly on to the bridge, and suddenly it drew itself up to a great height, and its wings were spread from wall to wall; but still Gandalf could be seen, glimmering in the gloom; he seemed small, and altogether alone: grey and bent, like a wizened tree before the onset of a storm.

From out of the shadow a red sword leaped
flaming. Glamdring [Gandalf's sword] glittered white in answer.

 There was a ringing clash and a stab of white fire. The Balrog fell back and its sword flew up in molten fragments. The wizard swayed on the bridge, stepped back a pace, and then again stood still.

You cannot pass!" he said.

 With a bound the Balrog leaped full upon the bridge. Its whip whirled and hissed.

"He cannot stand alone!" cried Aragon suddenly and ran back along the bridge. "Elendil!" he shouted. "I am with you, Gandalfi".

"Gondor!" cried Boromir and leaped after him.

At that moment Gandalf lifted his staff, and crying aloud he smote the bridge before him. The staff broke asunder and fell from his hand. A blinding sheet of white flame sprang up. The bridge cracked. Right at the Balrog's feet it broke, and the stone upon which it stood crashed into the gulf, while the rest remained, poised, quivering like a tongue of rock thrust out into emptiness.

With a terrible cry the Balrog fell forward, and its shadow plunged down and vanished. But even as it fell it swung its whip, and the thongs lashed and curled about the wizard's knees, dragging him to the brink. He staggered, and fell, grasped vainly at the stone, and slid into the abyss. "Fly, you fools!", he cried, and was gone.

The fires went out, and darkness fell. The company stood rooted with horror staring into the pit. Even as Aragon and Boromir came flying back the rest of the bridge cracked and fell.

With a cry Aragon roused them. "Come! I will lead you now," he called. "We must obey his last command, follow me...!"[75] (emphasis added).

In this story it took **all that Gandalf could do and give Gandalf's** willingness to give his all, those he led were saved from certain destruction. In this trilogy, Gandalf later returns from death with even greater powers to instruct, inspire and help the heroes finish their quest. However, these heroes **had to use all of their own efforts, to survive and overcome the obstacles and evils, which awaited them on their journey.**

At the end of the story, and after overcoming the enemy by destroying the ring of power which he sought, the heroes are able to go and live with Gandalf and other great beings in a place Tolkien called the Havens.

The analogy is clear. Whether Tolkien actually meant Gandalf to symbolize the Savior or not, is unimportant. The important thing is that this story is, as Tolkien might say, **applicable**.

Our Abyss

All of us face the great abyss of death and hell. Alma[2] had first-hand experience with the abyss. You will recall his words about the time he spent between the angel's reproof and his repentance:

> Nevertheless, after wading through much tribulations, repenting nigh unto death, the Lord in mercy hath seen fit to snatch me out of an everlasting burning, and I am born of God.
>
> My soul hath been redeemed from the gall of bitterness and bonds

of iniquity. **I was in the darkest abyss;** but now I behold the marvelous light of God. My soul was racked with eternal torment; **but I am snatched, and my soul is pained no more** (*BofM: Mosiah* 27:28-29; emphasis added).

Alma's friends, the sons of Mosiah, must have felt the pains of hell as well. Here is Ammon's description of their experience. Please note Ammon's description of God bringing him, and his brothers "...over that everlasting gulf of death and misery, even to the salvation of our souls".

> Who could have supposed that our God would have been so merciful as to have snatched us from our awful, sinful, and polluted state?
>
> Behold, we went forth even in wrath, with mighty threatenings to destroy his Church.
>
> Oh then, why did he not consign us to an awful destruction, yea, why did he not let the sword of his justice fall upon us, and doom us to eternal despair?
>
> Oh, my soul, almost as it were, fleeth at the thought. Behold, **he did not exercise his justice upon us, but in his great mercy hath brought us over that everlasting gulf of death and misery, even to the salvation of our souls** (*BofM: Alma* 26:17-20; emphasis added).

Alma's[2] grandson, Helaman, understood and taught the concept that the Savior had the power to keep us from being dragged "...down to the gulf of misery and woe...." Here are Helaman's words to his sons:

> And **he [Jesus Christ] hath power given unto him from the Father** to redeem them from their sins because of repentance; therefore he hath sent his angels to declare the tidings of the conditions of **repentance, which bringeth unto the power of the Redeemer**, unto the salvation of their souls.
>
> And now, my sons, remember, remember that **it is upon the rock of our Redeemer, who is Christ, the Son of God**, that ye must build your foundation; that **when the devil shall send forth his mighty winds, yea, his shafts in the whirlwind, yea, when all his hail and his mighty storm shall beat upon you, it shall have no power over you to drag you down to the gulf of misery and endless woe,** because of the rock upon which ye are built, which is a sure foundation, a foundation whereon if men build they cannot fall (*BofM: Helaman* 5: 11-12; emphasis added).

In these verses Helaman taught his sons that the word of God, meaning His scriptural record, would lead us "...across the everlasting gulf of misery...". As Mormon abridged the Record of Helaman, he added this commentary regarding the **word of God:**

> Yea, thus we see that **the gate of heaven is open unto all, even to those who will believe on the name of Jesus Christ, who is the Son of God.**
>
> Yea, we see that whosoever will may lay hold upon **the word of God [the Record], which is quick and powerful,** which shall divide asunder all the cunning and the snares and the wiles of the devil, and **lead the man of Christ in a strait and narrow course across that everlasting gulf of misery** which is prepared to engulf the wicked—
>
> **And land their souls, yea, their immortal souls, at the right hand of God in the kingdom of heaven**, to sit down with Abraham, and Isaac, and with Jacob, and with all our holy fathers, to go no more out (*BofM: Helaman* 3:28-30; emphasis added).

The Gulf of Misery

What did Mormon mean by his phrase in the above verse: "...that everlasting gulf of misery..."? According to Noah Webster one definition of the word *gulf* is:

...an abyss; a deep place in the earth...[76]

Therefore, we could substitute the word abyss for the word gulf in this verse. It would then read "...the everlasting abyss of misery..." Just as an abyss can stop our progression along a path, our unrepented sins stop our reunion with our Father in Heaven. This everlasting separation from God will cause great misery to those who choose not to return to Him.

The Word of God is a Weapon Against Evil

In this chapter about Bridges, we have reviewed a story from Tolkien's Trilogy. You will recall that a group of adventurers were guided by a great wizard named Gandolf. This Gandolf saved the lives of his colleagues by standing on a bridge and defeating a foe that they could not stand against.

The Book of Mormon verses quoted above not only contain similar imagery to the story of Gandolf in regards to a bridge across a gulf or abyss, and an enemy trying to interrupt progress along the path. There is another interesting similarity. In the story of Gandolf, he had a sword which demonstrated great power. These verses above from Helaman also describe a similar weapon.

This weapon is "quick and powerful". Also, it "...shall divide asunder all the cunning and snares and wiles of the devil." What is it that he is able to divide asunder all the cunning and snares and wiles of the adversary? It is: the word of God!"

The truth contained within the scriptures gives us knowledge and power whereby we can overcome the temptations of the adversary. As we consistently find truth and spiritual strength in the scriptures, we are able to cut through his snares which would entrap us.

In *The Book of Mormon*, we see examples of some of these snares. For example, in at least four cases, the Nephites were led away by deceptive leaders, who used words of flattery (*BofM: Alma* 46:1-7, 50:37, 61:4, *Helaman* 1:6-7). Knowing this, when we are flattered by someone, we are wise to watch out for ensnarement.

The Word of God is the Rod of Iron to Help Us Stay on the Path to our Father in Heaven

In the verses above, the word of God is used to represent more than just a weapon to overcome evil. The word of God will also lead us "...in a straight and narrow course across that everlasting gulf of misery..." (BofM: Helaman 3:28-30). In this analogy, Mormon was probably referring back to a dream that the prophet Lehi had described.

In this dream Lehi saw a path leading to the tree of Eternal Life. A rod of iron was along this path. Those who were traveling the path could hold on to the rod of iron in order to make their way to their goal. This rod of iron symbolized the word of God (*BofM: l Nephi* 15).

Therefore, to fully understand Mormon's imagery in *Helaman* 3:29, we should visualize a straight and narrow path or bridge leading across a gulf of misery which represents hell. We can visualize the traveler along the path holding onto a rod of iron, which helps him from falling off the path.

Also, in his other hand he wields the sword of truth or the word of God. With this sword he is able to fight off the adversary and eventually arrive "...at the right hand of God and the kingdom of Heaven..." (see *Helaman* 3:29-30). **Thus, the word of God is both our guide and our protection.**

There is also another use for our other hand. With one hand we hold onto the hand of God. With the other hand, we can hold onto a loved one, a friend, even a stranger to help them along the path. Also, at times, we will need to be helped by holding onto the hand of a person ahead of us on the path.

The Meaning of the Word of God

The word of God means more that just the scriptures. It also means the words of living prophets (see BofM: Jacob 2:8). Another meaning of the word of God is inspiration through the Holy Spirit (see *NewT: Ephesians* 6:17, 2 *Timothy* 3:16, 2 *Peter* 1:21).

The source of the word of God is our Savior Jesus Christ (see *NewT: Hebrews*

11:3, 1:1-3). One of the titles given to Jesus Christ by the apostle John is "The Word Of God" (see *NewT: John* 1:1-14, *Revelation* 19:13).

This title is appropriate, for all sources of inspiration, including: the scriptures, the words of the living apostles and prophets, and the whisperings of the Holy Spirit, have their source in Jesus Christ.

The Savior has made a bridge across this great gulf or abyss through His atonement and resurrection. He has also provided the word of God, which gives us a guide like a rod of iron to hold on to, and a sword of truth which can be used to conquer temptation, falsehood and to withstand the traps and snares set for us by the enemy of our souls.

Only the Power of Jesus Christ Can Bring Us Across the "Gulf Of Misery"

In order for us to get to the **"kingdom of Heaven"**, we must first get across the **"gulf of misery"**. Mormon speaks of the way across this gulf as being a "straight and narrow course". Now, what would you call a straight and narrow course across that everlasting "gulf of misery?" Could we not call such structure a **bridge**?

The power of Jesus Christ is our Bridge across this abyss or gulf of misery. He "hath power given unto him of the Father to redeem" us from the effects of our sins. Also, **He has prepared a way for us to make His power operative in our lives.** This power comes to those who will "believe on the name of Jesus Christ," and then repent. For it is **"...repentance, which bringeth unto the Power of the Redeemer, unto the salvation of their souls"** (*BofM: Helaman* 5:11).

The Only Source of the Power of Salvation

Helaman, a son of Alma[2], echoed the testimonies of the previous Record Keepers. He taught that only Jesus Christ has this power to save our souls. **Joseph Smith learned through revelation that a soul includes a body and spirit (see *D&C* 88:15). Therefore, only Christ has this power to save our spirits and our bodies.**

His power to resurrect our bodies is universal in its effect. The resurrection will come to all people as a free gift. Alma's missionary companion Amulek prophesied **"that all shall rise from the dead."** Amulek also taught that the Savior's atoning power to forgive our sins, is *not* a free gift to all. This power is reserved for those whose faith in Jesus Christ leads them to repent.

> And he shall come into the world to redeem his people; and **he shall take upon him the transgressions of those who believe on his name;** and these are they that shall have eternal life, and salvation cometh to none else.
>
> Therefore **the wicked remain as though there had been no redemption made,** except it be the loosing of the bands of death; for behold, **the day cometh that all shall rise from the dead** and stand before

God, and be judged according to their works (*BofM: Alma* 11:40-41).

The Only Way Across the Abyss

Jesus Christ's way is **the** way. We can either accept His power to atone for our sins or reject it. However there is **no other way** for us to be purified from the effects of our sins. For "there is no other way nor means whereby man can be saved", and there is no other way over **"the gulf of misery"** resulting from our sins and from death (*BofM: Helaman* 5:7, 12).

The Savior has already won the ultimate victory over sin and death. The question each of us must answer is this: will we travel His straight and narrow way, and we will choose to share in His victory?

The Enemy of Our Souls

Each of us has an enemy or adversary to our growth. It is important that we know a few things about him and understand some of his motivations and tactics. First, his name is Lucifer. Nephi referred to this being as "... the enemy of my soul" (see *BofM: 2 Nephi* 4:28).

He became the adversary, Satan, during the pre-mortal life. His Condition fell to Enemy and Treason, when he rebelled against Our Father in Heaven. In *The Power Formulas, Part Two*, we shall discuss the pre-mortal life in more detail.

Secondly, Satan now has great influence over many on the earth. Because of this influence Lucifer, or Satan, exercises considerable, but temporary, power. Third, he enlists help of others to try to destroy those who are resisting him. In the process, his servants are destroying themselves as well. Alma taught that:

> ...the devil will not support his children at the last day, but doth speedily drag them down to hell (*BofM: Alma* 30:60).

The fourth thing we need to know is that Satan is a real person. He is spirit being. One of his tactics is to try to convince us that he does not exist. Nephi commented on some of the tactics he uses to try to obtain power over us:

> For behold, at that day shall he **rage** in the hearts of the children of men, and s**tir them up to anger** against that which is good.
> And others will he **pacify, and lull** them away into carnal security, that they will say:
> All is well in Zion; yea, Zion prospereth, all is well—and thus the devil cheateth their souls, and leadeth them away carefully down to hell.
> And behold, **others he flattereth away**, and telleth them there is no hell; and **he saith unto them: I am no devil, for there is none**—and thus he whispereth in their ears, until he grasps them with his awful

chains, from whence there is no deliverance (*BofM: 2 Nephi* 28:20-22; emphasis added).

We learn this information about our adversary in *The Book of Mormon*. The fifth thing we need to know about Satan is his motivations for doing what he does. **One motivation was his desire to gain power without following Power Change, and doing what the Father and Son would have us do.** This will be discussed in greater detail in *The Power Formulas, Part Two*.

Another reason for his actions of opposition is to try to bring our Condition and Tone Level down to his. Nephi learned this fact from his father, Lehi, whom he here quoted:

And I, Lehi, according to the things which I have read, must needs suppose that an angel of God, according to that which is written, had fallen from heaven; wherefore, he became a devil, having sought that which was evil before God.

And because he had fallen from heaven, and had become miserable forever, he sought also the misery of all mankind (*BofM: 2 Nephi* 2:17-18; emphasis added).

Another of Satan's motivations is that he prefers evil to good. To those who do not have this preference for evil, it is very difficult to understand and to accept that beings exist who actually feel this way. Unfortunately, such beings exist among us on this earth as well.

We want to believe that people are good, because they start out that way. However, some choose to become evil. These individuals use our reluctance to see the evil in others,, to their advantage.

In *The New Testament*, the apostle John wrote of those who:

…loved darkness rather that light because their deeds were evil.
For everyone that doeth evil hateth the light, neither cometh to the light [Jesus Christ], lest his deeds should be reproved (*NewT: John* 1: 19-20; emphasis added).

Satan is the archetype, or father of those who love darkness rather than light. The Savior reproved a group of such individuals who later sought to take his life. The Savior confronted these men with their true character.

Ye are of your father the devil, and the lusts of your father ye will do. **He was a murderer from the beginning**, and abode not in the truth, because there is no truth in him. When he speaketh a lie, he speaketh of his own: for he is a liar, and the father of it (*NewT: John* 8:44; emphasis added).

THE POWER FORMULAS

The 90 Percent Rule

It is my observation that about 90 percent of the people I've met are trying to live good lives. Although they are not perfect, they are basically honest, and they try not to purposefully harm others. Unfortunately, if we live long enough, all of us will be harmed by one or more of the ten percent who love darkness rather than light.

Although it is difficult, *we need to not let these negative interactions with the ten percent influence how we feel about the 90 percent*. Keep a positive attitude about people, and realize that all people are God's children, and most of them have good intentions.

Also, we need to realize that even the 90 percent are going to make mistakes and commit sins. Some of their mistakes and sins are going to affect us. When this happens, don't be too critical, or assume that they are part of the ten percent. Usually, they are *not*.

We need to have forgiving hearts. This means we need to forgive everyone, including the ten percent. This does not mean we should not learn from negative experiences. We need to learn to weigh the risks versus the benefits in all our decisions. This includes decisions about *who* we will interact with, and *how* we will do so.

Also, never give up on people. Even those in the ten percent can change (see the parable of the prodigal son in *The Bible: Luke* 15:11-32, and see the story of Alma and the sons of Mosiah in *The Book of Mormon*). Their life experiences may produce enough pain and suffering in their lives that they will choose the light and reject the darkness. Like our Father in Heaven and His Son, Jesus Christ, we need to love everyone. Loving the 90 percent is not enough. We also need to love the ten percent. A favorite saying of mine is the motto of the Hard Rock Cafe: "Love all, serve all".

Satan and Contention

Finally, *The Book of Mormon* teaches that Satan is the great promoter of contention. The Savior taught this lesson to the Nephites:

> And according as I have commanded you thus shall ye baptize. And **there shall be no disputations among you**, as there have hitherto been; **neither shall there be disputations among you concerning the points of my doctrine**, as there have hitherto been.
>
> For verily, verily I say unto you, **he that hath the spirit of contention is not of me, but is of the devil, who is the father of contention, and he stirreth up the hearts of men to contend with anger, one with another** (*BofM: 3 Nephi* 11:28-29; emphasis added).

We shall discuss this further in *The Power Formulas, Part Two*, when we review about Satan and the Third Party Law.

The Savior Has Prepared a Way for Us to Escape the Awful Monster, Death and Hell

What would have become of us had the Savior not completed His atonement? Nephi taught that we would have become subject to our adversary, and that we would be "…in misery like unto himself". Fortunately, the Savior's "…power of the resurrection" provides a way for us to "…escape from the grasp of this awful monster, yea that monster death and hell".

> **O the wisdom of God, his mercy and grace!**
>
> **For behold, if the flesh should rise no more our spirits must become subject to that angel who fell from before the presence of the Eternal God, and became the devil, to rise no more. And our spirits must have become like unto him, and we become devils, angels to a devil, to be shut out from the presence of our God, and to remain with the father of lies, in misery, like unto himself;** yea, to that being who beguiled our first parents, who transformeth himself nigh unto an angel of light, and **stirreth up the children of men unto secret combinations of murder and all manner of secret works of darkness.**
>
> **O how great the goodness of our God, who prepareth a way for our escape from the grasp of this awful monster; yea, that monster, death and hell,** which I call the death of the body, and also the death of the spirit.
>
> And because of **the way of deliverance of our God**, the Holy One of Israel, [the Savior, Jesus Christ] this death, of which I have spoken, which is the temporal, shall deliver up its dead; which death is the grave.
>
> And this death of which I have spoken, which is the spiritual death, shall deliver up its dead; **which spiritual death is hell; wherefore, death and hell must deliver up their dead,** and hell must deliver up its captive spirits, and **the grave must deliver up its captive bodies, and the bodies and the spirits of men will be restored one to the other; and it is by the power of the resurrection of the Holy One of Israel** [Jesus Christ] (*BofM: 2 Nephi* 9:8-12; emphasis added).

The Savior Has the Ultimate Power of Survival, for Our Lives

The final thing we need to know about Satan is that there is a greater power than his. The Savior has already prevailed for us as He battled Lucifer during His premortal, and again during His earthly life. As a result of the Savior's incomprehensible suffering in the garden of Gethsemane, and culminating on the cross at Calvary, the Savior descended to the very bottom of the abyss **for us**.

In his letter to the saints of Ephesus, Paul wrote:

> although the Savior had ascended to Heaven, He had "... descended first into the lower parts of the Earth (*NewT: Ephesians* 4:10-11).

He returned from this experience with the power to keep us from being lost in that great chasm of sin and death. The effects of our sins include separation from God, and the misery of sorrow and of regret.

The Bridge over the abyss is the power of Jesus Christ. He obtained this power through his lineage, His obedience, His love and His atonement. His atonement required the best that was in Him, and **He was and is the best of our Father's children.** The Savior's overcoming both sin and death for us was truly *the best from the Best*!

Our Father prepared the Savior for his important mission. This truth was taught in *The Book of Mormon* by a prophet named Abinadi, and others.

> For were it not for the **redemption which he hath made for his people, which was prepared from the foundation of the world**, I say unto you, were it not for this, all mankind must have perished.
>
> But behold, the bands of death shall be broken, and **the Son reigneth, and hath power over the dead; therefore, he bringeth to pass the resurrection of the dead** (*BofM: Mosiah* 15:19-20; emphasis added).

In *The Power Formulas, Part Two,* we will also discuss how the Father did a **Power Formula** for Jesus Christ to prepare Him to be our Savior, "from the foundation of the world".

During His atonement, Jesus Christ overcame all of our enemies. These enemies would seek power over us, and thereby deprive us of our opportunities for freedom and progression. You will recall Joseph Smith's statement, quoted previously, that:

> **Salvation means a man's being placed beyond the power of all his enemies** (reference #46).

We must realize that men cannot, of themselves, overcome the obstacles of death and hell. However, the Savior has already overcome these obstacles for us. Earlier, we discussed that salvation is really survival in its highest sense. In this context then, the Savior has the ultimate power of survival, for only His power can bring us across the abyss, and only He can deliver us from the "...that monster, death and hell...".

Jesus Christ's Power of Atonement is the Source of Our Freedom and of Our Ability to Become a Cause Over Our Condition

Let's look briefly at some of the things which the Savior's atonement has accomplished for us. **First, because of His atonement, Jesus Christ is the source of our freedom. Nephi taught this great lesson:**

> Adam fell that **men might be; and men are, that they might have joy.**
>
> And the **Messiah cometh in the fullness of time, that he may redeem** the children of men from the fall. **And because that they are redeemed from the fall they have become free forever, knowing good from evil; to act for themselves and not to be acted upon**, save it be by the punishment of the law at the great and last day, according to the commandments which God hath given.
>
> **Wherefore, men are free** according to the flesh; and all things are given them, which are expedient unto man. And **they are free to choose liberty and eternal life, through the great Mediator of all men,** or to choose captivity and death, according to the captivity and power of the devil; for he seeketh that all men might be miserable like unto himself (*BofM: 2 Nephi* 2:25-27; emphasis added).

These verses teach that because of the Messiah, people have become free "to act for themselves and not be acted upon." This means that the Savior's atonement has made it possible for us to become a **cause** over our own condition.

Our Eternal Condition will be determined by our decisions to live "...according to the commandments which God hath given," or not. We will be subject only "... to the law at the great and last day...". Thus, **because of the Savior's winning the battle for our freedom, we will determine our own Eternal Condition. We will be the cause over our own situations, and Eternal Condition will not be the effect of circumstances, or of the will of others.**

Jesus Christ Has the Power to Resurrect Our Bodies

A second gift of the atonement is the resurrection of our bodies. The Record Keepers of *The Book of Mormon* taught plainly that our hope for overcoming the great abyss of death is centered in the power of resurrection, which the Savior holds. Jacob taught:

> Wherefore, beloved brethren, **be reconciled unto him [the Father] through the atonement of Christ, his Only Begotten Son, and ye may obtain a resurrection, according to the power of the resurrec-**

tion which is in Christ... (*BofM: Jacob* 4: 11; emphasis added).

Alma, later described the completeness and perfection of our bodily resurrection in this way:

> The soul shall be restored to the body, and the body to the soul; yea, and **every limb and joint shall be restored to its body; yea, even a hair of the head shall not be lost;** but all things shall be restored to their proper and perfect frame (*Alma* 40:23; emphasis added).

Amulek, a missionary companion to Alma, taught that the resurrection is universal and permanent.

> Now, there is a death [of our bodies], which is called a temporal death; and the death of Christ shall loose the bands of this temporal death, that **all shall be raised from this temporal death.**
>
> Now, behold, I have spoken unto you concerning the death of the mortal body, and also concerning the resurrection of the mortal body. I say unto you that **this mortal body is raised to an immortal body, that is from death, even from the first death unto life, that they can die no more; their spirits uniting with their bodies, never to be divided;** thus the whole becoming spiritual and immortal, that they can no more see corruption. (*BofM: Alma* 11:42, 45; emphasis added).

Jesus Christ Has the Power to Raise Our Spiritual Condition and Emotional Tone Level

As we have considered, a third blessing which comes to us because of Jesus Christ and His atonement, is His power to **raise our Emotional Tone Level, and Spiritual Condition from even the lowest levels.** This was shown by Alma's experience following his conversion. You will recall that, prior to his conversion, Alma had become an **Enemy** to the Lord's Church.

An angel visited Alma and his companions, who were the sons of king Mosiah. This angel made these young men aware of their true **Spiritual Condition**. Alma described his condition at that time as being in the "darkest abyss".

> My soul hath been redeemed from the gall of bitterness and bonds of iniquity. **I was in the darkest abyss; but now I behold the marvelous light of God. My soul was racked with eternal torment; but I am snatched, and my soul is pained no more** (*BofM: Mosiah* 27:29; emphasis added).

Also, in review, Alma later recounted this experience to his son, Helaman in this way:

> Oh, thought I, that I could be banished and become extinct both soul and body, that I might not be brought to stand in the presence of my God, to be judged of my deeds.
>
> And now, **for three days and for three nights was I racked, even with the pains of a damned soul.**
>
> And it came to pass that as I was thus racked with torment, while I was harrowed up by the memory of my many sins, behold, **I remembered also to have heard my father prophesy unto the people concerning the coming of one Jesus Christ, a Son of God, to atone for the sins of the world.**
>
> **Now, as my mind caught hold upon this thought, I cried within my heart: O Jesus, thou Son of God, have mercy on me,** who am in the gall of bitterness, and am encircled about by the everlasting chains of death.
>
> And now, behold, **when I thought this, I could remember my pains no more; yea, I was harrowed up by the memory of my sins no more.**
>
> **And oh, what joy, and what marvelous light I did behold;** yea, my soul was filled with joy as exceeding as was my pain! (*BofM: Alma* 36: 15-20; emphasis added).

In the previous chapter we reviewed the stories of Alma, and also of Ammon and his missionary brothers. In their lives we saw examples of the Savior's power to improve our emotional tone and **Spiritual Condition**. The life-changing power of Jesus Christ is still active. Many people now living have seen their lives changed because of the power of Jesus Christ.

Jesus Christ Has the Power to Forgive Our Sins Because of His Atonement

Because of His love for His Father and for us, Jesus Christ accomplished His atonement. His purpose in doing so was to obtain the power necessary to offer us a remission of our sins.

To the prophet Joseph Smith, Jesus Christ revealed further insights regarding His atonement. The Savior told the prophet that in taking upon Himself, our sins, the Savior "descended below all things…"[76], and that He had "suffered the pains of all men…"[77].

It is very difficult for us to describe or to comprehend what actually occurred during the Savior's atonement. Perhaps the best explanation of the Atonement is this one given by Elder James E. Talmage in his book, *Jesus the Christ*:

Christ's agony is unfathomable by the finite mind, both as to intensity and cause. The thought that he suffered through fear of death is untenable. Death to Him was preliminary to resurrection and triumphal return to the Father from whom He had come, and to a state of glory even beyond what He had before possessed; and, moreover, it was within His power to lay down His life voluntarily. **He struggled and groaned under a burden such as no other being who has lived on earth might even conceive as possible. It was not physical pain, nor mental anguish alone, that caused Him to suffer such torture as to produce and extrusion of blood from every pore; but a spiritual agony of soul such as only God was capable of experiencing. No other man, however great his powers of physical or mental endurance, could have suffered so; for his human organism would have succumbed and syncope [fainting) would have produced unconsciousness and welcome oblivion. In that hour of anguish Christ met and overcame all the horrors that Satan, "the prince of this world" could inflict.** The frightful struggle incident to the temptation immediately following the Lord's baptism was surpassed and overshadowed by **this supreme contest with the powers of evil.**

In some manner, actual and terribly real, though to man incomprehensible, the Savior took upon Himself the burden of the sins of mankind from Adam to the end of the world. Modern revelations assist us to a partial understanding of the awful experience. In March 1830 the glorified Lord, Jesus Christ, thus spake: **"For behold, I, God, have suffered these things for all, that they might not suffer if they would repent, but if they would not repent, they must suffer even as I, which suffering caused myself, even God, the greatest of all, to tremble because of pain, and to bleed at every pore, and to suffer both body and spirit: and would that I might not drink the bitter cup and shrink-nevertheless, glory be to the Father, and I partook and finished my preparation unto the children of men"** (*D&C* 19:16-19; compare 18:11).

From the terrible conflict in Gethsemane, Christ emerged a victor...the further tragedy of the night, and the cruel afflictions that awaited Him on the morrow, to culminate **in the frightful tortures of the cross, could not exceed the bitter anguish through which He had successfully passed**[78] (emphasis added).

As noted above and below, the Savior's suffering did not end in the Garden. As he experienced the physical suffering of the cross, the spiritual agony of Gethsemane returned. The Savior was about to reach the bottom of the abyss. He did so alone. As He completed this descent and started His assent from the abyss of suffering created by all of our sins, He gave a shout of triumph! Here is Talmage's account of these events:

> At the ninth hour, or about three in the afternoon, a loud voice surpassing the most anguished cry of physical suffering issued from the central cross, rending the dreadful darkness. It was the voice of the Christ: "Eloi, Eloi, Lama Sabachthani?", which is, being interpreted **"My God, my God, why hath thou forsaken me!"** What mind of man can fathom the significance of that awful cry? **It seems, that in addition to the fearful suffering incident to the crucifixion, the agony of Gethsemane had recurred, intensified beyond human power to endure. In that bitterest hour the dying Christ was alone, alone in most terrible reality. That the supreme sacrifice of the Son might be consummated in all its fullness, the Father seems to have withdrawn the support of His immediate Presence, leaving to the Savior of men the glory of complete victory over the forces of sin and death...**
>
> [Later] Fully realizing that He was no longer forsaken, but that His atoning sacrifice had been accepted by the Father, and that His mission in the flesh had been carried to glorious consummation, **He exclaimed in a loud voice of holy triumph; "It is finished."** In reverence, resignation, and relief, He addressed the Father saying; **"Father, into Thy hands I commend my spirit."** He bowed His head, and voluntarily gave up His life.
>
> Jesus the Christ was dead. His life had not been taken from Him except as He had willed to permit. Sweet and welcome as would have been the relief of death in any of the early stages of His suffering from Gethsemane to the cross, He lived until all things were accomplished as had been appointed. In the latter days the voice of the Lord Jesus has been heard affirming the actuality of His suffering and death, and the eternal purpose thereby accomplished. Hear and heed His words: **"For, behold the Lord your Redeemer suffered death in the flesh; wherefore he suffered the pain of all men, that all men might repent and come unto Him"** (*D&C* 18:11; emphasis added).[79]

In completing His atonement the Savior descended an abyss that equaled the depth of all human suffering combined! When He ascended from the abyss, He brought with Him the power to form a Bridge for us.

We can be spared the emotional torment described by Alma as "the pains of hell," and "the darkest abyss" if we repent and turn to the Savior (see *BofM: Alma* 37:13

THE POWER FORMULAS

and *Mosiah* 27:29). We could also call this abyss by another name: "...the valley of the shadow of death" (see *Psalms* 23:4).

If the Savior had not been willing to descend below all things in taking upon Himself the weight of sorrow and suffering caused by the sins of all mankind, He could not have obtained the power to bring us back into the presence of the Father. **It was in this darkest and deepest abyss that the power to become the Savior resided. He had to descend this abyss and experience the suffering of the atonement to claim this redeeming power.** He was the Son of God prior to the atonement. However, He became the Savior and Redeemer when He suffered and died for us.

The Savior suffered *only* for us, because he did not need to do it for Himself. He already had the power to resurrect His body, because of His lineage as the Son of the Immortal Father. Also, He was without sin. Therefore, He had no need to suffer for sin. **In other words, there was no abyss blocking His path back to the Father. The abyss He descended was mine and yours. Only He could finish this journey.**

The Savior Stands Between Us and Justice

You will recall that in Tolkien's story Gandolf stood between his friends and destruction. In like manner, the Savior stands between us and our enemies. Satan and his associates are the enemies of our souls. They desires that we fail. They work for our spiritual and physical destruction. If the Savior had not completed His atonement and resurrection, we would be come subject to Satan.

We noted earlier that Nephi wrote of the awful monster of death and hell. He also wrote that without the Savior:

> ...our spirits must have become devils, angels to a devil, to be shut out from the presence of our God, and to remain with the father of lies, in misery, like unto himself...
>
> O how great the goodness of our God, who prepareth a way for our escape from the grasp of this awful monster; yea, that monster, death and hell, which I call the death of the body, and also the death of the spirit (*BofM: 2 Nephi* 9:9-10).

Shortly before he was martyred, the great Nephite prophet, Abinadi, prophesied of the Savior. Included in this prophecy were these concepts:

> Yea, even so he shall be led, crucified, and slain, the flesh becoming subject even unto death, the will of the Son being swallowed up in the will of the Father.
>
> **And thus God breaketh the bands of death, having gained the victory over death; giving the Son power to make intercession for**

the children of men...

Having ascended into heaven, having the bowels of mercy; **being filled with compassion towards the children of men; standing betwixt them and justice; having broken the bands of death, taken upon himself their iniquity and their transgressions, having redeemed them, and satisfied the demands of justice** (*BofM: Mosiah* 15:7-9; emphasis added).

Webster's Dictionary defined betwixt as:

Between; in the space that separates two persons or things...[80]

One day, each of us will face judgment. The enemy of our souls will make his accusations and recite our sins. How will we respond?

A recent Christian song contains these lyrics:

Jesus Christ is our Savior and Deliverer. He literally stands betwixt us and justice. He has accepted the burden of our sins, and suffered for those sins. In doing so, He has met the demands of justice, and thwarted "... that monster, death and hell..."

The Savior Organized His Church So that We Could Help One Another Along the Path to Our Father

There is another analogy between the fantasy story of Gandalf, and the scriptural record of the Savior's mission. You will recall that after Gandalf had given his all to save the lives of his friends, Aragon stepped forward to lead. He inspired the others to "obey his last command," and to "follow me!"

The Savior did not leave his flock without a shepherd. His apostles, led by Peter, James and John were to feed His sheep. The Church organization, was built upon a foundation of apostles and prophets, Jesus Christ himself being the chief cornerstone. The apostles and prophets were to protect the saints from the "cunning" who would be lying "in wait to deceive" (see *NewT: Ephesians* 2:19-21 and 4:11-14).

The Savior does not intend for us to make the journey alone. He appointed leaders to guide us, and to receive revelation for His Church. With the restoration of His Church in these latter days, the Savior has once again called apostles and prophets.

Joseph Smith was ordained an apostle by Peter, James and John.[81] Since the time of Joseph Smith, there have been apostles and prophets directing the Church. These apostles and prophets lead under the inspiration of the Savior.

These apostles and prophets supervise local and regional priesthood leaders. Among the local priesthood leaders are bishops, who lead individual congregations.

Each member of the Church also has two home teachers assigned to watch over and to help them.

In addition, all members are given opportunities to participate and serve one another. In this way, the members of the Church are able to help one another along their journeys back to their Father in Heaven.

"All Things Which Are Good Cometh of Christ"

There are many other blessings brought into our lives **because of Jesus Christ and His atonement.** These blessings include:
1) "turning us from our iniquities" (*BofM: 3 Nephi* 20:26);
2) healing us spiritually and emotionally (*3 Nephi* 28:13);
3) He has the power to change our hearts, thereby making it possible for us to overcome addiction (*NewT: John* 8:34, 14:16; *BofM: Mosiah* 5:1-2);
4) He made it possible for us to receive help and inspiration through the gift of the Holy Ghost (*3 Nephi* 28:11);
5) As a result of His personal experience of mortality and the suffering which He endured for us, Jesus Christ knows by His own experience how to strengthen and help us (*BofM: Alma* 7:11-13);
6) He organized a Church, and empowered leaders to perform the ordinances of salvation and to teach and help us (*NewT: Ephesians* 2:19-21, 4:11-14).

In fact, as we consider our earth and our existence, we can see, as did Mormon, that **"...all things which are good cometh of Christ..."** (see *BofM: Moroni* 7:24; emphasis added).

There is No "Other Way" Over the Abyss

There is simply no "other way" around the Savior on the road to reaching our highest potential (see BofM: Moroni 3:17-19). The reason this is so is because our road to eternal life passes over the great abyss of death and sin. Each of us must face the reality that our bodies will die.

Also, each of us must face the fact that some of our actions have been harmful to ourselves and to others. Our bodies all must die, and our spirits have all been separated from our Father because of sin. **Death and sin are the obstacles—the abyss—which block our way.**

This separation from God is a condition called spiritual death. It is from this condition of spiritual death that we must be reborn or "born of God." As reviewed in the section about the **Spiritual Non Existence Formula**, spiritual rebirth occurs as we have faith in Jesus Christ, repent, are baptized for the remission of sin and receive the gift of the Holy Ghost.

When a person receives this gift of the Holy Ghost, he or she feels a partial reuniting with his or her Father in Heaven. This spiritual reuniting with our Father is the outcome and the meaning of the Savior's "at-one-ment..."[82]. We become "at one" with Him as His spirit touches us and changes our hearts.

The Bridge

L. Ron Hubbard spoke of "**A Bridge**" of training that people could take to improve their lives.[83] There is a Bridge which makes it possible for us to overcome physical death, and to be forgiven of our sins, thus overcoming spiritual death. **This Bridge is the resurrection and atonement provided by our Savior, Jesus Christ! Because of Him, we can gain the power to cross over the abyss of death and sin, which blocks the path back to our Heavenly Father.**

In addition to providing a bridge over the abyss, Jesus Christ has provided a guide, the Holy Spirit, to help us reach our destination.

The Grace of Jesus Christ is the Power Which Enables Us to Have Eternal Life

These blessings which come from the Savior to us, and which we could not obtain without Him, can be **described by a single word, Grace**. In a book about the far-reaching effects of the Savior's atonement, author Bruce C. Hafen gave this excellent explanation:

> The dictionary in the 1979 LDS [Latter-day Saint] edition of the *King James Bible*, under the heading "Grace," suggests that grace is needed not only because of our sins, but also because of our weaknesses and shortcomings:
>
> "It is through the grace of the Lord Jesus, made possible by his atoning sacrifice, that...individuals, through faith in the atonement of Jesus Christ and repentance of their sins, receive strength and assistance to do good works ... **This grace is an enabling power**... [that is needed] in consequence of the fall of Adam and also because of man's weaknesses and shortcomings. However, grace cannot suffice without total effort on the part of the recipient."
>
> ...In its fullness, this "gift" of grace is eternal life—being fully like God is "the greatest of all the gifts of God" (*D&C* 14:7). The term "at-one-ment" thus seems to mean not only being **with God, but being like God.**

This author also wrote of the Savior's power to heal the broken hearted.

> After his return from the wilderness of temptation, Jesus read to a

Sabbath congregation in Nazareth a passage from *Isaiah* 61, that stated a central theme of his ministry: "The Spirit of the Lord is upon me, because he hath anointed me to preach the gospel to the poor; he hath sent me to **heal the brokenhearted**, to preach deliverance to the captives, and recovering of sight to the blind, to set at liberty them that are bruised" (*NewT: Luke* 4:18; emphasis added).[84]

This grace is an everlasting power, which could be compared to a bridge. His grace bridges the great obstacles of sin and death, which stand in the way of our returning to be with our Father.

It is important that we keep the concept of grace in its proper perspective. For, although the Savior has provided the **bridge**, we must **decide** if we are going to cross over it. We do so by exercising our faith in Him, by repenting, being baptized and receiving the Holy Spirit.

Even after we have crossed the **bridge** by accepting the Savior and His atonement, we have a long and difficult path ahead of us. We must persist or "endure to the end in following the example of the Son of the living God ..." (*BofM: 2 Nephi* 31:16). It will take **our greatest effort** to walk the path, and we will need the guidance of the Holy Ghost.

Nephi gave us a great insight into how **our efforts and the Savior's atoning grace are both needed** for us to achieve our goal.

> For we labor diligently to write, to persuade our children, and also our brethren, to believe in Christ, and to be reconciled to God; **for we know that it is by grace that we are saved, after all we can do** (*BofM: 2 Nephi* 25:23; emphasis added).

Doing good works alone is not enough. Also, having faith alone is not enough. What we need is good works, which are born or motivated by our faith in Jesus Christ.

To end all doubt about the necessity of our **efforts or works and having faith in Jesus Christ**, here are the words of the Savior, Himself:

> **Not everyone that saith unto me, Lord, Lord, shall enter into the kingdom of heaven; but he that doeth the will of my Father which is in heaven...**
>
> **Therefore whosoever heareth these sayings of mine, and doeth them, I will liken him unto a wise man, which built his house upon a rock:**
>
> And the rain descended, and the floods came, and the winds blew, and beat upon that house; and it fell not: for it was founded upon a rock.
>
> And everyone that heareth these sayings of mine, and **doeth them**

not, shall be likened unto a **foolish man, which built his house upon the sand:**

And the rain descended, and the floods came, and the winds blew, and beat upon that house; and it fell: and great was the fall of it (*NewT: Matthew* 7:21,23-27; emphasis added).

The Book of Mormon is the Bridge Between Christianity and Scientology

In the previous chapters, examples have been cited to show that *The Book of Mormon* teaches principles like those of the **Power** and **Power Change Formulas**. A central message of this book is that *The Book of Mormon* is God's **Power Formula** for our lives. The Lord has inspired prophets to **make a record** for us (see *BofM: 1 Nephi:1-2, Mormon* 1:1).

However, *The Book of Mormon* is not Nephi's or Mormon's Record. Nor is it the Record of any other man. The Lord, through His final Record Keeper, Mormon, tells us that the Record contains "...my words unto you...".

And I exhort you to remember these things; for the time speedily cometh that ye shall know that I lie not, for ye shall see me at the bar of God; and the **Lord God will say unto you: Did I not declare my words unto you, which were written by this man...**(*BofM: Moroni* 10:27; emphasis added).

The Record was made by men, but their teachings come from the Lord. This is why *The Book of Mormon* contains God's **Power Formula**.

The Book of Mormon testifies that **Jesus is the Christ, The Eternal God** (see *BofM*: Title Page). This record teaches us to follow Him. The first Book of Mormon Record Keeper, Nephi, taught this principle in this way:

And now, my beloved brethren, **I know by this that unless a man shall endure to the end, in following the example of the Son of the living God, he cannot be saved** (*BofM: 2 Nephi* 31:16).

Those who are familiar with the principle of the **Power Change Formula** will recognize this same principle is contained in Nephi's instruction to follow "...the example of the Son of God".

In Chapter 3, we briefly discussed the eight dynamics as described by L. Ron Hubbard. *The Book of Mormon* supplies the essential data on the 8th Dynamic. This is "the dynamic of the Supreme Being" (see Chapter 3).

In summary, *The Book of Mormon* is a bridge between Christianity and Scientology for these reasons:

1) *The Book of Mormon* contains God's record and **Power Formula** for our lives;

2) It teaches us to do spiritual **Power Change** by following the example of Jesus Christ;
3) *The Book of Mormon* provides the essential knowledge about the Supreme Being, as mentioned in the 8th Dynamic. *The Book of Mormon* also teaches us His "...great plan of happiness..." (*BofM: Alma* 42:8).

The Atonement of Jesus Christ is the Bridge to Our Heavenly Father

Jesus Christ's powers of resurrection and atonement provide our bridge to eternal life with our Father. We must decide if we will cross the Bridge by gaining **faith** in Him, and by **doing** His will. There is no other way, and no other Bridge to our destination. Nephi testified that:

> **...this is the way; and there is none other way nor name** given under heaven whereby man can be saved in the kingdom of God. And now, behold, this is the doctrine of Christ, and the only and true doctrine of the Father... (*BofM: 2 Nephi* 31:21; emphasis added).

He Is The Way

The Savior testified that:

> **I am the way, the truth, and the life: no man cometh unto the Father, but by me** (*NewT: John* 14:6; emphasis-added).

What is the meaning of "the way"? Among Noah Webster's definitions are three, which seem to apply.

1) ... a passage;
3) course; direction of motion or travel;
10) manner of thinking, or behavior...[85]

Jesus Christ has blazed the road or passage leading to our Father in Heaven. He has provided the road map for our journey in His records. He also gives us current daily guidance through His servants, the apostles and prophets and through the guidance of the Holy Ghost. He has also shown us the way of thinking and behaving by His example. We are to follow His example and His way.

He is the Power

In addition to showing us the way, Jesus Christ also provides the power to us to return to our Father. After He had completed His resurrection and atonement, the

Savior taught the apostles that "**...all power** is given unto me in heaven and in earth" (see *NewT: Matthew* 28:18; emphasis added). "All power" includes the power to bring us across the great abyss of sin and death, and back into the presence of our Father in Heaven.

The Bridge

Jesus Christ has overcome all of our enemies and all of theobstacles to our being with, and being like Our Father in Heaven

This is why the Power of His Atonement and the Power of His Resurrection provides our Bridge across the Abyss of Sin and Death.

He is The Way, The Truth, The Life, And The BridgeTo Our Father In Heaven.

Chapter 10

Alma² Passed the Record to His Son Helaman², Teaching that God Shows His Power Through the Record

Alma² added much to the Record. Nearly one fifth of *The Book of Mormon* comes from Mormon's abridgement of Alma's writings. Also, Alma had a great influence on future Record Keepers. Of the final ten *Book of Mormon* Record Keepers, at least eight were direct descendants of Alma.

Alma's Power Formula with Helaman

When Alma gave the Record to his son Helaman, he took great care in training him. In doing so, Alma used actions like all four steps of the **Power Formula**. Alma taught Helaman to keep the Records "even as I have kept them."

> And now, my son Helaman, I command you that **ye take the Records**, which have been entrusted with me;
> And I also command you that ye **keep a record** of this people, **according as I have done**, upon the plates of Nephi, and **keep all these things sacred which I have kept, even as I have kept them;** for it is for a wise purpose that they are kept (*BofM: Alma* 37:1 & 2; emphasis added).

Alma Taught Helaman the Principle We Now Call Power Change

Alma was teaching his son, Helaman, to use the same principle, which is contained in the **Power Change Formula**. Alma's verbal and written instructions to Helaman included the phrase:

> I also command you that ye **keep a record** of this people, according **as I have done**.

The essence of the **Power Change Formula** is doing as your predecessor has done. This is what Alma told Helaman to do. Actually, Alma taught this principle to Helaman twice in one verse:

Keep a record of this people according as I have done...and...keep all these things sacred which I have kept, **even as I have kept them**.

Alma Also Used and Taught His Son using the Same Principles as the Power Formula

Through his example, Alma taught Helaman how to stay in communication with his successor, make, "or keep" a record, get the record to that successor, and then give him instructions to help him also be a successful record keeper. These four actions are identical to the four steps of the **Power Formula**!

The Book of Mormon prophets followed and taught these principles over, and over, and over again! In *Chapter 2*, we reviewed the many references of these ancient prophets to **making a record**. The question was asked: are these similarities in *The Book of Mormon* and the **Power Formula** references to making a record just coincidental? Chapter 2, contained this reason for my belief that their similarities are not just coincidental:

> It is possible that a casual reader may look at Nephi's first verses of *The Book of Mormon*, and also the words of Mormon about making a record, and see only a coincidence in their similarity to L. Ron Hubbard's **Power Formula**. However, as we look at *The Book of Mormon* as a whole, we see a consistent pattern of actions by the authors to make a record to preserve and to pass these writings on.
>
> As one Record Keeper finished he would prepare his successor. The way he prepared the next Record Keeper followed the pattern described in the **Power Formula. Therefore, the entire Book of Mormon was made by men who would make a record, and then got it into the hands of their successor.**
>
> Because of this consistency it becomes much more difficult to discount Nephi's and Mormon's references to making a record as being only coincidentally similar to the **Power Formula** (see *Chapter 2*, herein).

We have examined much evidence of these **Power Formula** patterns already. In the story of Alma and Helaman, we see yet even greater evidence that these similarities are not coincidental.

Alma's Instructions on Record Keeping Were the Most Complete in *The Book of Mormon*

As Alma prepared his son, Helaman, to receive the Record, he gave him the most complete set of instructions for Record Keepers in *The Book of Mormon*. These instructions are contained in the 37th chapter of *Alma*.

RECORD OF HELAMAN²

Pre-mortal Planning and Preparation Were Required to Bring Us *The Book of Mormon*

The Lord has shown great care in having *The Book of Mormon* Records preserved, and passed from one generation to another. He must have made plans from before the foundation of the world, to have such a Record made. He placed men in each generation who were capable of becoming His Record Keepers.

The Lord must have had very important purposes in doing so. Alma described these purposes as "great and eternal" and "wise" (*BofM: Alma* 37:7, 12).

Chapter 37 of Alma, explains some of the Lord's purposes for making the Record. We will now review these purposes.

The Lord's Purposes for Making *The Book of Mormon* Record

In the first twenty verses of the thirty-seventh chapter of his book, Alma was teaching his successors about the Record. In these verses, he referred seven times to the Lord's "purpose" or "purposes" in having the Record made. Alma also used the words "power" or "powerful" six times, in these same twenty verses.

These instructions could be compared to the fourth step of the **Power Formula**. In teaching Helaman his duties, Alma was doing all that he could to help him successfully occupy the "post" or calling of Record Keeper.

In addition, Alma's actions also incorporated all the others steps of the **Power Formula**. He maintained communication, and thereby he did not "disconnect" from Helaman. Alma also made a record, and got it into the hands of Helaman. We can learn a great deal from these verses and the Lord's purpose for *The Book of Mormon*. Next, we will consider some of the purposes one by one.

Purpose One, Bringing "About the Salvation of Many Souls"

Alma taught:

> Behold, it has been prophesied by our fathers, that they [the Records] should be kept and handed down from one generation to another, and be kept and preserved by the hand of the Lord until they should go forth unto every nation, kindred, tongue, and people, that they shall know of the mysteries contained thereon.
>
> Now ye may suppose that this is foolishness in me; but behold I say unto you, that **by small and simple things are great things brought to pass; and small means in many instances doth confound the wise.**
>
> And the Lord God doth work by means to bring about **His great and eternal purposes;** and by very small means the Lord doth con-

found the wise and **bringeth about the salvation of many souls** (*BofM: Alma* 37:4, 6, 7; emphasis added).

Purposes Two, Three and Four: Enlarging People's "Memory", Convincing Them of the "Error of Their Ways" and Providing Them "Knowledge of Their God Unto the Salvation of Their Souls" — Thereby, Providing the Lord's Cognitive Thinking Manual for Our Lives

Alma also taught:

> And now, it has hitherto been wisdom in God that these things should be preserved; for behold, **they have enlarged the memory of this people, yea, and convinced many of the error of their ways, and brought them to the knowledge of their God unto the salvation of their souls** (*BofM: Alma* 37:8; emphasis added).

Purpose Five, Six, Seven and Eight: The Record is Meant to be Used in Teaching the Gospel (Missionary Work); Bringing People to Repentance, and Thereby Leading People to "Rejoice"

> Yea, I say unto you, **were it not for these things that these records do contain**, which are on these plates, **Ammon and his brethren could not have convinced so many thousands of the Lamanites** of the incorrect tradition of their fathers; yea, **these records and their words brought them unto repentance; that is, they brought them to the knowledge of the Lord their God, and to rejoice in Jesus Christ** their Redeemer (*BofM: Alma* 37:9; emphasis added).

Purpose Nine: To Show the Lord's Power

Although even Alma did not know all of the Lord's purposes in producing *The Book of Mormon*, he did teach Helaman about one of these "wise" purposes. This purpose was to "...show forth His power unto future generations." This is accomplished as the sum of the above listed purposes. Here is Alma's reference to this purpose of the Lord in having the Record preserved and "kept sacred":

> And now remember, my son, that God has entrusted you with these things, which are sacred, which he has kept sacred, and also which he will keep and preserve **for a wise purpose** in him, **that he may show forth his power unto future generations.**
> ...For he **promised unto them that he would preserve these things for a wise purpose in him, that he might show forth his power unto**

future generations (*BofM: Alma* 37:14,18; emphasis added).

By way of review, the word **power** means "the ability to do or act," and "the capability of accomplishing something" (see reference #2). What has the Lord been able to accomplish through His Record? Verse 19 answers this question.

> And now behold, **one purpose hath he fulfilled**, even to the **restoration of many thousands of the Lamanites to the knowledge of the truth** [referring to those who had recently been converted by Ammon and other missionaries]; **and he hath shown forth his power in them** [the Records], **and he will also still show forth his power in them unto future generations; therefore they** [the Records] **shall be preserved.**
> Therefore I command you, my son Helaman, that ye be diligent in fulfilling all my words, and that ye **be diligent in keeping the commandments of God as they are written** (*BofM: Alma* 37:19-20; emphasis added).

The Lord Shows His Power by Producing Change in our Hearts and Lives

Here we see how the Lord has shown forth his power through these records. **He shows His power in the changes which occur in the lives of those who read, and then live by the teachings of His record.**

About 67 years after Alma, Samuel, a Lamanite prophet, spoke of how the Record brought about changes in the lives of the Lamanite converts of his day. Samuel taught how the Lord exercises His power to change lives through His scriptural records. These people's lives had been changed because they had been:

> **…led to believe the holy scriptures, yea, the prophecies of the holy prophets, which are written, which leadeth them to faith on the Lord, and unto repentance, which faith and repentance bringeth a change of heart unto them…**(*BofM: Helaman* 15:7; emphasis added).

In this verse Samuel outlined the sequence of how the scriptural records produced a change in peoples hearts. This process included the steps listed below:

1) **They were taught from the Record** by the missionaries;
2) **They believed in the Record and in the prophets who wrote it;**
3) This belief led to a **faith in the Lord, Jesus Christ, because the prophets and their records testify of Him;**
4) This **faith in the Lord led to repentance, which in turn led to:**

5) "**A change of heart**."

This change of heart is produced by the effect of the Holy Spirit upon people. People can change their minds, but it is only the Lord who can change their hearts (see BofM: Alma 5:6-14).

His Record Teaches Us How to Find His Life-Changing Power

The Lord's overall purpose in providing a Record for us is to enable us follow the Savior. He wants us to become like Him. Following Jesus Christ is **Spiritual Power Change**. In order to follow Him, we need a Record to guide our steps. *The Book of Mormon* is that Record.

Our journey to being with, and being like our Father may seem impossible to us now. In actuality, we are far along that path already. We have already made many important decisions in our pre-mortal spirit existence. This life is the final portion of our journey. It is though we are poised at the final base amp on Mt. Everest. We need to decide if we will finish our climb, or not.

We have been placed upon this earth with a physical body, and with our freedom to choose. We have also temporarily lost the memory of this pre-mortal existence. Therefore, we must search for, and locate, the path back to our Father.

This path is the one blazed by Jesus Christ. It is a path of love, service and of keeping the commandments of the Father. We enter the gate of this path as we are born of God, and thus come out of **Spiritual Non Existence**, in our relationship to our Father in Heaven. We have reviewed how this change occurs, through faith in Jesus Christ, repentance, baptism for the remission of sins, and then receiving the gift of the Holy Ghost.

The combination of our best efforts, and relying upon the Savior's power, are both necessary. We cannot do what He has done for us. However, we must do what we can do. Jesus Christ has walked the path, and made the Bridge over the Abyss of sin and death. The Savior has left us a Record, which provides a map, showing us the way. Our choice is simple. Will we follow Him, or not?

Helaman[2] Accepted Alma's Instructions, and Became the Next Record Keeper

Near the end of his life, Alma[2] called his sons to his side. He spoke to each son separately, giving advice, encouragement, and specific instructions. These instructions dealt with each son's own personal questions and challenges. In Chapter 45, Alma asked his son, Helaman, for a commitment to replace him as the Record Keeper. Here is Mormon's account of their conversation:

RECORD OF HELAMAN[2]

And it came to pass in the nineteenth year of the reign of the judges over the people of Nephi, that Alma came unto his son Helaman and said unto him: **Believest thou the words which I spake unto thee concerning those records which have been kept?** [see chapter 37, just reviewed].

And Helaman said unto him: Yea, I believe. And Alma said again: **Believest thou in Jesus Christ,** who shall come?

"And he said: **Yea**, I believe all the words, which thou hast spoken.

And Alma said unto him again: **Will ye keep my commandments?** [including Alma's commandments regarding the Record; see *BofM: Alma* 37:9-20].

And he said: **Yea, I will keep thy commandments with all my heart.**

Then Alma said unto him: **Blessed art thou; and the Lord shall prosper thee in this land** (*BofM: Alma* 45:2-8; emphasis added).

Helaman[2] accepted this challenge. He became the next Record Keeper. Helaman chronicled a period of great wars between the Lamanite and Nephite nations. Mormon's abridgment of Helaman[2]'s Records is found in Alma chapters 45 through 62.

Helaman also led an army of young Lamanites, whose families had been converted by Ammon and his companions. This small, but incredibly devoted, army turned the tide of the battle. Helaman and his 2,000 "stripling soldiers" probably saved the Nephite nation (see *BofM: Alma* 53).

Helaman[2] eventually gave the Records to his brother, Shiblon. Three years later, Shiblon gave them to Helaman[2]'s son, Helaman[3]. By the way, the first Helaman mentioned in *The Book of Mormon*, or Helaman[1], was a son of king Benjamin. This first Helaman lived about 50 years before Helaman[2].

Note that the account of these record transfers was made by Mormon, for it is written in the third person. Note also Mormon's reference to how the Record was "...written and sent forth among the children of men throughout the land".

And it came to pass in the commencement of the thirty and sixth year of the reign of the judges over the people of Nephi, **that Shiblon took possession of those sacred things [records], which had been delivered unto Helaman by Alma.**

And he was a just man, and he did walk uprightly before God; and he did observe to do good continually, to keep the commandments of the Lord his God ...

Therefore it became expedient for Shiblon to confer those sacred things, before his death, upon the son of Helaman, who was called Helaman, being called after the name of his father.

Now behold, **all those engravings which were in the possession**

of Helaman were written and sent forth among the children of men throughout all the land, save it were those parts which had been commanded by Alma should not go forth.

Nevertheless, **these things were to be kept sacred, and handed down from one generation to another; therefore, in this year, they had been conferred upon Helaman, before the death of Shiblon.**

And thus ended the account of Alma, and Helaman his son, and also Shiblon, who was his [Alma's] son (*BofM: Alma* 63:1-2, 11-13, 17; emphasis added).

The Power in the Lord's Power Formula

Alma's instructions to Helaman also teach us some very important truths. Among these truths are some of the Lord's purposes for having His servants make a record for us. The Lord uses this Record as an instrument to demonstrate His power to elevate and change our lives.

Our Father in Heaven and his Son, Jesus Christ, have the power to raise the Conditions of men and nations. **The Father and the Son not only have this power, they are the power to change lives.**

One means that they have helped us to improve our Condition is through inspiring their servants to "make a record" for us to follow. **As we read the Record, we develop faith in Jesus Christ. This faith leads us to repent. As we change through repentance, and as we are baptized for the remission of our sins, the Holy Spirit produces a great change in our hearts.**

As men and women are thus changed, their lives become living examples of the Lord's power. This is how the Lord "Shows Forth His Power" through His Record: *The Book of Mormon.*

Chapter 11

Helaman³ and His Sons Tried To Bring Their People Out Of Danger

Many Book of Mormon Records Have Been Published Previously

As noted in the previous chapter, when Helaman³ received the Records from his uncle, Shiblon, he had the engravings written down and sent forth "throughout all the land".

> Now behold, **all those engravings, which were in the possession Helaman, were written and sent forth among the children of men throughout all the land,** save it were those parts which had been commanded by Alma should not go forth (*BofM: Alma* 63:12).

These scriptural Records were not meant to be read only by future generations. The messages in these engraved Records were also designed to help the people who lived in the days of these prophet, Record Keepers. The contemporary use of the sacred record among the Nephites and Lamanites was also confirmed during the time of Helaman's grandfather Alma² who wrote:

> ...one purpose hath he fulfilled, even to the restoration of many thousands of the Lamanites to the knowledge of the truth (*BofM: Alma* 37:19).

As we look at this verse in *The Book of Mormon*, we see a printed letter reference next to this scripture. If one looks at the bottom of the page under verse 19, reference "a," "we are" referred to *Alma* 23:5. This chapter is an account of the missionary work performed by the sons of Mosiah, among the Lamanites. Thus, the sacred Records were used in the time of Alma and the sons of King Mosiah to teach the gospel. In this way "...many thousands..." were restored to the "...knowledge of the truth".

A Mission or a Kingdom?

Each of Mosiah's four sons could have followed their father as king. However

Ammon, Aaron, Omner and Himni preferred to do missionary work. For the next 14 years, these men taught the gospel to their brethren, the Lamanites. They had great success. One reason for their success was the Records, which they used in their teaching.

> And **thousands were brought to the knowledge of the Lord**, yea, thousands were brought to believe in the traditions of the Nephites; and **they were taught the Records and prophecies which were handed down even to the present time** (*BofM: Alma* 23:5; emphasis added).

About 80 years after Helaman published and distributed the writings of the Records, the Savior appeared on this continent. At this time, the Records were also being used to teach the people (see *BofM: 3 Nephi* 23). **Therefore, it is incorrect to think that the Record was first published in 1830. It appears that the prophets were routinely having the engraved Records written and distributed to their people.**

The writing being distributed to the Nephites and Lamanites would not have included Mormon's abridgment. Mormon lived much later. Rather, these Records were probably an unabridged collection of the Books of Nephi, Jacob, Omni, Mosiah, Alma, Helaman and the Old Testament scriptures which were contained on the brass plates. These published collections probably included the writings of all the Prophet/Record Keepers up until the time of each publication.

The reason we can make this assumption with some confidence is that Mormon reported that "all those engravings... were written and sent forth...throughout the land" (*BofM: Alma* 63:12). Mormon also taught that Aaron and his brethren "...taught the Records and prophecies which were handed down even to the present time" (*BofM: Alma* 23:4-5).

However, some sections of the Record were not meant for general distribution. Mormon indicated that Alma had instructed his descendants on which parts they were not to distributed:

> Now behold, all those engravings which were in the possession of Helaman were written and sent forth among the children of men throughout all the land, **save it were those parts which had been commanded by Alma should not go forth** (*BofM: Alma* 63:12).

The parts of the Record that Alma did not want to have distributed refered to how some of the people had formed secret combinations which promoted "...wickedness and...murders...". Alma did not want others "...to fall into darkness also, and be destroyed" (see *BofM: Alma* 37:27-32).

THE RECORD OF HELAMAN³ AND HIS SONS

The Book of Helaman

After receiving the plates from his uncle Shiblom, Helaman³ added his own teachings. He then passed the Record to his son Nephi² who added his own teachings to his father's Record. Nephi also included some teachings of a Lamanite prophet named Samuel. The teachings of Helaman³, Nephi², Samuel the Lamanite, and Mormon's commentary about this period make up *The Book of Helaman*.

Helaman's Sons Nephi and Lehi Spent Their Lives Teaching Others About the Savior

Nephi² and his brother Lehi⁴ devoted their lives to teaching the gospel. Their efforts helped many people. Mormon wrote about a mission of Nephi and Lehi to the Lamanites:

> And it came to pass that Nephi and Lehi did preach unto the Lamanites with such great power and authority, for they had power and authority, given unto them that they might speak, and they also had what they should speak given unto them—
> Therefore they did speak unto the great astonishment of the Lamanites, to the convincing them, insomuch that **there were eight thousand of the Lamanites who were in the land of Zarahemla and round about baptized unto repentance**, and were convinced of the wickedness of the traditions of their fathers (*BofM: Helaman* 5:18-19; emphasis added).

Although many responded to the preaching of Nephi and Lehi, the majority of people would not repent. As a result, the condition of the Nephite nation continued on a downward trend.

Nephi² Carried Out Actions Like Power Change for the Positions of Chief Judge and Record Keeper

Nephi² became the chief judge of the Nephite nation. Mormon wrote favorably of Nephi's leadership:

> And it came to pass in the fifty and third year of the reign of the judges, **Helaman died, and his eldest son Nephi began to reign in his stead.** And it came to pass that he did fill the judgment-seat with justice and equity; yea, **he did keep the commandments of God, and did walk in the ways of his father** (*BofM: Helaman* 3:37; emphasis added).

Of course, you will recognize the essential Power Change Formula action of

Nephi in this verse.

The central concept of Power Change is "don't change anything..." (see Reference #18). Please also note that Nephi² followed the same principle as that of the Power Change Formula. He did so by following both the commandments of God, and by "...walking in the ways of his father".

Prior to the change of their government to a representative form, the Nephites reckoned time from their departure from Jerusalem (see BofM: 2 Nephi 5:28). The Nephites reckoned time in this way for 509 years (BofM: Mosiah 29:44-47). For approximately the next one hundred years, the Nephites figured their calendar according to the reign of the judges. With the coming of the "night without darkness," which signaled the birth of the Savior, the Nephites changed to numbering their years to start "...from the coming of Christ..." (*BofM: 3 Nephi 2:4-8*).

No doubt, Nephi² was elected to be chief judge, rather than appointed. This policy of electing chief judges was started by Mosiah fifty-three years previously. You will note that the Nephites used this important event in their recording of time. The above verse is a good example of how they reckoned time prior to the birth of the Savior:

And it came to pass in the fifty and third year of reign of the judges...

Nephi² Found That His Three Hats Were One Too Many

Nephi² had three important "hats" of responsibility. These responsibilities were Record Keeper and the chief judge of the government. Also, although it is not specifically stated, Nephi was probably the leader of the Lord's Church.

Nephi² Passed the Hat of Government Leadership so He Could Teach the People Full Time

Nephi soon realized that he would have to give up the role of judge and concentrate all his efforts in teaching the people. He was trying to prevent the destruction of his people. Perhaps Nephi was following the example of Alma² who also gave up the judgment seat to devote his full time to trying to improve the **Spiritual Condition** of his people. Mormon engraved these words about Nephi's decision:

And it came to pass that in this same year, behold, **Nephi delivered up the judgment-seat to a man whose name was Cezoram**.

For as their laws and their governments were established by the voice of the people, and **they who chose evil were more numerous than they who chose good, therefore they were ripening for destruction, for the laws had become corrupted.**

Yea, and this was not all; they were a stiff necked people, insomuch that **they could not be governed by the law nor justice**, save it were to their destruction.

And it came to pass that **Nephi had become weary because of their iniquity; and he yielded up the judgment-seat, and took it upon him to preach the word of God all the remainder of his days, and his brother Lehi also, all the remainder of his days** (*BofM: Helaman* 5:1-4; emphasis added).

Examples of "Burnout" and How This Problem Was Handled in *The Book of Mormon*

In the verses quoted above, Mormon gave an interesting definition of a condition we now refer to as burnout. Mormon wrote that:

> ...Nephi had become weary because of their iniquity; and he yielded up the judgment seat... (*BofM: Helaman* 5:4).

We see this same reaction in the lives of many people in our time. This is a particular problem for law enforcement officers. My father, who was a police detective, taught me that officers of the law have to deal with the dark side of life including crime, people's hatred, cruelty to each other and violence on a regular basis. Being exposed to these experiences takes a toll on those who are trying to help and protect others.

Alma[2] also experienced something of a burnout in his position as the Nephite chief judge. By the way, the Nephite system of government, although based on freedom and democracy, was unlike ours. The difference was this: as far as we can discern from *The Book of Mormon*, the chief judge was also their chief executive, or as we would say in the United States, their president. Therefore, he carried two heavy burdens. These were being both the head of the judiciary and of the executive branches of the government.

We don't know for certain of there were a legislative branch of government among the Nephites. However, according to Moron's commentary found in *Alma* 4:16, the chief judge who replaces Alma when he resigned had "...power to enact laws...and put them in force..." as well. No wonder these individuals could become "...sorely grieved...", and "...very sorrowful..." (in other words, burned out (see *BofM: Alma* 4:7, 15).

Mormon observed that because of the pride, the wickedness, the despising of others, and the inequity of the Nephite people, Alma and many others were "...sorely grieved..." (*BofM: Alma* 4:6-16). Mormon also wrote that Alma:

> ...began to be very sorrowful; nevertheless the Spirit of the Lord did not fail him...(*BofM: Alma* 4:15).

THE POWER FORMULAS

It is interesting to see how Alma, and Nephi responded to their similar situations. They both left the positions, which were completely causing their weariness and sorrow. However, rather than retiring, both Alma and Nephi turned their full attention to correcting the causes of the problems they were seeing in their society. They devoted themselves to improving the **Spiritual Condition** of their people, by teaching them the gospel of Jesus Christ.

We can learn a cure for burnout from the examples of Alma and Nephi. The three things that Alma and Nephi did were:

1) They changed their environment by turning over some of their responsibilities to someone else;
2) They maintained a closeness to the Spirit of the Lord;
3) They became involved in valuable service designed to help other people.

Those who suffer burnout in our time could consider these three actions to overcome problems in their own lives.

Nephi[2] Had Been Trained by His Father Who Used Actions Like Those of the Power Formula

Lehi and Nephi followed the words of their father, Helaman. Helaman's actions of preparing a Record, passing it to his sons and giving them help through personal instructions were in perfect alignment with the steps of the **Power Formula.**

Please note how Helaman used the Record of king Benjamin to teach his sons. Helaman also quoted part of Amulek's testimony of Jesus Christ. Amulek was a missionary companion of Alma[2]. Here are some of Helaman's instructions to his sons:

> For **they remembered the words which their father Helaman spake unto them. And these are the words which he spake:**
> Behold, my sons, I desire that ye should remember to keep the commandments of God; and I would that ye should declare unto the people these words...
> **O remember, remember, my sons, the words which king Benjamin spake unto his people; yea, remember that there is no other way nor means whereby man can be saved, only through the atoning blood of Jesus Christ,** who shall come, yea, remember that he cometh to redeem the world.
> And remember also the words which Amulek spake unto Zeezrom, in the city of Ammonihah; for he said unto him that the Lord surely should come to redeem his people, but that he should not come to redeem them in their sins, but to redeem them from their sins.
> And **he hath power given unto him from the Father to redeem**

them from their sins because of repentance; therefore he hath sent his angels to declare the tidings of **the conditions of repentance, which bringeth unto the power of the Redeemer, unto the salvation of their souls** (*BofM: Helaman* 5:5, 6, 9-11: emphasis added).

In the chapter on Benjamin, we referred to his teaching that there was "no other name given nor any other way nor means whereby salvation can come unto the children of men, only in and through the name of Christ" (*BofM: Mosiah* 3:1-7). Helaman here used the Record of Benjamin to teach his sons these central truths about the Savior and His Power:

1) Where His power comes from (His Father);
2) What He can do with it (Redeem us by paying the penalties for our sins);
3) The limits of this redeeming power (it cannot help those who will not come "unto the Power of the Redeemer";
4) **How the Savior's redeeming power is activated in our lives (through our faith in Him, and "...because of repentance...";**
5) **The Savior sends angels to His prophets, who in turn teach us by making a Record of these life-changing truths.**

Nephi and Lehi were two of the Lord's representatives at this time. They endeavored to bring people to the power of Jesus Christ through teaching faith and repentance. Nephi and Lehi had received the Lord's "power and authority...that they might speak in behalf of the Lord" (see *BofM: Helaman* 5:18-19).

This is an example of how the Savior delegates His power to men on the earth. Through such individuals He is able also to bring about the change in our hearts. Such changes come as we love and seek the truth. Inspired leaders, like Nephi and Lehi, have, "what they should speak given unto them."

We can feel the life-changing influence of the Lord's Spirit, both as we read His records, and as we listen to His authorized and inspired representatives. **As the Lord's earthly representatives teach by the power of the spirit, they are actually living Records of the truth.**

How the Lord Teaches Moral Truths

I. He teaches His prophets:
 1) Directly (see *BofM: Helaman* 10:1-12);
 2) Through Angels (see *Helaman* 13:7-11);
 3) Through previous scriptures (see *Helaman* 5:9-11);
 4) Through the Holy Ghost (see *Helaman* 4:40).
II. We receive truth through:
 1) The previous prophets [scriptures] (see *BofM: Alma* 14:1);

2) Through living prophets and apostles (see *BofM: Helaman* 13);
3) Through each other (see *BofM: Alma* 4:7, 15:13);
4) Through the Holy Spirit (see *BofM: Mosiah* 5:1-5);
5) We can also receive truth through angels or directly from the Lord Himself. However, the information given to individuals is for their personal benefits or meant to benefit those they serve. The Lord reveals directions for the Church as a whole only through His apostles and prophets (see *BofM: Alma* 32:33; *D&C* 43:1-7, 1:1-17, 38).

The "More Part", Meaning the Majority of the Nephites Rejected Their Living Prophets

Unfortunately, only a minority of the Nephite people who heard Nephi and Lehi chose to avail themselves of the blessings of repentance.

Samuel, the Lamanite Prophet

We do not know the background of Samuel's early life. However, we know that he was called of the Lord to declare repentance to the Nephites. This represented a change in the common pattern. Usually, the Nephites were the more righteous of the two groups, and they usually sent missionaries to the Lamanites.

However, at this time, a righteous Lamanite group was in a higher **Spiritual Condition** than many of the Nephites. These verses describe the mission of Samuel, the prophet:

> And now it came to pass in the eighty and sixth year, the Nephites did still remain in wickedness, yea in great wickedness, while the Lamanites did observe strictly to keep the commandments of God, according to the law of Moses.
>
> And it came to pass that in this year there was one Samuel, a Lamanite, came into the land of Zarahemla, and began to preach unto the people. And it came to pass that he did preach, many days, repentance unto the people, and they did cast him out, and he was about to return to his own land.
>
> But behold, the voice of the Lord came unto him, that he should return again, and prophesy unto the people whatsoever things should come into his heart (*BofM: Helaman* 13:1-3, emphasis added).

Samuel Prophesied of the Savior's Birth, Death and Resurrection

In addition to teaching a message of repentance, Samuel prophesied at length regarding the signs and wonders which would occur on this continent at the times of the Savior's birth and death. Samuel prophesied of two signs which would be shown to those on this continent, indicating the Savior's birth. These signs were to be the appearance of a new star, and a night without darkness.

Samuel also prophesied of the events, which would accompany the Savior's death. Among these prophecies were: three days of darkness, and then the resurrection of many, following the Savior's resurrection. Here are these prophecies:

> And behold, again, another sign I give unto you, yea, **a sign of his death**.
>
> But behold, as I said unto you concerning another sign, a sign of his death, behold, in that day that he shall suffer death the sun shall be darkened and refuse to give his light unto you; and also the moon and the stars; and **there shall be no light upon the face of this land, even from the time that he shall suffer death, for the space of three days, to the time that he shall rise again from the dead.**
>
> And **many graves shall be opened, and shall yield up many of their dead; and many saints shall appear unto many** (*BofM: Helaman* 14:14, 20, 25; emphasis added).

When the Savior appeared to the people on the American continent, He referred to this prophecy by Samuel and its fulfillment. We will review this incident in the next chapter.

In the case of Samuel, the Lamanite prophet, some of the Nephites even sought to take his life. Mormon recorded that Samuel taught the Nephites while standing on the top of their city wall. Here is Mormon's account of these events:

> But **the more part of them did not believe in the words of Samuel**; therefore when they saw that they could not hit him with their stones and their arrows, they cried unto their captains, saying: Take this fellow and bind him, for behold he hath a devil; and because of the power of the devil which is in him we cannot hit him with our stones and our arrows; therefore take him and bind him, and away with him.
>
> And as they went forth to lay their hands on him, behold, he did cast himself down from the wall, and did flee out of their lands, yea, even unto his own country, and **began to preach and to prophesy among his own people.**
>
> And behold, he was never heard of more among the Nephites; and thus were the affairs of the people.
>
> And thus ended also the eighty and seventh year of the reign of the judges, **the more part of the people remaining in their pride and**

wickedness, and the lesser part walking more circumspectly before God (*BofM: Helaman* 16:6-8, 10; emphasis added).

The Spiritual Condition of the Majority of the Nephites Declined

At this point, it would be good to recall king Mosiah's warning when he first instituted a representative form of government:

> Now it is not common that the voice of the people desireth anything contrary to that which is right; but it is common for the lesser part of the people to desire that which is not right; therefore this shall ye observe and make it your law to do your business by the voice of the people.
>
> And **if the time comes that the voice of the people doth choose iniquity, then is the time that the judgments of God will come upon you; yea, then is the time he will visit you with great destruction** even as he has hitherto visited this land (*BofM: Mosiah* 29:26-27; emphasis added).

The **Conditions** of the majority of these people were leading them toward destruction. You will recall that Nephi² had cited the serious problems of the **majority** of his people as a reason for giving up the government seat and to preach full time (see *BofM: Helaman* 5:1-4). Also, note in this verse, how the **Spiritual Condition** of these people affected their laws:

> And it came to pass that in this same year, behold, Nephi delivered up the judgment seat to a man whose name was Cezoram.
>
> For as their laws and their governments were established by the voice of the people, and **they who chose evil were more numerous than they who chose good, therefore they were ripening for destruction, for the laws had become corrupted** (*BofM: Helaman* 5:1-2).

Within about one generation, this destruction occurred for many. Those who were more righteous would survive. They would also be privileged to experience the greatest single event in the Record—the appearance of the Savior to the people on this continent. However, the Recording of those events, both sorrowful and joyous, would fall to the next Record Keeper, Nephi³.

Before we turn to the Record of Nephi³, it is well for us to consider Mosiah's warning again. If opinion polls can be believed, it appears that on moral, even life or death issues such as abortion, the majority opinion in our nation is approaching or already past the danger point.

As a result, some of our laws have also "...become corrupted".

If we do not learn from the downfall of the Nephites, and if the **Spiritual Condition** of the integrity of the people of our nation continues to decline, we should not expect to escape the "great destruction" which they brought upon themselves.

THE POWER FORMULAS

Chapter 12

Nephi² Gave "Charge Unto His Son," Nephi³, Who "Did Keep the Records in His Stead"

The Record Keepers Were Also Very Successful Parents

It is amazing that these Record Keepers were able to complete their difficult missions, and raise such outstanding children as well! When Helaman gave his son Nephi² the Records, it was the tenth time that the Records had been passed from father to son.

Also, father-to-son transmission of the Record would occur four more times. Of the twenty-two record transfers in *The Book of Mormon*, fifteen were from father to son. This is a remarkable example of raising righteous children.

In addition, four of these exchanges were between brothers. These exchanges were: Nephi¹ to Jacob, Amaron to Chemish, Helaman² to Shiblon, and Amos² to Ammaron. In only three of these transfers, there is no evidence of a familial relation between the Record Keepers. These three were: Amaleki to Benjamin, Mosiah to Alma² and Ammaron to Mormon.

The Power Formula Between Nephi² and Nephi³

Now, turning to the story of Nephi³. Perhaps no Record Keeper in *The Book of Mormon* lived to see a greater period of contrast than did Nephi³. His life spanned from a very low point in the **Spiritual Condition** of the Nephite civilization to the highest point of their society. This apex of Nephite and Lamanite culture was initiated by the visit of Jesus Christ to these people. Thirty-three years prior to the Savior's visit, Nephi³ received this "charge" to keep the Record from his father, Nephi²:

> And Nephi[2], the son of Helaman, had departed out of the land of Zarahemla, **giving charge unto his son Nephi[3], who was his eldest son, concerning the plates of brass, and all the Records** which had been kept, and all those things which had been kept sacred from the departure of Lehi out of Jerusalem.
> Then he departed out of the land, and whither he went, no man knoweth; and **his son Nephi did keep the Records in his stead**, yea,

the Record of this people (*BofM: 3 Nephi* 1:2-3; emphasis added).

It is significant to note that Nephi³ received the Record from his father in the same year that the Savior was born in Bethlehem of Judea. This was the year A.D. 1. The **Spiritual Condition** of the majority of the Nephite and Lamanite peoples had continued to deteriorate.

Eventually, those who did not believe the prophets began to persecute those who did. These unbelievers, recalling Samuel's prophecy of a night that would "...not be darkened...," threatened the believers with death, if this prophecy was not fulfilled. Mormon wrote:

> But there were some who began to say that the time was past for the words to be fulfilled, which were spoken by Samuel, the Lamanite.
>
> And they began to rejoice over their brethren, saying: Behold the time is past, and the words of Samuel are not fulfilled; therefore, your joy and your faith concerning this thing hath been vain.
>
> And it came to pass that they did make a great uproar throughout the land; and the people who believed began to be very sorrowful, lest by any means those things which had been spoken might not come to pass.
>
> But behold, they did watch steadfastly for that day and that night and that day which should be as one day as if there were no night, that they might know that their faith had not been in vain.
>
> **Now it came to pass that there was a day set apart by the unbelievers, that all those who believed in those traditions should be put to death except the sign should come to pass, which had been given by Samuel the prophet.**
>
> Now it came to pass that when Nephi³, the son of Nephi², saw this wickedness of his people, his heart was exceedingly sorrowful (*BofM: 3 Nephi* 1:5-10).

Nephi³ was greatly concerned for his people, and he prayed in their behalf. His prayer was answered with this assurance, from the Lord:

> Lift up your head and be of good cheer; for behold, the time is at hand, and on this night shall the sign be given, and **on the morrow come I into the world, to show unto the world that I will fulfill all that which I have caused to be spoken by the mouth of my holy prophets.**
>
> And it came to pass that the words which came unto Nephi were fulfilled, according as they had been spoken; for behold, at the going down of the sun there was no darkness; and the people began to be astonished because there was no darkness when the night came (*BofM: 3 Nephi* 1:13, 15).

Jesus Christ is Jehovah

In these verses, The Savior, Jesus Christ, identifies that **He** is the one who has been speaking to the prophets:

> ...I will fulfill all that which **I have caused to be spoken by the mouth of my holy prophets** (*BofM: 3 Nephi* 1:13, emphasis added).

The God known as Jehovah prior to His birth became known as Jesus Christ when He came to earth. He was coming to fulfill the prophecies, which He had given to these ancient prophets. When the Savior later appeared to the Nephites, He announced that the Law of Moses had been fulfilled, and that it was He who had given the law.

> And he said unto them: Marvel not that I said unto you that old things had passed away, and that all things had become new.
> Behold, I say unto you that the law is fulfilled that was given unto Moses.
> **Behold, I am he that gave the law, and I am he who covenanted with my people Israel;** therefore, the law in me is fulfilled, for I have come to fulfill the law; therefore it hath an end (*BofM: 3 Nephi* 15:5; emphasis added).

During His visit to the ancient American inhabitants, Jesus Christ also taught:

> Arise and come forth unto me, that ye may thrust your hands into my side, and also **that ye may feel the prints of the nails in my hands and in my feet, that ye may know that I am the God of Israel, and the God of the whole earth, and have been slain for the sins of the world** (*BofM: 3 Nephi* 11:14; emphasis added).

In his book, ***Jesus the Christ***, James E. Talmage wrote about the meaning of the word **Jehovah**, and the identity of this Being:

> **Jehovah** is the Anglicized rendering of the Hebrew, **Yahweh or Jahveh, signifying the Self-existent One, or The Eternal.** This name is generally rendered in our English version of the Old Testament as LORD, printed in capitals. The Hebrew, **Ehyeh, signifying I Am**, is related in meaning and through derivation with the term **Yahweh or Jehovah**; and herein lies the significance of this name by which the Lord revealed Himself to Moses when the latter received the commission to go into Egypt and deliver the children of Israel from bondage: "Moses said unto God, Behold, when I

come unto the children of Israel, and shall say unto them, The God of your fathers hath sent me unto you; and they shall say to me, What is his name? What shall I say unto them? And God said unto Moses, I AM THAT I AM; and he said, Thus shall thou say unto the children of Israel, I AM hath sent me unto you." In the succeeding verse the Lord declares Himself to be "the God of Abraham, the God of Isaac, and the God of Jacob." While Moses was in Egypt, the Lord further revealed Himself, saying "I am the LORD: and I appeared unto Abraham, unto Isaac, and unto Jacob, by the name of God Almighty, but by my name JEHOVAH was I not known to them." The central fact connoted by this name, **I Am, or Jehovah**, the two having essentially the same meaning, is that of existence or duration that shall have no end, and which, judged by all human standards of reckoning, could have had no beginning; the name is related to such other titles as **Alpha and Omega**, the first and the last, the beginning and the end."

Jesus, when once assailed with question and criticism from certain Jews who regarded their Abrahamic lineage as an assurance of divine preferment, met their abusive words with the declaration: **"Verily, verily, I say unto you, Before Abraham was, I am."** The true significance of this saying would be more plainly expressed were the sentence punctuated and pointed as follows: "Verily, verily, I say unto you, **Before Abraham, was I AM"; which means the same as had He said-Before Abraham, was I, Jehovah**[86] (emphasis added).

In his notes to this chapter in *Jesus the Christ*, James E. Talmage further wrote regarding the identity of Israel's God by quoting the words of another of the Lord's modern servants, Franklin D. Richards:

> Jesus Christ, the God of Israel—That Jesus Christ was the same Being who called Abraham from his native country, who led Israel out of the land of Egypt with mighty miracles and wonders, who made known to them His law amid the thunderings of Sinai, who delivered them from their enemies, who chastened them for their disobedience, who inspired their prophets, and whose glory filled Solomon's temple, is evident from all the inspired writings, and in none more so than in the Bible.
> **His lamentation over Jerusalem in the New Testament evidences that, in His humanity, He had not forgotten His former exalted position: "O Jerusalem, Jerusalem thou that killest the prophets, and stonest them which are sent unto thee, how often would I have gathered thy children together,...and ye would not!" (Matthew**

23:37) From *Compendium Of The Doctrines Of the Gospel*, by Franklin D. Richards and James A. Little[87] (emphasis added).

Jesus Christ is a Separate Being from Our Father in Heaven

We should not be confused about the relationship of the Father and the Son. Jesus Christ is Jehovah, but He is not our Heavenly Father. James E. Talmage explained this concept in this way:

> The name **Elohim** is of frequent occurrence in the Hebrew texts of the Old Testament, though it is not found in our English versions. In form the word is a Hebrew plural noun; but it connotes the plurality of excellence or intensity, rather than distinctively of number. It is expressive of supreme or absolute exaltation and power. **Elohim**, as understood and **used in the restored Church of Jesus Christ, is the name-title of God the Eternal Father, whose firstborn Son in the spirit is Jehovah—the Only Begotten in the flesh, Jesus Christ...**
>
> A general consideration of scriptural evidence leads to the conclusion that **God the Eternal Father has manifested Himself to earthly prophets or revelators on very few occasions, and then principally to attest the divine authority of His Son, Jesus Christ**[88] (emphasis added).

Apostle Talmage also wrote about the trial of Jesus, prior to His crucifixion. Take special note of the final phrase of this commentary.

> The first question put to Him was, "Art thou the Christ? Tell us." The Lord made dignified reply: "If I tell you, ye will not believe: and if I also ask you, ye will not answer me, nor let me go. Hereafter shall the Son of man sit on the right hand of the power of God." Neither did the question imply nor the answer furnish cause for condemnation. The whole nation was looking for the Messiah; and if Jesus claimed to be He, the only proper judicial action would be that of inquiring into the merit of the claim. The crucial question followed immediately: "Art thou then the Son of God? And he said unto them, Ye say that I am. And they said, what need we any further witness? For we ourselves have heard of his own mouth" (*NewT: Luke* 22:66-71). **Jehovah was convicted of blasphemy against Jehovah**[89] (emphasis added).

THE POWER FORMULAS

Jehovah, Who is Jesus Christ, Has Saved Many of His Followers from Early Physical Death

We know that many times in *The Old Testament*, Jehovah's power was used to Deliver His followers. Perhaps the best known example of His Deliverance is when He worked the miracle of parting the Red Sea, through His servant, Moses. Because of this miraculous intervention, His people were delivered from death or bondage at the hands of Pharaoh and his armies (see *OldT: Exodus* 14).

During His mortal ministry, the Savior delivered many individuals from physical death. These would include those critically ill people whom He healed, and those whom He raised from the dead. These included the daughter of Jairus (see *NewT: Mark* 4:41), the only son of a widow in the city of Nain (see *NewT: Luke* 7:15), and Lazarus (see *NewT: John* 11:1-44). He also saved a woman from being stoned to death (see *NewT: John*: 8). Jesus Christ also saved His apostles from being taken and possibly crucified when He was arrested (see *NewT: John* 18:7-9).

Many prophets have written of His future deliverance of His people when He comes again in His glory. Zechariah, in particular, speaks of how He will preserve his people in Jerusalem from destruction (see *OldT: Zechariah* 14:1-9). Christians refer to this appearance as the Second Coming of Jesus Christ.

Jesus Christ was Born as a Deliverer

Also, from Nephi's[3] account we learn that at the very moment of his birth, Jesus Christ delivered or saved many of His followers here upon the American continent. This occurred because of the manifestation of God's power in the attending miracle of the night without darkness. As a result of this miracle, which fulfilled Samuel's prophecy, the lives of the Savior's followers on this continent were spared. Here is Mormon's account:

> And it came to pass that the words which came unto Nephi were fulfilled, according as they had been spoken; for behold, **at the going down of the sun there was no darkness;** and the people began to be astonished because there was no darkness when the night came.
>
> And there were many, who had not believed the words of the prophets, who fell to the earth and became as if they were dead, for they knew that **the great plan of destruction which they had laid for those who believed in the words of the prophets had been frustrated;** for the sign which had been given was already at hand.
>
> And it came to pass that **there was no darkness in all that night, but it was as light as though it was mid-day.** And it came to pass that the sun did rise in the morning again, according to its proper order; and **they knew that it was the day that the Lord should be born,**

because of the sign which had been given (*BofM: 3 Nephi* 1:15,16,19; emphasis added).

This Miracle Brought Change in Condition of Both Those Who Accepted, and Those Who Rejected It

The miracle of a night without darkness had a marvelous effect upon many people. As a result of this wonderful sign, many people had a change of heart. They became receptive to the teachings of Nephi[3] and other missionaries.

> And it came to pass that Nephi went forth among the people, and also many others, baptizing unto repentance, in the which there was a great remission of sins. And thus the people began again to have peace in the land (*BofM:3 Nephi* 1:23).

Unfortunately, many others would not believe and repent. **Perhaps the reason many did not believe was because they did not want to repent.** Soon the clouds of spiritual darkness began to gather again. During the next 33 years, while the Savior was dwelling among His fellowmen on the other side of the earth, ethics and spiritual conditions deteriorated among the majority of the Nephites and Lamanites.

It is as though the miracle of the night without darkness had a negative effect on some of these people. The effect of this miracle on those who would not believe was the opposite to the effect of the miracle on those whose hearts were softened and changed. **When light comes to one who does not want that light, their rejection of the light will actually leave that person in greater darkness.**

You may recall another example of this truth in the lives of Laman and Lemuel. These rebellious older brothers of Nephi[1], witnessed more than one miracle. They had even seen an angel. However, they refused to have faith in, or to obey the Lord. Six-hundred years later these rebellious Nephites and Lamanites failed to learn a lesson from the negative examples of Laman and Lemuel.

Organized Crime is Not New

As the ethics and spiritual condition of these groups continued to deteriorate, crime became an increasing problem. Soon an organized band of robbers began to plague these nations. These robbers became so powerful that they could actually declare open war on the nations around them. Isn't it interesting how these events sound so much like the news we hear out of many nations in our own day. Here is an example of organized crime among *The Book of Mormon* peoples.

> And it came to pass in the commencement of the fourteenth year [14 A.D.], **the war between the robbers and the people of Nephi did con-**

tinue and did become exceedingly sore; nevertheless, the people of Nephi did gain some advantage of the robbers, insomuch that **they did drive them back out of their lands into the mountains and into their secret places.**

And thus ended the fourteenth year. And in the fifteenth year they did come forth against the people of Nephi; and because of the wickedness of the people of Nephi, and their many contentions and dissensions, the Gadianton robbers did gain many advantages over them.

And thus ended the fifteenth year, and thus were the people in a state of many afflictions; and the sword of destruction did hang over them, insomuch that they were about to be smitten down by it, and this because of their iniquity (*BofM: 3 Nephi* 2:17-19).

The Nephites were blessed with two leaders who responded appropriately to this dangerous situation. The first of these leaders was Lachoneus. He was the chief judge, and he was also a "great prophet." Lachoneus selected a man of equal abilities, named Gidgiddoni, to lead the Nephite army.

These men prepared the Nephites to defend themselves. Because of their fortifications, their gathering to a central defensible location, and because of their foresight in storing provisions for a seven year period, the Nephites eventually prevailed in this war. This is perhaps one of history's great examples of how to defend against siege warfare. Mormon, who was also a military commander, observed:

> And the robbers could not exist save it were in the wilderness, for the want of food; for **the Nephites had left their lands desolate, and had gathered their flocks and their herds and all their substance, and they were in one body.**
>
> Therefore, there was no chance for the robbers to plunder and to obtain food, save it were to come up in open battle against the Nephites; and the Nephites being in one body, and having so great a number, and **having reserved for themselves provisions, and horses and cattle, and flocks of every kind, that they might subsist for the space of seven years, in the which time they did hope to destroy the robbers from off the face of the land**; and thus the eighteenth year did pass away.
>
> And notwithstanding the threatenings and the oaths which Giddianhi [the leader of the army of robbers] had made, behold, the Nephites did beat them, insomuch that they did fall back from before them (*BofM: 3 Nephi* 4:3, 4, 12).

THE RECORD OF NEPHI[3]

Pride Proved to be More Difficult to Conquer Than an Invading Army

This victory over the robber's army did not solve the underlying problem of many Nephites. This was the problem of pride.

> But it came to pass in the twenty and ninth year there began to be some disputings among the people; and **some were lifted up unto pride and boastings because of their exceedingly great riches,** yea, even unto great persecutions;
> Now the cause of this iniquity of the people was this—Satan had great power, unto the stirring up of the people to do all manner of iniquity, and to the **puffing them up with pride, tempting them to seek for power,** and authority, and riches, and the vain things of the world.
> And thus Satan did lead away the hearts of the people to do all manner of iniquity; therefore they had enjoyed peace but a few years.
> **Now they did not sin ignorantly, for they knew the will of God concerning them, for it had been taught unto them; therefore they did willfully rebel against God** (*BofM: 3 Nephi* 6:10,15,16,18; emphasis added).

Although the Nephites had been able to conquer an external enemy, many could not deal with their own **internal enemy of pride**. As a result, divisions, contentions, secret combinations and conspiracies occurred. The Nephite chief judge was murdered, as were many prophets who tried to teach the people. Mormon described the condition of these people, in this way:

> Now all this was done, and there were no wars as yet among them; and all this iniquity had come upon the people because they did yield themselves unto the power of Satan.
> And **the regulations of the government were destroyed,** because of the secret combination of the friends and kindreds of those who murdered the prophets.
> And they did cause a great contention in the land, insomuch that the more righteous part of the people had nearly all become wicked; yea, **there were but few righteous men among them** (*BofM: 3 Nephi* 7:5-7).

Nephi[3], the Record Keeper, was among the prophets who tried to prevent the people from bringing about their own destruction. Also, his brother, Timothy, was one of the prophets who was killed while trying to teach the people. However, Nephi[3] raised Timothy from the dead. Both of these men were later called to be among the Savior's twelve ancient American disciples (see *BofM:3 Nephi* 7:17-19, 19:4).

Nephi had some success, but many people persisted on the course leading to destruction. This decline eventually led to a period of great disasters in the form of earthquakes, fires and other upheavals. This destruction came at the same time the Savior was being crucified on a hill called Golgotha, outside the city of Jerusalem.

On this continent many of the more wicked people died in these disasters. The remainder of the people found themselves enveloped in an atmosphere of thick darkness.

Before we describe the Savior's visit to these people, we will first review a few of Mormon's commentaries on this period. As Mormon read, Nephi³'s account and then engraved an abridged version of Nephi's book onto his plates, Mormon added many valuable personal insights.

Mormon Explained Why He Decided to Make a Record

You will recall from Chapter 1, Mormon's reference to making a record. This quote came from the first verse of his personal account, *Mormon* 1:1. It was during his abridgement of the writing of Nephi³ (the *Book of Third Nephi*) that Mormon explained his reasons for abridging the writings of other Record Keepers. Please notice how many times he refers to **the Record**, or **making a Record** in these verses:

> Therefore I have **made my Record** of these things according to the Record of Nephi, which was engraven on the plates, which were called the large plates of Nephi.
>
> And behold, I do **make the Record** on plates, which I have made with mine own hands.
>
> And behold, I am called Mormon, being called after the land of Mormon, the land in which Alma did establish the church among the people, yea, the first church, which was established among them after their transgression.
>
> Behold, I am a disciple of Jesus Christ, the Son of God. I have been called of him to declare his word among his people, that they might have everlasting life.
>
> And it hath become expedient that I, **according to the will of God**, that the prayers of those who have gone hence, who were the holy ones, should be fulfilled according to their faith, should **make a record** of these things which have been done—
>
> Yea, **a small record** of that which hath taken place from the time that Lehi left Jerusalem, even down until the present time.
>
> Therefore I do **make my record** from the accounts, which have been given by those who were before me, until the commencement of my day;
>
> And then I do **make a record** of the things, which I have seen with mine own eyes.

THE RECORD OF NEPHI³

And I know **the record which I make** to be a just and **a true record**; nevertheless there are many things which, according to our language, we are not able to write (*BofM: 3 Nephi* 5: 10-18; emphasis added).

It is remarkable that in these 10 verses, Mormon makes reference to the Record 10 times! In these verses, Mormon also twice used the indented phrase found in the **Power Formula**: "...make a record". Additionally, when Mormon later added his own writings to the abridgment of the Records of others, the very first thing he wrote was:

And now I, Mormon, **make a record** of the things which I have both seen and heard, and call it *The Book of Mormon* (*BofM: Mormon* 1:1, emphasis added).

Also, as discussed at the beginning of this book, Nephi¹, the first, author and record keeper of the engraved metal plates which were later translated into *The Book of Mormon*, began his writings with the same phrase:

I, Nephi, ...make a record..." (*BofM: 1 Nephi* :1).

Perhaps you are thinking that its just a coincidence that L. Ron Hubbard's **Power Formula** and *The Book of Mormon*, both contain the phrase: "make a record". However, here is a challenge: if you think this is coincidental, name another book witten over 100 years before L. Ron Hubbard's time that contains this phrase **four times**.

The common use of this phrase, and the many other examples of the principles of the **Power and Power Change Formulas** are found within *The Book of Mormon* are present, not as a result of chance or coincidence. Rather, these concepts are similar, because they both share the same stream and source of truth. The source of all truth is our Father in Heaven. The stream of His truth flows through Jesus Christ, and the Holy Spirit, to us by way of inspiration and revelation.

The Book of Mormon is God's verification that the principles found in the **Power and Power Change Formulas** are true principles.

Also, conversely, the fact that the principles of **The Power and Power Change Fomulas** are found throughout *The Book of Mormon* is God's verification to those who accept the teachings of L. Ron Hubbard that *The Book of Mormon* is a true Book of Scripture from God.

When you understand these facts, it then behooves you to act. The actions needed are to read, pray about and then follow God's teachings as found in *The Book of Mormon*, and in The Church which publishes this Book of Scripture: The Church of Jesus Christ of Latter-day Saints.

THE POWER FORMULAS

The Actions Required by The Source

The actions that our Father in Heaven expects of us can be summarized as listed below:

1) Have faith in your Father in Heaven, in His Son Jesus Christ and in the Holy Ghost. Faith is a belief strong enough to inspire hope an action.

2) Repent of all your sins, all those past, present and future.

3) Be baptized for the remission of your sins, by one holding God's priesthood authority in The Church of Jesus Christ of Latter-day Saints.

4) Actively receive the Gift of the Holy Ghost, who brings a mighty change of heart away from sin, and who brings the ability to love like God loves.

5) Receive the ordinances and make the covenants with God that are available in God's Holy Temples (see *Super Power* for more on this).

6) Endure to the end of your life in doing good, and sharing your love by following the example of Jesus Christ (see *2nd Nephi* chapter 31).

The Result of These Actions

When you have carried out the above actions, the eventual result will be Eternal Life, which means living with and becoming like God. It also means living with our families, in the presence of Gode. Eternal life is the prize we need to keep our eyes on. It doesn't end—it can't get any better than this.

Please make Eternal Life your goal and aim to do what needs to be done to achieve the goal.

It is my testimony to you that these concepts are true. These truths answer the question posed by people who had just learned of Jesus Christ by listening to His apostles. Their question was this, "...men and brethren, what shall we do?..." (see *New Test. Acts Chapter 2*, especially verses 37 and 38, but please read the entire chapter).

Now you know what need to be done. It is time to act. Please do.

For help see the *Afterword*.

In Making His Abridged Record, Mormon was Fulfilling God's Will, and Fulfilling the Prayers of Previous Record Keepers

Now please focus on verse fourteen. In this verse, Mormon tells two reasons why he made his record:

> And it hath become expedient that I, **according to the will of God, that the prayers of those who have gone hence, who were the holy ones, should be fulfilled according to their faith**, should **make a record** of these things which have been done... (*BofM: 3 Nephi* 5:14; emphasis added).

We can see that Mormon's two reasons for **making a record** were: 1) because it was **"according to the will of God;"** and 2) **to fulfill "the prayers of those who have gone hence, who were holy ones."**

Perhaps you can recall some of the hopes and prayers of the previous Record Keepers. Throughout the Record, these Record Keepers had prayed that their testimonies would be preserved to bless future generations. Here are two examples, which Mormon undoubtedly read as he reviewed the writings of these Record Keepers. First we will recall Jacob's words of hope that his Record would be read by many of his brethren.

> And I, Jacob, saw that I must soon go down to my grave; wherefore, I said unto my son Enos:
>
> Take these plates. And I told him the things which my brother Nephi had commanded me, and he promised obedience unto the commands. And I make an end of my writing upon these plates, which writing has been small; and to the reader I bid farewell, **hoping that many of my brethren may read my words**. Brethren, adieu (*BofM: Jacob* 7:27; emphasis added).

This next prayer was by his Jacob's son, Enos. Please note how the Lord acknowledged that Enos was not the first to pray that the Record would be preserved to help future generations.

> And I had faith, and **I did cry unto God that he would preserve the Records; and He covenanted with me that he would bring them forth unto the Lamanites in his own due time.**
>
> And I, Enos, knew it would be according to the covenant, which he had made; wherefore my soul did rest.
>
> **And the Lord said unto me: Thy fathers have also required of me this thing;** and it shall be done unto them according to their faith; for their faith was like unto thine (*BofM: Enos* 1:16-18; emphasis added).

Mormon must have realized the great responsibility, which he had been given. Certainly he must have wanted to **make a record** for his Heavenly Father, for his people, for those who had preceded him as Record Keepers and for those of future generations

Like these earlier Record Keepers, Mormon also prayed that the Record would be preserved, and that it would help his brethren. As Mormon finished his abridgement he offered this prayer in the section titled "The Words Of Mormon":

> And **my prayer to God is concerning my brethren**, that they may once again come to the knowledge of God, yea, the redemption of

Christ; that they may once again be a delightsome people.

And now I, Mormon, proceed to finish out my record, which I take from the plates of Nephi...

And they were handed down from king Benjamin, from generation to generation until they [the small plates] have fallen into my hands. **And I, Mormon, pray to God that they may be preserved from this time henceforth. And I know that they will be preserved; for there are great things written upon them...** (*BofM: Words of Mormon* 1:8, 9, 11; emphasis added)

As mentioned in Chapter 3, these concerns for the preservation of the Records, and concern for the people of future generations, were a unifying desire of the *The Book of Mormon* Record Keepers. It became Mormon's privilege and responsibility to complete his abridgement, as he expressed it: "...to finish out my record...". In doing so, he fulfilled the prayers of the previous Record Keepers, whom he described as "holy ones." We shall look at Mormon's work in greater detail in a later chapter.

After inserting his explanation of why he was making of the Record, Mormon again returned to abridging the account of Nephi[3]. Please note how he made this transition from his personal commentary to abridging the records of Nephi[3].

Therefore I do **make my record** from the accounts which have been given by those who were before me, until the commencement of my day;

And then I do **make a record** of the things, which I have seen with mine own eyes.

And I know the **Record, which I make to be a just and a true record;** nevertheless there are many things which, according to our language, we are not able to write.

And now **I make an end of my saying, which is of myself** *[editorial comments, written in the first person]*, **and proceed to give my account of the things which have been before me** [Mormon returns to his [*third person*] abridgement of Nephi's[3] record] (*BofM: 3 Nephi* 5:16-19).

Chapter 13

Nephi's Account of the Visit and Teachings of Jesus Christ are the Heart of *The Book of Mormon* Record

Mormon Also Wrote of Great Natural Disasters Which Occurred on This Continent

Unfortunately, as Mormon returned to the story of Nephi^3's time, he returned to a story of many people who were headed for sorrow, and for sudden death. You will recall that the prophet Samuel had predicted that signs would occur on this continent when the Savior died in Jerusalem. These signs included a period of darkness lasting three days and great earthquakes on this continent. These national disasters came as a result of the extremely low spiritual condition of the people.

Those who survived these disasters were the more righteous portion of the population.

Conversely, for those who had been more wise, a time of great joy was approaching. The Savior would appear to those who survived these disasters. These people would receive the Lord's **Power Formula**, which is His gospel, directly from their Savior.

Jesus Christ Appeared to the People of Ancient America

Mormon prefaces the account of the Savior's appearance by describing the situation of the people who had survived the destructions. These people had gathered to the temple in a place they called Bountiful. The time was approximately six weeks after the Savior's resurrection.[90]

> And now it came to pass that there were a great multitude gathered together, of the people of Nephi, round about the temple which was in the land Bountiful; and they were marveling and wondering one with another, and were showing one to another the great and marvelous change which had taken place.
> And they were also conversing about this Jesus Christ, of whom the sign had been given concerning his death (*BofM: 3 Nephi* 11:1-2).

THE POWER FORMULAS

Our Father in Heaven Introduced His Son Jesus Christ

As the people were conversing, they heard a voice "as if it came out of heaven." At first they did not understand what they were hearing, perhaps because they were so overcome by the way they felt. For the voice was:

> ...not a harsh voice, neither was it a loud voice; nevertheless, and notwithstanding it being a small voice **it did pierce them that did hear to the center, insomuch that there was no part of their frame that it did not cause to quake; yea, it did pierce them to the very soul, and did cause their hearts to burn** (*BofM: 3 Nephi* 11:3; emphasis added).

It must have been a truly amazing experience for these people. They were among the very few in the history of the world to actually hear the voice of the Father! Down through the ages the Father has made His will known through His Son, Jesus Christ. Almost the only time the Father has spoken to men and women, is when He is introducing His Son, and testifying of the Son's divine authority. This was one of these introductions.

In the case of these Nephites, it took three times before they could recover from the profound emotional experience of hearing the voice of their Father, and actually "open their ears" and understand His words.

> And again the third time they did hear the voice, and did open their ears to hear it; and their eyes were towards the sound thereof; and they did look steadfastly towards heaven, from whence the sound came.
>
> And behold, the third time they did understand the voice, which they heard; and it said unto them:
>
> **Behold my Beloved Son, in whom I am well pleased, in whom I have glorified my name hear ye him** (*BofM: 3 Nephi* 11:5-7; emphasis added).

In *Part Two* of the *Power Formulas*, we shall look at these introductions in detail. The Father's introductions are actually part of the **Power Formula**-like actions, which God the Father has used for His Son.

These introductions are actually testimonies of the Savior's divinity, authority and mission. As such, these introductions fulfill the fourth principle of the **Power Formula**, which is doing all you can to help someone assume a "post" meaning a position. The Savior defined the position He had received from the Father when He later taught the people that:

> **...I am the God of Israel and the God of the whole earth, and have been slain for the sins of the world** (see *BofM: 3 Nephi* 11:14).

THE RECORD OF JESUS CHRIST

The People Saw, Heard and Touched Their God

What could possibly be more wonderful than hearing the Father's voice? Meeting His Son! These people were about to **see, hear and actually touch their God! First they saw:**

> **...a Man descending out of heaven;** and he was clothed in a white robe; and he came down and stood in the midst of them; and the eyes of the whole multitude were turned upon him, and they durst not open their mouths, even one to another, and wist [understood] not what it meant, for they thought it was an angel that had appeared unto them (*BofM: 3 Nephi* 11:8; emphasis added).

Here in the space of just a few minutes these people had **another** overwhelming experience. At first, the people did not realize who He was. Although they had heard the Father introduce Him as "My beloved Son," they thought that "it was an angel that had appeared unto them."

The Savior must have known of their confusion, for He re-introduced Himself. **Next, these people heard Him speak:**

> ...saying: **Behold, I am Jesus Christ, whom the prophets testified shall come into the world** (*BofM: 3 Nephi* 11:9-10).

Please note that **Jesus Christ testified of the prophets who had testified of Him.** There could be no doubt that these prophets and Record Keepers had spoken the truth, for the Lord immediately acknowledged them, and validated their testimonies of Him! In doing so, the Savior was actually using a **Power Formula**-like action for His prophet leaders among these people.

Jesus Christ then defined the purpose of His mission with these words:

> **...I am the light and the life of the world; and I have drunk out of that bitter cup which the Father hath given me, and have glorified the Father in taking upon me the sins of the world, in the which I have suffered the will of the Father in all things from the beginning** (*BofM: 3 Nephi* 11: 11; emphasis added).

The Savior Sustained His Father's Will in All Things

When one looks up the word "suffered" in the 1828 edition of Noah Webster's *American Dictionary of the English Language*, it is interesting to note that this word does not necessarily mean experiencing pain. **"Suffered" also means to allow, and to have "supported" or "sustained"**.[91] In the above verse, when the Savior said that He had "suffered the will of the Father in all things from the beginning," This means that

He has always "supported and sustained" the Father.

It was the Father's will that the Son should take upon Himself "the sins of the world". The Savior experienced incomprehensible physical and spiritual suffering during His atonement. However, in the above verse "suffered" means more than experiencing pain.

We can reach this conclusion because of the additional phrase "in all things from the beginning." The period of the Savior's actually physical and spiritual suffering cannot be described by these terms. **The Savior is saying here that He sustained or supported the will of His Father in all things from the beginning.**

Why the Savior is the Instrument of the Father's Power

We can also observe that **although the Father had already introduced the Son,** Jesus also told these people that He was the Son of God. His relationship to the Father was that of the "First Born" Spirit Child and the "Only Begotten" in the flesh (see *NewT: Colossians* 1:15; *John* 1:14).

Jesus Christ is a Sustainer, Glorifier and Witness of the Father. He is also a Perfect Example of the Father. It is through the Savior that the Father **accomplishes His will and plan.** Jesus Christ is the Instrument through which the Father exercises His power.

It does us no good to look elsewhere for the power of God. We cannot bypass Jesus Christ to get to the Father. Our Father in Heaven has made it clear that we are to **"hear ye Him"** (see *BofM: 3 Nephi* 11:7 and *NTest. Matthew* 17:1-5). Our choice is simple—we can hear the Savior and receive the truth, and the power of God, or we can choose not to hear Him and not receive His truth, nor receive His power in our lives.

Peter understood this when he answered the Lord's question at a time when many of his disciples were forsaking Jesus. The Savior asked the twelve apostles, "will ye also go away?" Peter speaking for the twelve, and indeed for all mankind, answered:

> **...Lord, to whom shall we go? Thou hast the words of eternal life** (see *NewT: John* 6:66-69).

There truly is no one else we can go to. Only our Savior, Jesus Christ, has the words, and the power of eternal life. Like these ancient Americans, and all people of all ages, **we must choose to "hear Him"!**

Jesus Christ's Teachings and Actions Provided a Power Formula for His Followers

As the Savior taught these people, the life-changing power of these experiences kept building. Their God was about to have them come forward and actually touch Him! Before we review this next marvelous experience, we will review how the Savior used actions equivalent to those of the **Power Formula** to help these people.

King Benjamin was one who used and taught the principles like those of the **Power Formulas** (see Chapter 5, King Benjamin and the **Power Formulas**). However, an even greater example of the use of these principles is found in the Savior's teachings to these people.

While visiting these people, Jesus taught them similar principles to those of the **Power** and **Power Change Formulas**. For example, He taught about the importance of a Record being made and passed to future generations. In this way, He was teaching the principles of an ongoing **Power Formula**. He wanted His teachings to also benefit those of future generations.

Jesus Christ and the Power Formula Step 1: Not Disconnecting

We will begin by reviewing the paraphrased steps of the **Power Formula**. The first step is: **"don't disconnect..."**[92] This means that when a person has achieved great success in their position, he or she should **continue to communicate with those around them.**

It also means that highly successful people should not allow themselves to become proud and look down upon others. You will recall how king Benjamin set such a fine example of not disconnecting from his people.

In the book of *Third Nephi*, Chapter 11, the Savior made an appearance to the people of the new world. It is extremely important that **following the introductions by His Father, and by Himself,** the first thing the Savior did was to teach the principle of not disconnecting. Here is how He did this:

> **And it came to pass that the Lord spake unto them saying:**
> **Arise and come forth unto me,** that ye may thrust your hands into my side, and also that ye may feel the prints of the nails in my hands and in my feet, **that ye may know that I am the God of Israel, and the God of the whole earth, and have been slain for the sins of the world.**
>
> And it came to pass that the multitude went forth, and thrust their hands into His side, and did feel the prints of the nails in his hands and in his feet; and this **they did do, going forth one by one until they had all gone forth, and did see with their eyes and did feel with their hands, and did know of a surety and did bear record,** that it was He, of whom it was written by the prophets, that should come.
>
> And when they had all gone forth and had witnessed for themselves, they did cry out with one accord, saying:
>
> Hosanna! Blessed be the name of the Most High God! And they did fall down at the feet of Jesus, and did worship Him (*BofM: 3 Nephi* 11:13-17; emphasis added).

Jesus also testified of the power He had received from His Father, when He taught

THE POWER FORMULAS

these people that: "I am the God of Israel, and the God of the whole earth." The first thing He did after establishing who He was, and establishing **His Condition of Power**, was to not disconnect. Not only did He not disconnect, He actually "connected" in a physical and spiritual way with His followers. Each person came "forth one by one" to meet and touch their God!

Regarding this remarkable event, Robert J. Matthews, the former Dean of Religious Education at Brigham Young University, has written perceptively:

> There were about 2,500 persons who saw and *felt his physical body on that occasion (see 3 Nephi* 17:25). Even at three or four seconds each, "one by one," that would take several hours. The passage we have just read is one of the greatest scriptural records in our possession. It is clear that "showing" himself involved more than having them merely look. It was sight, sound, touch, and a witness of the Spirit.[93]

It is amazing to realize how much time the Savior spent meeting each person individually. Even at four seconds per person, it would have taken over two hours and 46 minutes. It's much more likely that it took significantly **longer** than this for everyone to see and touch Him. Probably, the better part of the day, or at least one half of a day was spent in **making contact** with these 2,500 people.

What was the reaction of these blessed people? They all now **knew**, for a surety, of His reality and love. This is how they described their experiences with the Savior:

> And the multitude did see and hear and **bear record; and they know that their record is true for they all of them did see and hear, every man for himself;** and they were in number about two thousand and five hundred souls; and they did consist of men, women, and children (*BofM: 3 Nephi* 17:25).

The Savior's Visit Produced a 200-Year-Long Condition of Peace and Spiritual Power Among His Followers

Even more impressive was the effect of this wonderful experience, and His teachings upon these people. During the Savior's visit, He completed all of the actions we now call the **Power Formula**. For nearly two hundred years their society remained in a condition of peace, prosperity and enlightenment. In other words, the condition of these people was one of **Spiritual Power**. Mormon later wrote of this wonderful time, in this way:

> And it came to pass that the thirty and fourth year passed a way, and also the thirty and fifth, and behold the disciples of Jesus had formed a Church of Christ in all the lands round about. And as many

as did come unto them, and did truly repent of their sins, were baptized in the name of Jesus; and they did also receive the Holy Ghost.

And it came to pass in the thirty and sixth year, the people were all converted unto the Lord, upon all the face of the land, both Nephites and Lamanites, and **there were no contentions and disputations among them, and every man did deal justly one with another.**

And it came to pass that there was no **contention in the land, because of the love of God, which did dwell in the hearts of the people.**

And there were **no envyings, nor strifes, nor tumults, nor whoredoms, nor lyings, nor murders, nor any manner of lasciviousness; and surely there could not be a happier people** among all the people who had been created by the hand of God.

There were **no robbers, nor murderers,** neither were there Lamanites, nor any manner of -ites; but **they were in one, the children of Christ, and heirs to the kingdom of God** (*BofM: 4 Nephi* 1:1-2, 15-17; emphasis added).

Here we see **another** example of how the Lord demonstrates His power in the lives of people, by changing their hearts, and turning them from their iniquities. In short, we see how the people and their society went into a **Condition of Spiritual Power**, as a result of their experience with the Savior. This unparalleled change in the lives of these people began with the Savior "connecting" with each of them.

We shall also see in the next chapter that there is evidence that at least some of these people actually lived longer as a result of their improved **Spiritual Condition**.

Jesus Taught the People to Not Disconnect from Others

In later teachings, The Savior reminded the people that He had asked them to come to Him. He taught that they should treat others as He had treated them. In other words, He taught them to not disconnect. This is the first principle of the **Power Formula**. The Savior gave both an example, and this instruction in this principle:

And behold, ye shall meet together oft; and **ye shall not forbid any man from coming unto you when ye shall meet together, but suffer [allow] them that they may come unto you and forbid them not;**

But ye shall pray for them, and **shall not cast them out;** and if it so be that they come unto you oft ye shall pray for them unto the Father, in my name.

Therefore, **hold up your light that it may shine unto the world. Behold I am the light which ye shall hold up that which ye have seen me do.** Behold ye see that I have prayed unto the Father, and ye all have witnessed.

And ye see that I have commanded that none of you should go away, but rather have commanded that ye should come unto me, that ye might feel and see; even so shall ye do unto the world; and whosoever breaketh this commandment suffereth himself to be led into temptation (*BofM: 3 Nephi* 18:22-25; emphasis added).

Did you note that the Savior also taught the principle of **Power Change?** After reminding them of His example, He taught His people to do as He had done. He said: "...even so shall ye do...".

Pride is a Cause of Disconnecting from Others

The teachings above constitute a plain warning against disconnecting. The Savior also explained the consequence of breaking this **commandment**. The result of disconnecting is that people suffer (allow) themselves to be led into temptation.

Unrighteous pride harms our communications and our relationships with others. One of those we alienate by behaving in this way is the Holy Ghost. We then lose His companionship. Without the assistance of the Holy Ghost, our **ever-present temptations become more difficult to resist.**

Also, as we give into one temptation, two bad things happen to us. First, we isolate or disconnect ourselves even more from the Holy Ghost, and **thereby weaken our power to resist temptation**. Secondly, as we give into temptation, we put ourselves into an environment where **we are likely to find more temptation.** For these reasons, temptations increase as people disconnect from others because of pride.

The net result from losing the companionship of the Holy Ghost, and having more temptation, is that our **Spiritual Condition** is headed down, unless and until we repent.

What it Means to be Proud

It is interesting to realize that the words, pride and proud have come to represent positive virtues in our society. We hear such phrases as "proud sponsor of the Olympic Games," or "proud to be an American." It is difficult, but we must correct our misunderstanding of what it means to be proud, for in the Lord's view pride is **not** a good thing. There are no scriptural references that show pride as being a positive attribute.

Noah Webster gave these excellent definitions of the word *proud,* and why it is harmful to ourselves and to others when we allow ourselves to become proud:

1) Having inordinate self-esteem; possessing a high or unreasonable conceit of one's own excellence, either of body or mind. A man may be proud of his person, of his talents, of his accomplishments or of his achievements. **He may be**

proud of anything of which to which he bears some relation. He may be proud of his country, his government, his equipage, of whatever may, by association, gratify his esteem of himself. He may even be proud of his religion or of his church. **He can concede that any thing excellent or valuable, in which he has a share, or to which he stands related, contributes to his own importance, and this conception exalts his opinion of himself...**

2) Arrogant; haughty...(emphasis added).[94]

When we speak of **"not disconnecting"**, we are really speaking of a **warning against unrighteous pride. Pride causes disconnection from others, because we start to think of ourselves as being better than they are.**

As reviewed above, pride also leads us into temptation and into counter survival acts. Another name for a counter survival act is a sin. We can come to the conclusion that sin is counter survival by reading Paul's description of the outcome of unrepented sins:

> For **the wages of sin is death, but the gift of God is eternal life through Jesus Christ Our Lord** (*NewT: Romans* 6:23).

Pride, Disconnection, Separation and Death

Unrighteous pride leads to **separation** or **disconnection** from others, including our Father in Heaven. Pride also lowers our survival potential, and leads us towards death, both physical and spiritual. Physical death is a **separation** or **disconnection** of the body and spirit. Spiritual death is a **separation** or **disconnection** of ourselves from God.

We Offend God When We Disconnect from His Children

As we exclude and pull away from people, we offend the Father and Son because They love everyone. Jesus Christ reminded us in *The New Testament* that "inasmuch as ye have done it unto one of the least of these my brethren, ye have done it unto me" (see *NewT: Matthew* 25:31-40). Usually this verse is thought of in terms of positive values, such as love and service. However, this maxim also applies to our negative attitudes and actions as well.

Another consequence of pride is that those who are afflicted with it, render themselves unable to acknowledge the power of the Father and the Son. They seek to become a power unto themselves. As stated in the preface, the gospel of Jesus Christ is *the* **Power Formula** for our lives. We receive spiritual power by believing, loving and following our Father in Heaven and His Son, Jesus Christ.

Spiritual power flows from our Father, through His Son Jesus Christ, and then through the Holy Ghost to us. Even our limited power or ability to do and accomplish things here upon the earth comes from God. King Benjamin taught this con-

THE POWER FORMULAS

cept as he gave his final message, or **Power Formula**, to his people.

We will compare Benjamin's teachings about not disconnecting with those given about 160 years later by the Savior. We can see similarities in the teachings of the Savior and of His servant, Benjamin. **This is because the Savior was the source of inspiration for Benjamin.**

Here are some of Benjamin's teachings about the subjects of how we should treat others, and about the source of our power to live:

> And behold, I tell you these things that ye may learn wisdom; that ye may learn that **when ye are in the service of your fellow beings ye are only in the service of your God** (*BofM: Mosiah* 2:17; emphasis added).
>
> I say unto you that if ye should serve him who has **created you from the beginning, and is preserving you from day to day, by lending you breath, that ye may live and move and do according to your own will, and even supporting you from one moment to another**—I say, if ye should serve him with all your whole souls yet ye would be unprofitable servants.
>
> And now, in the first place, **he hath created you, and granted unto you your lives,** for which ye are indebted unto him.
>
> And secondly, he doth require that ye should do as he hath commanded you; for which if ye do, he doth immediately bless you; and therefore he hath paid you. And **ye are still indebted unto him, and are, and will be, forever and ever; therefore, of what have ye to boast?** (*BofM: Mosiah* 2:21, 23, 24; emphasis added).

Benjamin also quoted the teachings of an angel, regarding our dependence upon God, and concerning our treatment of our fellowmen.

> And also, ye yourselves will succor [give help to] those that stand in need of your succor; ye will administer of your substance unto him that standeth in need; and **ye will not suffer that the beggar putteth up his petition to you in vain, and turn him out to perish.**
>
> **Perhaps thou shalt say: The man has brought upon himself his misery; therefore I will stay my hand, and will not give unto him of my food, nor impart unto him of my substance that he may not suffer, for his punishments are just**—
>
> **But I say unto you, O man, whosoever doeth this the same hath great cause to repent;** and except he repenteth of that which he hath done he perisheth forever, and hath no interest in the kingdom of God.
>
> **For behold, are we not all beggars? Do we not all depend upon the same Being, even God, for all the substance which we have,** for

both food and raiment, and for gold, and for silver, and for all the riches which we have of every kind? (*BofM: Mosiah* 4: 16-19; emphasis added).

The sin of pride is present when a person is unwilling to allow others to participate or unwilling to share of their abundance with those who are in need of help. Christ taught these people that they would lead themselves into temptation by refusing to have compassion for others.

The Savior referred to His own behavior as a guide for his followers to use in their relations with others. He expected his followers to treat their fellow men like He had treated them. His words on this subject are worthy of another consideration.

> And ye see that I **have commanded that none of you should go away, but rather have commanded that ye should come unto me, that ye might feel and see;** *even so shall ye do* **unto the world; and whosoever breaketh this commandment suffereth himself to be led into temptation** (*BofM: 3 Nephi* 18:25; emphasis added).

As we become successful, we may become proud if we don't understand and acknowledge the Source of our success. We become successful by following true principles. The Father and the Son are the Source of all true principles. Because They are the Source of our power of life and the Source of all true principles, how can we accurately take all the credit for our successes? We should acknowledge Them as our Source of **life**, truth, and success.

There seems to be a connection between realizing our dependence upon God, and how we treat others. As we realize our dependence upon God, we learn humility. **When our pride has been replaced with humility, we are then ready to treat others with compassion.** As we develop compassion we find ourselves connecting with others rather than disconnecting from them.

To avoid pride, we need to avoid comparing ourselves to other people. We should evaluate our progress by another Standard. In one of His sermons to these ancient Nephites, Jesus set our true goal or Standard:

> **Therefore I would that ye should be perfect even as I, or your Father who is in heaven is perfect** (*BofM:3 Nephi* 12:48; emphasis added).

When we compare ourselves to these Standards, we learn humility, rather than pride. We can then, with the help of the Holy Ghost, align ourselves with the Father and the Son. In this way, we are prepared to receive **Their power**.

There is a reason why we have spent this much time reviewing the first principle of the **Power Formula**, or not disconnecting. If we do not understand and follow this principle, we will not need the other principles of the **Power Formula**. There will be no need for us to make a Record or to get it into the hands of a successor. This is because **if we fail on this principle of not disconnecting, we will not be in a condition of spiritual power for long!**

Jesus Christ and Power Formula Step 2: Making a Record

The second step in the **Power Formula** is to "...make a record..."[96].

It is amazing to note that a large percentage of the book of Third Nephi has to do with the Savior's teaching the people and having them record His words. In addition, He gave them the words of other prophets, that these might also be added to the Record, which He was preparing for them, and for us.

While teaching these people, Jesus placed a great priority on the Record. He performed a quality control check on the Records to make certain that they were complete and accurate. We will review how the Savior checked the Record shortly.

Jesus Christ foresaw that the Record would be very important in showing forth His power through changing the lives of those who would read it. With this in mind, as we read the book of Third Nephi, it becomes apparent how important it was to the Savior that His Record be complete.

The Savior corrected Nephi[3] for not recording the fulfillment of an important prophecy made by Samuel, the Lamanite prophet. He specifically directed Nephi to repair this omission. Here are the Savior's words of instruction to His Record Keeper, Nephi:

> Therefore give heed to my words; **write the things which I have told you;** and according to the time and the will of the Father they shall go forth unto the Gentiles.
>
> And whosoever will hearken unto my words and repenteth and is baptized, the same shall be saved. Search the prophets, for many there be that testify of these things.
>
> And now it came to pass that when Jesus had said these words he said unto them again, after he had expounded all the scriptures unto them which they had received, he said unto them: **Behold, other scriptures I would that ye should write, that ye have not.**
>
> And it came to pass that he said unto Nephi: **Bring forth the record which ye have kept.**
>
> And when **Nephi had brought forth the records, and laid them before him, he cast his eyes upon them and said:**
>
> Verily I say unto you, **I commanded my servant Samuel,** the Lamanite, **that he should testify unto this people, that at the day that the Father should glorify his name in me** [meaning the day of Jesus Christ's resurrection] that there were **many saints who should arise from the dead,** and should appear unto many, and should min-

THE RECORD OF JESUS CHRIST

ister unto them. And he said unto them: **Was it not so?**

And his disciples answered him and said: **Yea, Lord, Samuel did prophesy according to thy words, and they were all fulfilled.**

And Jesus said unto them: **How be it that ye have not written this thing, that many saints did arise and appear unto many** and did minister unto them?

And it came to pass that **Nephi remembered that this thing had not been written.**

And it came to pass that **Jesus commanded that it should be written; therefore it was written** according as he commanded.

And now it came to pass that when Jesus had expounded all the scriptures in one, which they had written, he commanded them that they should teach the things which he had expounded (*BofM: 3 Nephi* 23:4-14; emphasis added).

By reviewing and correcting the Record, The Savior demonstrated that it was **His record. In fact, He really didn't need to look** at the Record at all. He already knew, or could find out, what it contained without actually looking at it. **The act of reviewing the Record served as a witness, and as a symbol, that it was His Record! What greater testimony could we have of the importance of** *The Book of Mormon*?

It is also important to note that in verse 4, **the Savior directed Nephi to make a Record of His teachings to the people. By having His servants write down His teachings, the Savior fulfilled the action we now call Step 2 of the Power Formula "...make a record...".**

The Book of Mormon Record Serves as Another Witness of Christ's Power to Resurrect Others, as Well as Himself

As noted above, the Savior instructed Nephi[3] to add the fulfillment of the prophecy of Samuel to the Record. This was a very important prophecy because its fulfillment gave another witness, along with *The Holy Bible*, of the Savior's power to resurrect others, as well as Himself. This is a strong witness.

The Lord has established the law a witnesses, which states that in "the mouth of two or three witness shall every word be established" (*NewT: 2 Corinthians* 13:1).

We have one witness of the Savior's power of resurrection in *The Holy Bible*. Matthew recorded that after the Savior's resurrection:

...the graves were opened; and **many bodies of the saints which slept arose,**

And came out of the graves a**fter his resurrection, and went into**

the holy city, and appeared unto many (*NewT: Matthew* 27:52-53; emphasis added).

In ***The Book of Mormon***, we have a second witness that the Savior's resurrection brought about the resurrection of others.

> Verily I say unto you, I commanded my servant Samuel, the Lamanite, that he should testify unto this people, that at the day that the Father should glorify his name in me that there were **many saints who should arise from the dead, and should appear unto many, and should minister unto them. And he said unto them: Was it not so?**
> **And his disciples answered him and said: Yea, Lord, Samuel did prophesy according to thy words, and they were all fulfilled** (*BofM:3 Nephi* 23:9-10).

The Resurrections of Our Bodies will be Literal, Perfect, Permanent, and Universal

The resurrection which Jesus initiated was to become a universal occurrence. The scriptures contain witnesses which lay to rest any question about the nature of man following this life. The eternal nature of man is that our bodies will all be resurrected and our spirits will re-enter these perfect and immortal bodies.

In an earlier section of the Record, Alma's missionary companion, Amulek, taught these great truths regarding the resurrection: it will be **universal, perfect and permanent**. Here are Amulek's teachings on this important subject:

> Now, there is a death which is called a temporal [bodily] death; and the death of **Christ shall loose the bands of this temporal death, that all shall be raised from this temporal death.**
> **The spirit and the body shall be reunited again in its perfect form;** both ...
> Now, **this restoration shall come to all,** both old and young, both bond and free, both male and female, both the wicked and the righteous; and even **there shall not so much as a hair of their heads be lost; but every thing shall be restored to its perfect frame...**
> Now, behold, I have spoken unto you **concerning the death of the mortal body, and also concerning the resurrection of the mortal body.** I say unto you that this mortal body is raised to an immortal body, that is from death, even from the first death unto life, that **they can die no more; their spirits uniting with their bodies, never to be divided;** thus the whole becoming spiritual and immortal, that they can no more see corruption [death] (*BofM: Alma* 11:42-45; emphasis

added).

Nephi[1] also wrote of the resurrection, and about the source of this wonderful blessing:

> **O how great the goodness of our God, who prepareth a way for our escape from the grasp of this awful monster; yea, that monster, death and hell,** which I call the death of the body, and also the death of the spirit [separation from the Father].
> And **because of the way of deliverance of our God, the Holy One of Israel [the Savior, Jesus Christ],** this death, of which I have spoken, which is the temporal, shall deliver up its dead; which death is the grave.
> And this death of which I have spoken, which is the spiritual death, shall deliver up its dead; which spiritual death is hell; wherefore, death and hell must deliver up their dead, and hell must deliver up its captive spirits, and **the grave must deliver up its captive bodies, and the bodies and the spirits of men will be restored one to the other; and it is by the power of the resurrection of the Holy One of Israel [the Savior, Jesus Christ]** (*BofM: 2 Nephi* 9:10-12; emphasis added).

It is the **power of Jesus Christ** which brings us out and across the abyss of sin and death. Only the Savior can deliver us from "the awful monster death and hell." We also learn from these verses that our spirits will not go into other bodies, as in the doctrine of reincarnation.

One may choose to believe or reject these testimonies of the resurrection. However, these witnesses are plain. **We cannot misunderstand them. The resurrection of others, besides the Savior, was seen on two continents, and two Records were made by these two independent groups of witnesses.**

Jesus Christ Added Some of the Words of His Servants Isaiah and Malachi to the Record

In Chapter 24 of *Third Nephi*, Jesus Christ taught or quoted His prophecy which He gave through His servant Malachi, in *The Old Testament*. The Savior was basically **reading this into the Record** so that the people in the new world would have it in their scriptures.

Malachi was an Old Testament prophet who had lived **after** Lehi and his family had left the old world. Therefore, they did not have Malachi's writings on the brass plates, which they brought with them. This is another reason why the Savior gave these same revelations to the Nephites.

Great lessons are taught in these chapters including prophecies regarding the

Lord's second coming in glory. The law of tithing is also taught.

In addition, Malachi made a great prophecy regarding the work of Elijah the prophet.

> Behold, I will send you Elijah the prophet before the coming of the great and dreadful day of the Lord;
> **And he shall turn the heart of the fathers to the children, and the heart of the children to their fathers,** lest I come and smite the earth with a curse (*BofM: 3 Nephi* 25:5-6; emphasis added; see also *OldT: Malachi* 4).

On April 3, 1836, Malachi's prophecy was fulfilled in the first Temple of the modern age. Here is the Prophet Joseph Smith's record of this event:

> The veil was taken from our minds, and the eyes of our understanding were opened.
> We saw the Lord standing upon the breastwork of the pulpit, before us; and under his feet was a paved work of pure gold, in color like amber.
> His eyes were as a flame of fire; the hair of his head was white like the pure snow; his countenance shone above the brightness of the sun; and his voice was as the sound of the rushing of great waters, even the voice of Jehovah, saying: I am the first and the last; I am he who liveth, I am he who was slain; I am your advocate with the Father.
> Behold, your sins are forgiven you; you are clean before me; therefore, lift up your heads and rejoice.
> Let the hearts of your brethren rejoice, and let the hearts of all my people rejoice, who have, with their might, built this house to my name.
> For behold, I have accepted this house, and my name shall be here; and I will manifest myself to my people in mercy in this house.
> Yea, I will appear unto my servants, and speak unto them with mine own voice, if my people will keep my commandments, and do not pollute this holy house.
> Yea the hearts of thousands and tens of thousands shall greatly rejoice in consequence of the blessings which shall be poured out, and the endowment with which my servants have been endowed in this house.
> After this vision had closed, another great and glorious vision burst upon us; for Elijah the prophet, who was taken to heaven without tasting death, stood before us, and said:
> Behold, the time has fully come, which was spoken of by the mouth

of Malachi—testifying that he [Elijah] should be sent, before the great and dreadful day of the Lord come—

To turn the hearts of the fathers to the children, and the children to the fathers, lest the whole earth be smitten with a curse—

Therefore, the keys of this dispensation are committed into your hands; and by this ye may know that the great and dreadful day of the Lord is near, even at the doors (*D&C* 110:1-9 and 13-16).

The prophecy has been fulfilled. Elijah has appeared to men on the earth again. The appearance of Elijah has led to the great Family History and Temple building programs of the Church of Jesus Christ of Latter-day Saints. What better description could we have of the work of family history, than to describe it as "the turning of the heart of the children to their fathers"?

The Savior also quoted from Isaiah's prophecies. *Third Nephi Chapter 22* and *23* contains prophecies about the latter-day gathering of Israel, and the re-establishment of the Lord's kingdom.

The Savior felt that these particular teachings and prophecies were important enough to be taught to these ancient Americans, and to be added to their record. These teachings were for their benefits as well as ours. **In these teachings we have a second witness of many important doctrines and prophecies.**

Jesus Taught His Doctrine in the New World as He Had Taught it in the Holy Land

The Savior not only quoted from His revelations to these prophets, He also gave many of His own teachings to His followers on this continent, as he had in the Holy Land. Among the teachings which He gave to both groups is the sermon now commonly called the Sermon on the Mount. The teachings in *Chapters 13, 14* and *15* of *Third Nephi* are very similar to those in *Matthew* 5, 6, and 7.

These teachings give us two witnesses of His doctrine. There are a few interesting differences between the two accounts. One important difference is seen as we compare *Matthew* 5:48 with *3 Nephi* 12:48.

The Holy Bible:

Be ye therefore perfect, **even as your Father which is in heaven is perfect** (*NewT: Matthew* 5:48; emphasis added).

The Book of Mormon:

Therefore I would that ye should be perfect even as I, or your Father who is in heaven is perfect (*BofM:3 Nephi* 12:48; emphasis added).

Please consider this question: why was Jesus' teaching different when He taught the Nephites than when He taught those in the Holy Land? The answer to this question is one of the main topics of *The Power Formulas, Part Two*. Therefore, we will more fully answer this question in *Part Two*. However, a brief answer is that the first statement was made **by the Savior prior to His atonement and resurrection. His later teaching to the Nephites came after these great events.**

Therefore, His teaching that His followers should become perfect like His Father came prior to His completing His mission, and thus prior to His completing **Power Change** with His father. The later teaching to His Nephite followers that they should be perfect as **He and His Father are perfect,** came after He had completed **Power Change** with the Father. With the completion of His earthly mission, He became like His Father in perfection, and in power.

Jesus Added to the Record to Fulfill His Father's Will that We Receive These Teachings

We might ask, **Why did the Savior go through this rather lengthy quotation of scriptures? He did so for the same reason that He did everything else, to fulfill His Father's will**. He explained this truth with these words:

> And he saith: **These scriptures, which ye had not with you, the Father commanded that I should give unto you;** for it was wisdom in Him that they should be given unto future generations (*BofM:3 Nephi* 26:2; emphasis added).

This is evidence that the Father was also greatly concerned about how the Record was being made. As the Savior carried out his **Power Formula**, He was doing so under the direction of the Father. Both the Father and the Son wanted the Record to contain the necessary information to allow the future generations to return to the Father by following Jesus Christ.

Mormon Was Inspired in Selecting Which of the Savior's Teaching to Include in His Abridgement

The Savior continued to teach the people and have them record His teachings. Not all of His words were included by Mormon in his abridged Record. Here is Mormon's commentary regarding the teachings that he chose to include as he abridged the Savior's teachings from the Record of Nephi[3]:

> And he [Jesus] did expound all things, even from the beginning until the time that he should come in his glory—yea, even all things which should come upon the face of the earth...

> And now **there cannot be written in this book even a hundredth part of the things which Jesus did truly teach unto the people;**
>
> **But behold the plates of Nephi do contain the more part of the things which he taught the people** (*BofM:3 Nephi* 26:3, 6-7; emphasis added).

Evidently, there were many, many things which the Savior taught which were not engraved by Mormon on his abridged record. As Mormon was engraving or writing the Savior's words from Nephi's plates to his abridged plates, he was inspired to know what to include.

> And these things have I written, which are **a lesser part** of the things which he taught the people...
>
> And **when they shall have received this, which is expedient that they should have first, to try their faith, and if it shall so be that they shall believe these things** [*The Book of Mormon*] **then shall the greater things be made manifest unto them.**
>
> **And if it so be that they will not believe these things, then shall the greater things be withheld from them, unto their condemnation.**
>
> **Behold, I was about to write them, all which were engraven upon the plates of Nephi, but the Lord forbade it, saying: I will try the faith of my people.**
>
> **Therefore I, Mormon, do write the things which have been commanded me of the Lord.** And now I, Mormon, make an end of my sayings, and proceed to write the things which have been commanded me (*BofM: 3 Nephi* 26:8-12; emphasis added).

The Lord wants us to receive all truth. However, we must first be receptive to the **basics** of His gospel message before He makes the remainder of His teachings known to us. Isaiah, an Old Testament prophet, spoke of how the Lord gives knowledge to us, "Line upon line and precept upon precept." (*OldT: Isaiah* 28:10).

Mormon here tells us who the real editor of these plates was. He wrote the things "which have been commanded me of the Lord." Also, he teaches that we should not expect to see all of the Lord's revelations and doctrines in *The Book of Mormon*. There is, however, sufficient truth and revelation, that if we receive it, and live by the truth, we will receive the gift of the Holy Ghost.

The inspiration of the Holy Ghost will then bring more and more truth. Also, those who accept and obey the gospel of Jesus Christ, as contained in *The Book of Mormon*, will then have access to additional modern scripture, and the words of living prophets and apostles. In addition, these people will also be able to receive the Lord's instructions and ordinances which are available only in His Holy Temples.

Mormon's words bring to mind some of Alma's teachings to a lawyer named Zeezrom. This man had been contending with Alma and Amulek as they were preaching. It is interesting to note that Zeezrom later became converted and joined Alma in the work of teaching the gospel as a missionary. Alma explained how the Lord dispenses the truth based upon our receptiveness and obedience:

> And now Alma began to expound these things unto him, saying: **It is given unto many to know the mysteries of God; nevertheless they are laid under a strict command that they shall not impart only according to the portion of his word which he doth grant unto the children of men, according to the heed and diligence which they give unto him.**
>
> And therefore, he that will harden his heart, the same receiveth the lesser portion of the word; and **he that will not harden his heart, to him is given the greater portion of the word, until it is given unto him to know the mysteries of God until he know them in full** (*BofM: Alma* 12:9-10; emphasis added).

The Lord inspired Alma to teach that He (the Lord) **gives us knowledge according to our desire for knowledge, and according to our diligence in living by the truth we have already received. At a later time, Alma expressed that he would have loved to have taught everything to everyone.** However, he realized that the Lord would not force His word upon those who didn't want it, and who were not yet prepared to receive it. Here are Alma's words:

> **O that I were an angel, and could have the wish of mine heart,** that I might go forth and speak with the trump of God, with a voice to shake the earth, and cry repentance unto every people!
>
> Yea, **I would declare unto every soul, as with the voice of thunder, repentance and the plan of redemption,** that they should repent and come unto our God, **that there might not be more sorrow upon all the face of the earth.**
>
> But behold, I am a man, and do sin in my wish; for I ought to be content with the things which the Lord hath allotted unto me.
>
> I ought not to harrow up in my desires, **the firm decree of a just God, for I know that he granteth unto men according to their desire,** whether it be unto death or unto life; yea, I know that **he allotteth unto men,** yea, decreeth unto them decrees which are unalterable, **according to their wills, whether they be unto salvation or unto destruction** (*BofM: Alma* 29: 1-4; emphasis added).

Alma's zeal is a natural and common feeling among missionaries. Therefore, the **feelings** Alma expressed in these verses are another internal witness of the truthfulness of *The Book of Mormon*. These are the words of someone who had experienced missionary work.

Also, if we considered the context of these verses, and read the previous verses, we will see that it was a time of much sorrow, following a war, which had cost many lives. The nation was feeling great sorrow over the deaths of so many loved ones. So, it is understandable, and completely appropriate, that Alma would be trying to help people "...that there might not be more sorrow...". This, too, is an internal evidence that *The Book of Mormon* was written by ancient prophets who had experienced these events and these *emotions*, rather than by Joseph Smith.

Jesus Christ and the Third Step of the Power Formula

The third step of the **Power Formula**, paraphrased, is to get the Record "...into the hands..." of the person who is going to follow you.[97] The Savior had a great way of getting the Record into the hands of those who would head the Church. Jesus Christ had His servant, the prophets Nephi[3] write His teachings. Also, after He had reviewed the Records, the Savior returned them to Nephi[3].

In this way, Jesus fulfilled immediately both the second and third steps of the **Power Formula** by making the Record, and getting it into the hands of those who would lead His Church. Undoubtedly, the Record, or a portion of it, was written and distributed to the people by His disciples.

Jesus Christ and the Fourth Step of the Power Formula

The final step in the **Power Formula** is to: "do all you can do to make the post occupiable."[98]

First, we need to define the "post" that the Savior has prepared for His followers. We have considered the Savior's teaching to these people, that they should: "...be perfect," even as He and The Father are perfect. Later, the Lord taught these disciples that they could become "even as I am" (*BofM: 3 Nephi* 28:10). Our potential is to become perfect beings. We will then be like the Savior in love, knowledge and power. This is the post that His gospel **Power Formula** prepares us for.

If we tried to make a list of everything that the Savior has done to help us accomplish this goal, we would never be able to finish it. However, we will review a short list of what the Savior has done to help us occupy this post of becoming like Him and His Father. Jesus Christ has provided:

1) The Earth, which allows us to obtain a physical body;
2) All truth;
3) Freedom;
4) The Resurrection;

5) The Atonement, which makes forgiveness of sins possible;
6) His scriptural Records;
7) His Church;
8) His servants, the apostles and prophets;
9) His Witness and Guide, the Holy Ghost;
10) His personal visitation and introduction to His Father, when we are sufficiently prepared.

Perhaps the best way to make a list of all He has done to help us occupy our post as sons and daughters of God is to summarize as did Moroni, that "every good gift cometh of Christ" (*BofM: Moroni* 10: 18; emphasis added).

Jesus Christ Used Principles Like Those of the Power Formula, on Three Levels

The Savior, like king Benjamin, used principles similar to the **Power Formula** on more than one level. You may recall how king Benjamin had first, acknowledged and empowered the next king, Mosiah. Then, He assisted everyone else.

The Savior followed this same pattern. Immediately after His appearance and, after having the people come to Him, He called for the current Record Keeper, Nephi³, to come forward. In view of all the people there present, the Savior gave Nephi³ power.

> And it came to pass that **he spake unto Nephi (for Nephi was among the multitude) and he commanded him that he should come forth.**
> And Nephi arose and went forth, and bowed himself before the Lord and did kiss his feet.
> And the Lord commanded him that he should arise. And he arose and stood before him.
> And the **Lord said unto him: I give unto you power** that ye shall baptize this people when I am again ascended into heaven (*BofM: 3 Nephi* 11:18-21; emphasis added).

"I Give Unto You Power"

When Nephi had come to Him, the Savior's very first words to him were, **"I give unto you power."** The Savior also chose eleven others and gave them power as well.

> And again **the Lord called others, and said unto them likewise; and he gave unto them power** to baptize (*BofM: 3 Nephi* 11:22; em-

Another Name for God's Power is the Priesthood

This power and authority to perform sacred ordinances, such as baptism, is called the **priesthood**. The priesthood has two divisions or levels. The first level of the priesthood, known as the Aaronic Priesthood, includes the authority to baptize.

Jesus Christ later gave these twelve disciples the higher, or Melchizedek Priesthood, which included the power to actually bestow the gift of the Holy Ghost upon those who had exercised their faith in Jesus Christ by repenting and being baptized.

It is interesting to note that the account of this ordination was not included in Mormon's abridgment of Third Nephi's writings. The Lord inspired Mormon's son, Moroni, to later add this information in his concluding book. Here is Moroni's account of Christ giving His disciples this power of the higher priesthood:

> **The words of Christ, which he spake unto his disciples, the twelve whom he had chosen, as he laid his hands upon them—**
> And he called them by name, saying: Ye shall call on the Father in my name, in mighty prayer; and after ye have done this **ye shall have power that to him upon whom ye shall lay your hands, ye shall give the Holy Ghost;** and in my name shall ye give it, for thus do mine apostles.
> Now Christ spake these words unto them at the time of his first appearing; and the multitude heard it not, but the disciples heard it; and on as many as they laid their hands, fell the Holy Ghost (*BofM: Moroni* 2:1-3; emphasis added).

In ordaining the twelve disciples on this continent, the Savior was actually organizing His Church among them. In doing so He followed the pattern which He had used among His saints in the Holy Land.

The Savior's Three New World Power Formulas

The Savior went on to give instructions which were written down into **Records** or **Power Formulas** for: 1) Nephi[3] as the prophet leader of His Church and as the Record Keeper, 2) the 12 disciples as leaders in His Church, and 3) all the members of His Church. We shall also see in the *Power Formula Parts Two and Three*, that the Savior repeated this pattern during the two other times He has established His Church upon the earth. These were during the time of Peter in *The New Testament*, and again when He restored His Church through the prophet Joseph Smith.

THE POWER FORMULAS

A Comparison of the Power Formula-Like Actions of King Benjamin and Jesus Christ

We have reviewed some of the similarities between Benjamin's **Power Formula**-like actions for his successor, Mosiah, and the Savior's **Power Formula**-like actions for Nephi and the other eleven disciples. Now let us compare Benjamin's admonition for the people to follow his successor, Mosiah, with the Savior's admonition for these people to follow the twelve disciples. First, we will review Benjamin's words. You will recall that at the time of this discourse, king Benjamin was advanced in years.

> For even at this time, my whole frame doth tremble exceedingly while attempting to speak unto you; but the Lord God doth support me, and hath suffered [allowed] me that I should speak unto you, and hath commanded me that I should **declare unto you this day, that my son Mosiah is a king and a ruler over you.**
>
> And now, my brethren, I would that ye should do as ye have hitherto done. As ye have kept my commandments, and also the commandments of my father, and have prospered, and have been kept from falling into the hands of your enemies, even so **if ye shall keep the commandments of my son, or the commandments of God which shall be delivered unto you by him, ye shall prosper in the land, and your enemies shall have no power over you** (*BofM: Mosiah* 2:30-31; emphasis added).

This was how Benjamin used an action like **Step 4 of the Power Formula**, which is "do all you can do to make the post occupiable." Benjamin helped Mosiah to assume his position as the leader of his people. In addition to being a **Power Formula** action for his successor, Mosiah, Benjamin's instructions to "...keep the commandments of my son..." was a **Power Change Formula** for those who would soon be looking to Mosiah as their king and spiritual leader. Please note the similarity to **how the Savior did the same thing for Nephi[3], and the other eleven disciples, who would lead His Church.**

> And it came to pass that when Jesus had spoken these words unto Nephi, and to those who had been called, (now the number of them who had been called, and received power and authority to baptize, was twelve) and behold, **he stretched forth his hand unto the multitude, and cried unto them, saying: Blessed are ye if ye shall give heed unto the words of these twelve whom I have chosen from among you to minister unto you, and to be your servants; and unto them I have given power** that they may baptize you...(*BofM: 3 Nephi* 12:1; emphasis added).

We should not be surprised that the thoughts and actions expressed by Benjamin and Jesus were so much alike. Benjamin was inspired and commanded "by the Lord God" [Jesus Christ] to encourage the people to support and follow their new leader, Mosiah (see *BofM: Mosiah* 2:30).

In like manner, the Savior taught His people that they were to follow Nephi and the other eleven disciples who were the earthly leaders of His Church.

The Savior told these people that they would be "Blessed" if they gave "heed unto the words of these twelve whom I have chosen from among you." In doing so, He completed the same actions as described in **the fourth step in the Power Formula**, for the leaders of His Church, by doing all He could to make their posts or positions as leaders in His Church "occupiable".

At the same time, Jesus Christ taught these people the essential action of **Power Change** following the example of those in **Power**.

The Savior Did a Power Formula for Every Member of His Church

The Savior, through His teachings, His records, His Church and through the guidance provided by the gift of the Holy Ghost, made it possible for every member of His Church to follow Him. In this way, and as noted above, Jesus Christ carried out the essential actions now described in the **Power Formula** on three levels. First, He did a specific **Power Formula** for Nephi. Second, He did a **Power Formula** for all of His 12 disciples who were to be the leaders of His Church in the New World. Then third, the Savior made it possible for each member of His Church to achieve a **Condition of Spiritual Power**, through following His example.

In summary, the Savior's actions produced the equivalent of a **Spiritual Power Formula** for his followers in this way:

1) The Savior met and connected perfectly with these people (Step 1 of the **Power Formula**);
2) He made a Record by instructing His servant Nephi to add His teachings to the plates, and by personally reviewing of the Record (Step 2 of the **Power Formula**);
3) The Record was given back to Nephi, who was the spiritual leader of these people, and this Record was made available to teach the members of The Church of Jesus Christ, (Step 3 of the **Power Formula**);
4) The Savior spent His time with these people, teaching them, organizing His Church, their training and empowering their leaders to help them and making it possible for the members of His Church to receive the guiding Gift of the Holy Ghost, thereby doing all that He could to help them become the heirs of God (Step 4 of the **Power Formula**).

Jesus Christ Taught the Principle of the Power Change Formula: "...the Works Which Ye Have Seen Me Do, That Shall Ye Also Do..."

The Savior also taught a principle we can equate with the **Power Change Formula**. This principle was for each person to follow His example as closely as they could. In other words, we are to do "the works which ye have seen me do."

> Now this is the commandment: **Repent,** all ye ends of the earth, and **come unto Me and be baptized** in My name, that ye may **be sanctified by the reception of the Holy Ghost**, that ye may stand spotless before Me at the last day.
>
> Verily, verily, I say unto you, this is My gospel; and ye know the things that ye must do in My Church; **for the works which ye have seen Me do that shall ye also do; for that which ye have seen Me do even that shall ye** *do (BofM: 3 Nephi* 27:20-21; emphasis added).

After His departure, the members of His Church were to then also follow the teachings of His chosen 12 disciples, thereby continuing to do Power Change with the Savior (see *BofM: 3 Nephi* 12:1).

If we had been asked to try to put in words how the Savior might have taught the principle of **Power Change**, we could not have done so any better than this!

Later, the Savior also taught this principle, not just in the terms of what we should *Do,* but also in terms of what we can *Be*. At this time He was speaking to the twelve disciples. However, this principle applies to all who follow the Savior.

> ...Therefore, **what manner of men ought ye to be? Verily I say unto you, even as I am** (*BofM:3 Nephi* 27:27; emphasis added).

Jesus Christ Taught That it is Possible to: "...Be Even as I Am, and I Am Even As the Father"

What will be the ultimate condition of someone who does **Power Change** by following the Savior? What would such a person be like? The Savior taught three of his disciples, and, again by inference all of us, that **it is possible to become even as He and His Father are.** Here are His words:

> And for this cause [bringing people to Christ] ye shall have fullness of joy; and ye shall sit down in the kingdom of my Father; yea, your joy shall be full, even as the Father hath given me fullness of joy; **and ye shall be even as I am, and I am even as the Father...** (*BofM: 3*

Nephi 28:10; emphasis added).

Mormon also taught this same principle in a epistle he wrote to his son Moroni. He concluded his letter by teaching about the importance of "**Charity**," which he defined as "**the pure love of Christ**." Mormon wrote that those who have this crowning virtue would be the "**true followers of His [the Father's] Son Jesus Christ**". Mormon concluded that those who follow the Savior, and who have this pure love of Christ "**shall be like him**" (*BofM: Moroni* 7:46-48).

The Savior's words were very plain. He did not say that those who follow Him will just live with Him. **Rather, He taught that it is possible to live with Him, and to become "even as" He and the Father are. This is the condition that awaits those who will do Power Change by following Jesus Christ.**

Those who accomplish this goal will be like the Savior and His Father, in knowledge, perfection, love and in the power to do good. They will have accomplished the Savior's commandment to be:

> ...perfect even as I, or your Father who is in Heaven is perfect"
> (*BofM: 3 Nephi* 12:48; emphasis added).

Jesus Accomplished His Great Work Among the Nephites in a Three-Day Period

Jesus Christ visited and taught these people, including the children, for a period of three days. Chapters 11 through 18 of Third Nephi discuss the events and teachings of His first day with them. As you might expect, there was an increase in the size of the multitude and great excitement and anticipation for His visit on the second day.

> And now it came to pass that when Jesus had ascended into heaven, the multitude did disperse, and every man did take his wife and his children and did return to his own home.
>
> And **it was noised abroad among the people immediately,** before it was yet dark, that the multitude had seen Jesus, and that he had ministered unto them, and **that He would also show Himself on the morrow unto the multitude.**
>
> **Yea, and even all the night it was noised abroad concerning Jesus; and insomuch did they send forth unto the people that there were many, yea, an exceedingly great number, did labor exceedingly all that night, that they might be on the morrow in the place where Jesus should show himself unto the multitude** (*BofM: 3 Nephi* 19:1-3; emphasis added).

THE POWER FORMULAS

The Savior Instituted the Sacrament Among His Followers on This Continent

Some of His teachings of the second and third days' visits are recorded in Chapters 20 through 26 of *Third Nephi*. It is interesting to note that the Savior administered the ordinance of the sacrament on both the first and second days (see chapters 18 and 20). Perhaps the reason for this was to allow those who had not been present on the first day to also receive this blessing. Also, perhaps the Lord was employing repetition to teach the importance of this ordinance.

The sacrament is an ordinance in which the members of His Church recommit themselves to **following Jesus Christ by remembering Him and keeping His commandments. As they do, they are promised to have His Spirit to be with them always** (see *BofM: Moroni* 4 and 5). Mormon reported that even after His third day of visiting them, He continued to appear to these people often. Also, the Savior often administered the sacrament to them.

> Therefore, I would that ye should behold that **the Lord truly did teach the people, for the space of three days; and after that he did show himself unto them oft, and did break bread oft, and bless it, and give it unto them** (*BofM: 3 Nephi* 26:13; emphasis added).

Jesus Healed Their Sick and Prayed for the People

Jesus also healed their sick, blessed their children and prayed to His Father for these people. This prayer was so powerful that Nephi, the Record Keeper, was unable to record this prayer, or the joy these people experienced at "... the time we heard Him pray for us unto the Father" (*BofM: 3 Nephi* 17:17).

This chapter is an extremely important one, for it allows us to glimpse the love which Jesus Christ has for all of us. This prayer was similar to the Savior's great intercessory prayer, which is in the 17th chapter of *John's* gospel in *The Holy Bible*. In both of these prayers, we are privileged to see how the Savior functions in His role as our advocate with the Father.

In a modern revelation to the prophet Joseph Smith, the Savior revealed how He pleads for us with our Heavenly Father. Here is this amazing insight into His love for each of us and into why we call Him our Savior:

> **Listen to him who is the advocate with the Father, who is pleading your cause before him—**
> **Saying: Father, behold the sufferings and death of Him who did no sin, in whom thou wast well pleased; behold the blood of thy Son which was shed, the blood of Him whom Thou gavest that Thyself might be glorified;**
> **Wherefore, Father, spare these My brethren that believe on**

My name, that they may come unto Me and have everlasting life (*D&C* 45:3-5, emphasis added).

The significance and meaning of His Intercessory prayer in the New Testament will be reviewed in *The Power Formulas, Part Two*.

Mormon Concluded His Abridged Record of the Savior's Visit by Saying Jesus Christ Had "Shown Forth His Power"

Please note Mormon's final comment about the Savior's visits to the multitude prior to His ascension to His Father.

> Therefore, I would that ye should behold that the Lord truly did teach the people, for the space of three days; and after that He did show Himself unto them oft, and did break bread oft, and bless it, and give it unto them.
>
> And it came to pass that after He had ascended into heaven—the second time that He showed himself unto them, and had gone unto the Father, after having healed all their sick, and their lame, and opened the eyes of their blind and unstopped the ears of the deaf, and even had done all manner of cures among them, and raised a man from the dead, **and had shown forth His power unto them,** and had ascended unto the Father—(*BofM: 3 Nephi* 26: 13, 15; emphasis added).

This a fitting conclusion to the Record of the Savior's visit to the people of the ancient America. He truly had given them His Gospel. We have equated His Gospel with His Power Formulas. In teaching them His Gospel Power Formula Jesus Christ had "shown forth his power unto them"!

The Results of the Savior's Visit

Following the Savior's visits, the twelve disciples went out and began a great missionary effort. Their efforts produced wonderful success. One reason for their success was the multitude who had absolute knowledge of the Savior's existence. This multitude could now testify with great power to others, who may have not seen the Savior, and to their own children, grandchildren and great grandchildren.

Chapter 27 and *28* of *Third Nephi* contain the Savior's teachings and blessings to the leaders of His Church. Apparently, these teachings were not delivered to the multitude. Rather, He taught the twelve separately on these occasions.

These two chapters are among the greatest in the Record. In these chapters He counseled the twelve on many matters, including these: The name of His Church; the meaning of His gospel; the standard of behavior He expected of His leaders; what gives His Father and Himself joy; how His followers could obtain this same fullness of joy; and finally, that His followers could become "...even as I am..." (*BofM: 3 Nephi* 28:10).

The teachings of Jehovah, who is Jesus Christ, which are contained in the book of Third Nephi constitute the heart of His Gospel, and His Power Formula: *The Book of Mormon.*

It was Nephi's great privilege and responsibility to record these teachings from the Savior. It was Mormon's privilege and responsibility to abridge Nephi's record to transfer it onto his plates. It was Joseph Smith's privilege and responsibility to translate the Record from these plates, and to publish it.

It is our privilege and responsibility to read the Record, choose faith in Jesus Christ, repent of our sins, be baptized into His Church, receive the Gift of the Holy Ghost by the laying on of the hands of those who hold His priesthood, and then endure to the end of our lives in "...following the example of the Son of God" (see *BofM 2nd Nephi* 31:15-16). As we do these things, we are doing **Power Change** with God!

Our Father in Heaven, His Son Jesus Christ, and the Holy Ghost have made it possible for us to receive these blessings through Their scriptural Records. These Records, including *The Book of Mormon*, are Their **Power Formulas** to us.

By now, if your heart is open to His influence, you will be feeling, and thereby knowing, that these things are true. As you know, you need to **Do**, so you can be what the Lord wants you to be. What is it that He wants for you? The Savior has answered this question when He taught that "...ye shall be even as I am, and I am even as the Father..." (*3 Nephi* 27:10). This, then, is the purpose for God's **Power** and **Power Change Formulas**!

Chapter 14

Nephi⁴, Amos¹ Amos² and Ammaron Recorded a Period of Spiritual Power and Then Decline

Nephi³ kept the Record and was the chief disciple and the head of the Church among the Nephites and Lamanites following the Savior's Ascension. Next, the Record was kept by Nephi's³ son, Nephi⁴. We are told very little about the life of Nephi⁴. We do know that he lived to see a wonderful time of peace and happiness among the people.

Mormon abridged 285 years of their Record into only four pages. For about 165 of these years, the **Condition** of their society could only be described as being one of **Spiritual Power**. We discussed the effect of the Savior's visit previously, but it is worth reviewing because the **Condition** of this society is an example for all societies to try to achieve.

> **And there were no envyings, nor strifes, nor tumults, nor whoredoms, nor lyings, nor murders, nor any manner of lasciviousness; and surely there could not be a happier people among all the people who had been created by the hand of God.**
>
> There were no robbers, nor murderers, neither were there Lamanites, nor any manner of -ites; but **they were in one, the children of Christ, and heirs to the kingdom of God.**
>
> And how blessed were they! For the Lord did bless them in all their doings; yea, even **they were blessed and prospered** until an hundred and ten years had passed away; and the first generation from Christ had passed away, and **there was no contention** in all the land (*BofM:4 Nephi* 1: 16-19).

This society was the ideal one described in the aims of Scientology. It was a society with no insanity, crime or war. They got to this high **Condition** through living the Father's **Gospel Power Formula**, taught by the Savior Jesus Christ, and by the leaders He chose and prepared.

THE POWER FORMULAS

Following the Savior's Visit the Next Four Record Keepers Survived to Very Advanced Ages

As we look at the timetable of the Record Keepers, an amazing fact becomes evident. Not only did these Record Keepers live in a time of great happiness, peace and prosperity, they also **lived longer** following the Savior's visit! Nephi[4] kept the Records from approximately 35 A.D. to 111 A.D., or 76 years. His son, Amos[1], then kept the Records for 84 years, before passing them to his son, Amos[2].

Amos[2] kept the Records longer than anyone else. He had them from 194 A.D. to 305 A.D., which was an amazing **111 years.** Even if he received them at the very early age of 20, this would mean that he survived for 131 years.

Also, when Amos[2] passed the Records on, **it was to someone of his own generation: his brother Ammaron.** Ammaron kept the Records for an additional 19 years. It is very significant that, **at least for these Record Keepers, their survival increased as the Condition of their society improved.** Here is Mormon's account of the first two of these transfers of the Record.

> And it came to pass that Nephi [Nephi[4]], **he that kept this last record, (and he kept it upon the plates of Nephi) died,** and his son Amos kept it in his stead; and he kept it upon the plates of Nephi [large plates of Nephi] also.
> And **he kept it eighty and four years...**
> And it came to pass that **Amos died also**, (and it was an hundred and ninety and four years from the coming of Christ) and **his son Amos kept the Record in his stead**; and he also kept it upon the plates of Nephi; and it was also written in the book of Nephi [the *Fourth Book of Nephi*], which is this book (*BofM:4 Nephi* 1:20-21; emphasis added).

Unfortunately, during the time of Amos[2], the Condition of his society deteriorated. We will now consider why this decline occurred.

Pride Leads to a Disconnection and Violation of the Power Formula

Mormon explained the cause of the decline of this society.

> And now, in this two hundred and first year there began to be among them those who were **lifted up in pride**, such as the wearing of costly apparel, and all manner of fine pearls, and of the fine things of the world. And from that time forth they did have their goods and their substance no more common among them. And **they**

began to be divided into classes; and they began to build up churches unto themselves to get gain, and began to deny the true church of Christ (*BofM: 4 Nephi* 1:24-26 emphasis added).

As mentioned previously, pride leads to a disconnection from others. An example of disconnection is seen in Mormon's comment about these people being "divided up into classes". You will recognize that such actions were a violation of the **Power Formula** Step 1, which includes the phrase, "don't disconnect"[99].

As these people violated principles like those of the **Power Formula**, this made it impossible to do **Spiritual Power Change** with the Savior. The **Spiritual Condition** of their society began to go down. Soon the people were not even functioning at the **Spiritual Non Existence** level.

If we think about it, before we can do **Power Change** by following Jesus Christ, we need to start by being born of God. This was identified earlier as the **Spiritual Non Existence Formula**.

You will recall that being born of God includes:

1) Having faith in Jesus Christ;
2) Repentance;
3) Baptism for the remission of sin;
4) Receiving the gift of the Holy Ghost.

Before people can receive and follow the Spiritual Power Change Formula, we need to first complete the Spiritual Non Existence Formula.

For about 200 years after the Savior's visit, the people followed Him. This is what led to a time of great success and peace. After this wonderful time and in a relatively short time, the **Condition** of many fell well below **Spiritual Non Existence** to **Enemy** and **Treason**. The more wicked part of the people organized themselves again into bands of robbers.

These bands of robbers had from, time to time, afflicted the Nephites and Lamanites. Eventually, these robbers again became strong enough to actually make war on the government. These ancient bands of robbers required their members to take oaths to bind themselves to secrecy, and to a life of criminal activity.

Ammaron Hid the Record and Selected Mormon to be the Next Record Keeper

As the **Condition** of these nations deteriorated, the time came when Amos[2] needed to pass the Record on as well. He did transfer the Record to his brother Ammaron, who then hid the Record for a time.

And it came to pass that after three hundred and five years had

passed away, (and the people did still remain in wickedness) Amos died; and his brother, Ammaron, did keep the Record in his stead.

And it came to pass that **when three hundred and twenty years had passed away, Ammaron, being constrained by the Holy Ghost,** did hide up the Records which were sacred—yea, **even all the sacred records which had been handed down from generation to generation,** which were sacred—even until the three hundred and twentieth year from the coming of Christ.

And he did hide them up unto the Lord that they might come again unto the remnant of the house of Jacob according to the prophecies and the promises of the Lord. And **thus is the end of the Record of Ammaron** (*BofM: 4 Nephi* 1:47-49; emphasis added).

The **Spiritual Condition** of the people had deteriorated to the point where Ammaron could no longer insure the safety of the Records. Therefore, he was inspired to actually hide these records for safekeeping.

It may be that there were not any grown men worthy of being entrusted with the Records at this time. Rather than turning the Records over to an adult, Ammaron selected a ten-year-old boy named Mormon. Next, we will review the life of Mormon, and how he came to **"make a record"** of God's **Power Formula** for us.

Chapter 15

Mormon Was Chosen to "Make a Record" for Us

Ammaron could see, by inspiration, that Mormon had been chosen by the Lord to be the next Record Keeper. These are Mormon's introductory words to his **first-person** record. Previous to his personal Record, Mormon had been writing in the third person with quotes from the previous prophets as he abridged their Records.

In these verses, Mormon explained how he came to receive the plates and **make a record**.

> And now I, Mormon, **make a record** of the things which I have both seen and heard, and call it *The Book of Mormon*.
>
> And about the time that Ammaron hid up the Records unto the Lord, he came unto me, (I being about **ten years of age, and I began to be learned somewhat** after the manner of the learning of my people) and Ammaron said unto me: **I perceive that thou art a sober child, and art quick to observe;**
>
> Therefore, when ye are about twenty and four years old I would that ye should remember the things that ye have observed concerning this people; and when ye are of that age go to the land Antum, unto a hill which shall be called Shim; and there have I deposited unto the Lord all the sacred engravings concerning this people.
>
> And behold, ye shall **take the plates of Nephi unto yourself,** and the remainder shall ye leave in the place where they are; and **ye shall engrave on the plates of Nephi all the things that ye have observed concerning this people.**
>
> And I, Mormon, being a descendant of Nephi, (and my father's name was Mormon) **I remembered the things which Ammaron commanded me** (*BofM: Mormon* 1:1-5; emphasis added).

Ammaron's Power Formula for Mormon

Ammaron here gave Mormon his instructions, which could be equated with a **Power Formula**. Please note that Mormon was instructed to eventually "...take the plates..." and to "...engrave on the plates of Nephi all the things that ye have observed concerning this people." Ammaron's actions were the same as described in the four steps of the **Power Formula,** in these ways:

1) He communicated with Mormon (Step 1);
2) He made a record (Step 2);
3) He told Mormon how and when to take possession of the Records (Step 3);
4) He instructed Mormon in what he should do with the Record (Step 4).

Mormon was Selected by the Lord to Compile the Record

Mormon must have truly been an amazing person. He became a prophet, an inspired writer and editor of sacred writings, a great military leader and a wonderful father.

We shall observe in the following pages how he preserved his people from destruction many times. In fact, his nation would have survived, if the people had followed Mormon's military leadership and his spiritual counsel, and had taken advantage of the time which Mormon gave them to repent! (*BofM: Mormon* 3:2-3).

As we look at Mormon's many accomplishments, it becomes apparent he was selected by His Father in Heaven for his important role of preparing the Record.

Parallels Between Mormon and Joseph Smith, and Between Mormon and Nephi

There are an interesting parallels in the lives of Mormon and Joseph Smith. Both of these men were selected by the Lord while in their youth to perform an important work related to the His Record. Both Joseph and Mormon were not allowed to receive the plates at first. They were required to wait for a period before they actually received the Record. Also, both of them retrieved the Record from hills where they had been deposited.

We can also see an interesting parallel between Mormon and Nephi. In Chapter 1, we demonstrated that both Nephi and Mormon started their books by telling us that they were going to **make a record**. Also, we saw that Nephi's **Spiritual Condition** must have been one of **Power**. In review, please note Nephi's humble way of telling us his **Spiritual Condition**:

> I, Nephi, **having been born of goodly parents, therefore I was taught somewhat in all the learning of my father;** and having seen many afflictions in the course of my days, nevertheless, **having been highly favored of the Lord in all my days; yea, having had a great knowledge of the goodness and the mysteries of God, therefore I make a record of my proceedings in my days** (*BofM: 1 Nephi* 1:1; emphasis added).

Mormon's introduction to his personal record shows indications that he, like

Nephi, was also in a **Spiritual Condition** of power. In addition, Mormon was similar to Nephi in another way: he was very humble. Here is Mormon's humble explanation of why the Lord selected him to **make a record**:

> And now I, Mormon, **make a record** of the things which I have both seen and heard, and call it *The Book of Mormon*.
> And about the time that Ammaron hid up the Records unto the Lord, he came unto me, (I being about ten years of age, and **I began to be learned somewhat after the manner of the learning of my people) and Ammaron said unto me: I perceive that thou art a sober child, and art quick to observe...**
> And I, being fifteen years of age and being **somewhat of a sober mind, therefore I was visited of the Lord, and tasted and knew of the goodness of Jesus** (*BofM: Mormon* 1:1, 2, 15; emphasis added).

Please also note Mormon's humble understatement that he was of "...*somewhat* of a sober mind..." and "...learned *somewhat*... (emphasis added)".

Also, as we read verse 15, we learn that Mormon was "visited of the Lord" at age 15. This is another parallel between the lives of Mormon, Nephi and Joseph Smith. The Father and the Son appeared to Joseph when he was 14 years of age.

As a young man, Nephi had a vision in which he saw the Lord (*BofM: 1 Nephi* 11). The lives of Nephi and Mormon were similar in another way. Both of these men made two records. Each made a personal account, and also each abridged the writings of others.

Mormon abridged the writings of the Record Keepers of Nephi's large set of plates (Benjamin through Ammaron). Nephi abridged the writings of his father, Lehi (*BofM: 1 Nephi* 1:16-17; 8:29; 9;1).

It is even possible that Mormon learned how to abridge the Records of others by studying the Records of Nephi. Indeed, the similarities between the opening statements of Nephi and Mormon suggest that Mormon patterned his record keeping style after Nephi. Nephi and Mormon were also similar in that their peoples looked upon them as protectors and deliverers (*BofM: Jacob* 1:10; *Mormon* 5:1).

Mormon was Selected by His People to Lead Their Armies While in His Sixteenth Year

Mormon must have been an amazing lad because he was also selected by his people to be their military leader while he was still a young man.

> And it came to pass in that same year [about 327-328 A.D.] there began to be a war again between the Nephites and the Lamanites. And notwithstanding I being young, was large in stature; therefore **the peo-**

ple of Nephi appointed me that I should be their leader, or the leader of their armies.

Therefore it came to pass that **in my sixteenth year I did go forth at the head of an army of the Nephites,** against the Lamanites; therefore three hundred and twenty and six years had passed away (*BofM: Mormon* 2:1-2; emphasis added).

Mormon Found a Power Formula for His Post as Nephite Military Commander, in The Record

In regard to his age at the time of his military appointment, Mormon's life parallels that of a previous Nephite military leader named Moroni[1]. About 500 years prior to Mormon's time, Moroni was also appointed to be the "chief captain" over the Nephite armies. Also, like Mormon, his appointment came a very young age (see *BofM: Alma* 43:7).

Mormon faced a task nearly identical to Moroni's. He was called upon to defend his people with an inferior force, and in the same geographical location. As he abridged the book of Alma, Mormon had the opportunity to study Moroni's life and military tactics. It is probable that Mormon used Moroni's example as a **Power Formula** for his post as the Nephite military commander.

Mormon had great respect for general Moroni (see *BofM: Alma* 48:11-17). Perhaps this is why Mormon chose to name his son Moroni. This is another internal evidence of the truthfulness of *The Book of Mormon*.

As the military leader of his nation, Mormon would also be responsible for training other military leaders of his people. His record indicates the names of twelve such commanders, including his son Moroni[2] (see *BofM Mormon* 6:12-14 and *Moroni* 9:6). Is it not likely that Mormon used the lessons he learned from Moroni and other preceeding Nephite generals to train the leaders under him?

In Mormon's writings, we can find over 200 references to the causes, tactics *and factors of war. To my mind, this is absolute proof that The Book of Mormon* must have been written by a military leader, like Mormon.

Joseph Smith was in his mid twenties when he translated the metal plate records, which contained *The Book of Mormon*. Joseph Smith had no military experience or background. He, therefore, would have neither the knowledge or the disposition to include 200 plus factors of military science in a fictitious record, even if he wanted to do so.

Mormon's Four Pursuits

Mormon was a very special individual. He probably prolonged the survival of his nation by decades. However, even a great individual can't save those who will not be helped. Mormon's life seems to have been devoted to four pursuits. These were:

1) Raising his family;
2) Endeavoring to preserve his people physically by serving as their military leader;
3) Endeavoring to preserve his people spiritually by calling upon them to repent;
4) Abridging the large plates of Nephi, and adding the small plates of Nephi, and his own writings to the compiled Record.

In the second and third of these pursuits, Mormon probably found little success or joy, because his people would not be helped. However, he must have had great satisfaction in preparing the Record, and in his family.

Mormon Fought for His Nation's Survival

Even with Mormon's help, the Nephites were barely able to withstand their enemies. In order to survive, it became necessary for them to retreat on many occasions. Here is Mormon's account of one of these periods:

> And it came to pass that in the three hundred and twenty and seventh year the **Lamanites did come upon us with exceedingly great power,** insomuch that they did frighten my armies; therefore they would not fight, and **they began to retreat towards the north countries...**
>
> ...Thus there began to be a mourning and a lamentation in all the land because of these things, and more especially among the people of Nephi.
>
> And it came to pass that when I, Mormon, saw their lamentation and their mourning and their sorrow before the Lord, my heart did begin to rejoice within me, knowing the mercies and the long-suffering of the Lord, therefore supposing that he would be merciful unto them that they would again become a righteous people.
>
> But behold this my **joy was vain, for their sorrowing was not unto repentance, because of the goodness of God; but it was rather the sorrowing of the damned,** because the Lord would not always suffer them to take happiness in sin.
>
> And **they did not come unto Jesus with broken hearts and contrite spirits, but they did curse God, and wish to die. Nevertheless they would struggle with the sword for their lives.**
>
> And it came to pass that my sorrow did return unto me again, and **I saw that the day of grace was passed with them, both temporally and spiritually;** for I saw thousands of them hewn down in open rebellion against their God, and heaped up as dung upon the face of the land. And thus three hundred and forty and four years had passed away

(*BofM: Mormon* 2:3, 11-15; emphasis added).

We can see that as the Nephite nation's **Spiritual Condition** deteriorated, their survival potential had a corresponding drastic decline. This verse indicates that rather than repent and live, these people chose to "...curse God and wish to die". This decrease in survival potential is a reflection of their decreasing **Spiritual Condition** and **Emotional Tone Level**.

Mormon Retrieved the Hidden Record

These retreats were interspersed with a few temporary victories. During one retreat, the Nephite people were near the hill where Ammaron had deposited the Record. Mormon took this opportunity to retrieve the metal plates which contained the Record.

> And now, the city of Jashon was near the land where Ammaron had deposited the Records unto the Lord, that they might not be destroyed. And behold I **had gone according to the word of Ammaron, and taken the plates of Nephi,** and did **make a record** according to the words of Ammaron (*BofM: Mormon* 2: 17; emphasis added).

Mormon Used the Same Principles as the Power Change Formula by Following Ammaron's Instructions

We have noted also how Ammaron used actions like those of the **Power Formula** to eventually transfer the Record to Mormon. In this verse we have evidence that Mormon followed Ammaron's instruction. Mormon states here that he "did **make a record...according to the words of Ammaron.**" This is yet another example of a *Book of Mormon* Record Keeper following his predecessor's example and instruction. This is also the action described in the **Power Change Formula**. Please also note another reference by Mormon that he did **"make a record"**.

Mormon Felt Great Sorrow for His People

Like Jacob, from an early age, many of Mormon's days were days of sadness. He watched as his own people refused a course which would have prevented their destruction. He could see where their non-survival actions were leading them. Mormon is another example of a person, who like Jacob and the Savior, suffered great sorrow because of others.

However, even with all of the earthly troubles and sorrows, Mormon still found hope in knowing that he would be "lifted up at the last day". Here is his account of the emotional effect that these sad experiences had upon Mormon:

...I did forbear to make a full account of their wickedness and abominations, for behold, **a continual scene of wickedness and abominations has been before mine eyes ever since I have been sufficient to behold the ways of man.**

And woe is me because of their wickedness; for **my heart has been filled with sorrow because of their wickedness, all my days; nevertheless, I know that I shall be lifted up at the last day** (*BofM: Mormon* 2:18-19; emphasis added).

Mormon Prevented the Destruction of His Nation—for a Time, by Stopping A Retreat

When it was appropriate, Mormon employed the tactic of retreat. However, he realized that at other times a retreat could spell disaster. In these verses, we see an instance of Mormon urging his people "with great energy" to "stand boldly and fight for their wives and children...".

> And it came to pass that in this year **the people of Nephi again were hunted and driven.** And it came to pass that we were driven forth until we had come northward to the land which was called Shem.
>
> And it came to pass that we did fortify the city of Shem, and **we did gather in our people as much as it were possible, that perhaps we might save them from destruction.**
>
> And it came to pass in the three hundred and forty and sixth year they began to come upon us again.
>
> And it came to pass that **I did speak unto my people, and did urge them with great energy, that they would stand boldly before the Lamanites and fight for their wives, and their children, and their houses, and their homes.**
>
> And my words did arouse them somewhat to vigor, insomuch that **they did not flee** from before the Lamanites, but **did stand with boldness against them.**
>
> And it came to pass that we did contend with an army of thirty thousand against an army of fifty thousand. And it came to pass that **we did stand before them with such firmness that they did flee from before us.**
>
> And it came to pass that when they had fled we did pursue them with our armies, and did meet them again, and **did beat them; nevertheless the strength of the Lord was not with us; yea, we were left to ourselves,** that the Spirit of the Lord did not abide in us; therefore **we had become weak like unto our brethren** [who were their Lamanite enemies] (*BofM: Mormon* 2:20-26; emphasis added).

THE POWER FORMULAS

Mormon Tried to Raise the Spiritual Condition of His People

It appears that, due mainly to Mormon's efforts, his nation was able to enjoy peace for another decade. However, this victory did not lead to any change in attitudes or conditions of these people. Even so, their condition was still not hopeless. **These people could have survived had they listened to the Lord, and to His prophet Mormon.**

> And it came to pass that the **Lamanites did not come to battle again until ten years more had passed away.** And behold, I had employed my people, the Nephites, in preparing their lands and their arms against the time of battle. And it came to pass that the Lord did say unto me: Cry unto this people—**Repent ye, and come unto me, and be ye baptized, and build up again my Church, and ye shall be spared.**
>
> And I did cry unto this people, but it was in vain; and **they did not realize that it was the Lord that had spared them, and granted unto them a chance for repentance.** And behold they did harden their hearts against the Lord their God (*BofM: Mormon* 3:1-3; emphasis added).

Mormon was a Success, Even Though His Nation was Destroyed

Please note that Mormon had succeeded in this way: **he preserved his nation long enough for them to have a final "...chance for repentance...".** In actuality, it was the Lord, who, through Mormon's efforts, granted this people many chances for repentance. Mormon not only saved them from being defeated, he also tried to get them to repent. What could one man do more for his people? He truly was a success!

Here is an example of how an individual can be in a much higher condition than his group. Mormon's **Condition of Power,** both in spiritual matters, and as a military leader, prolonged the survival of his nation for a time. During this time he tried to raise the **Spiritual Condition** of the nation. However, his people did not respond, and soon they were under attack again.

> And it came to pass that I did cause my people that they should gather themselves together at the land Desolation, to a city which was in the borders, by the narrow pass which led into the land southward.
>
> And there we did place our armies, that we might stop the armies of the Lamanites, that they might not get possession of any of our lands; therefore we did fortify against them with all our force.
>
> And it came to pass that in the three hundred and sixty and first year the Lamanites did come down to the city of Desolation to battle

against us; and it came to pass that in that year we **did beat them, insomuch that they did return to their own lands again.**

And in the three hundred and sixty and second year they did come down again to battle. **And we did beat them again,** and did slay a great number of them, and their dead were cast into the sea (*BofM: Mormon* 3:5-8, emphasis added).

In this battle, Mormon employed a similar tactic as general Moroni had used about 500 years earlier. He used the geography of the area to help the defense of his nation. This was done by placing his armies by a "narrow pass" to curtail the Lamanite's advances. Moroni[1] had also defended a narrow pass (see *BofM: Alma* 50:13).

Pride and a Desire For Revenge Led to the Downfall of the Nephites

Under Mormon's guidance, the Nephites won the two defensive victories mentioned above. However, the people were not satisfied. They became **proud** in their victories, and they wanted **revenge**.

> And now, **because of this great thing which my people, the Nephites, had done, they began to boast in their own strength, and began to swear before the heavens that they would avenge themselves** of the blood of their brethren who had been slain by their enemies.
>
> And they did swear by the heavens, and also by the throne of God, that they would go up to battle against their enemies, and would cut them off from the face of the land.
>
> And it came to pass that **I, Mormon, did utterly refuse from this time forth to be a commander and a leader of this people, because of their wickedness and abomination.**
>
> Behold, I had led them, notwithstanding their wickedness **I had led them many times to battle, and had loved them,** according to the love of God which was in me, **with all my heart; and my soul had been poured out in prayer unto my God all the day long for them; nevertheless, it was without faith, because of the hardness of their hearts.**
>
> And **thrice have I delivered** them out of the hands of their enemies, and **they have repented** not of their sins.
>
> And when they had sworn by all that had been forbidden them by our Lord and Savior Jesus Christ, that they would go up unto their enemies to battle, and avenge themselves of the blood of their brethren, behold the voice of the Lord came unto me saying:
>
> Vengeance is mine, and I will repay; and **because this people repented not after I had delivered them, behold, they shall be cut off**

from the face of the earth (*BofM: Mormon* 3:9-15; emphasis added).

Mormon Refused to Lead the Nephites in a War of Aggression and Revenge

The Lord would not allow Mormon to lead the people in an offensive war of vengeance. Mormon had "thrice delivered them out of the hands of their enemies, and they have repented not of their sins." His calling was to defend his people. He had no desire for conquest, or bloodshed.

Mormon Wrote His Personal Record or Journal in Distinct Sections

If we look carefully at these verses, we can see a change in Mormon's writings. In verse twelve of Chapter 3, and in the preceding chapter, Mormon had been writing in the **past tense**. In the next verse, Mormon changed the tense of his writings from **past to present**.

This change in tense is an indication that Mormon was writing at this time. He began by writing about previous experiences. Next, he wrote about events that were happening, at the **present** time, to him and his people. Later in this chapter, we see Mormon writing to those who would received his words, in the **future**.

For those of you who keep a journal, please think for a minute of how you make your entries. Many of us who keep a journal or diary do not make entries every day. Therefore, when we write, we often include events of the past which have occurred since our last entry. Usually, we will then write about our present experiences or thoughts. Often we will conclude our journal entry by writing about our plans for the future, (thanks to my wife, Karla, for this insight).

As we read Mormon's personal account, we are in effect reading his journal. In his personal Record, Mormon repeatedly used the same style or pattern of past, present and future writing. How could a modern writer, such as Joseph Smith, have incorporated this journal style of writing into a fictional work?

It is much more likely that Mormon's Record was written this way because Mormon was writing about **his past, his present and about the future.** This is another internal evidence of the truthfulness of *The Book of Mormon*.

For a time, Mormon would not participate in the great wars. During this time, he worked on the third great pursuit of his life, **making a record for us**.

> And it came to pass that I utterly refused to go up against mine enemies; and I did even as the Lord had commanded me; and I did stand **as an idle witness to manifest unto the world the things which I saw and heard, [past tense] according to the manifestations of the Spirit which had testified of things to come**.

Therefore **I write unto you, [present tense] Gentiles, and also unto you, house of Israel,** [future tense] when the work [the publication of *The Book of Mormon*, and the restoration of the Church of Jesus Christ to the earth] shall commence, that **ye shall be about to prepare to return to the land of your inheritance** (*BofM: Mormon* 3:16-17; emphasis added).

Two of Mormon's Prophecies

It is interesting to note that in verse 17 above, Mormon gives a prediction as to the time frame when the Record would be translated and be published. Mormon wrote, "Therefore I write unto you, Gentiles [meaning, the world at large], and also unto you, house of Israel, when the work shall commence, [the publishing of *The Book of Mormon* and the restoration of Christ's Church] that ye shall be about to prepare to return to the land of your inheritance." This was a prophecy of the return of the descendants of Israel to their homeland.

In 1841, eleven years after *The Book of Mormon* was published and the Church was established, one of the twelve apostles of the Church, Orson Hyde, was sent to the Holy Land, by the Prophet Joseph Smith. In an article about this mission, David B. Gailbraith has written:

> ...during April [1841] conference [of The Church of Jesus Christ of Latter-day Saints], **the Prophet [Joseph Smith] commissioned Elder Hyde [one of the twelve apostles of the Church] to go to Palestine and there dedicate that land for the return of the Jewish people.** After a long and arduous trip fraught with suffering and personal sacrifice, Elder Hyde arrived in Jerusalem on Sunday, 24 October, 1841. Elder Hyde climbed the Mount of Olives and offered a heavenly inspired dedicatory prayer.
>
> In one of the prayers opening paragraphs Elder Hyde focused on these themes: 1) The gathering of Judah, 2) The building of Jerusalem, 3) The rearing of a temple..."[100]

In 1979, the Orson Hyde Memorial Park was constructed in Jerusalem. To my understanding, this park is located on the Mount of Olives, where Elder Hyde delivered his prayer.

We know now that within a little over a century of Orson Hyde's visit, the Jewish people had gathered and formed the nation of Israel. Since Mormon's prophecy was so accurate, it is important that we look at another one of his prophecies. This prophecy applies to each one of us.

And these things doth the Spirit manifest unto me; therefore **I write**

> **unto you all**. And for this cause I write unto you, that ye may know that **ye must all stand before the judgment-seat of Christ, yea, every soul who belongs to the whole human family of Adam; and ye must stand to be judged of your works, whether they be good or evil;**
>
> And **also that ye may believe the gospel of Jesus Christ, which ye shall have among you...**
>
> **And I would that I could persuade all ye ends of the earth to repent and prepare to stand before the judgment-seat of Christ** (*BofM: Mormon* 3:20-22; emphasis added).

When he found he could not help his own people to repent, Mormon turned his attention to helping those who would live in later generations. In these verses, Mormon listed three reasons or purposes for his writing to **future** readers. He wrote, "For this cause I write unto you:

[1] "...That ye may know that ye all must stand before the judgment seat of Christ...";
[2] We will be judged for works, "...whether they be good or evil...";
[3] We all need to "...repent and prepare to stand before the judgment-seat of Christ."

Many, the world over, are responding to Mormon's message.

The Way of Revenge Failed, and the Nephites were Overthrown

As might be expected, the Nephites war of revenge was not successful. Soon they were fleeing for their lives again.

> And it came to pass that the three hundred and sixty and sixth year had passed away, and the Lamanites came again upon the Nephites to battle; and yet **the Nephites repented not of the evil they had done, but persisted in their wickedness continually.**
>
> And it is impossible for the tongue to describe, or for man to write a perfect description of the horrible scene of the blood and carnage which was among the people, both of the Nephites and of the Lamanites; and every heart was hardened, so that they delighted in the shedding of blood continually.
>
> And the Lamanites did not come again against the Nephites until the three hundred and seventy and fifth year.
>
> And in this year they did come down against the Nephites with all their powers; and they were not numbered because of the greatness of their number.

And from this time forth did **the Nephites gain no power over the Lamanites,** but began to be swept off by them even as a dew before the sun.

And now **I, Mormon, seeing that the Lamanites were about to overthrow the land, therefore I did go to the hill Shim, and did take up all the Records which Ammaron had hid up unto the Lord** (*BofM: Mormon* 4:10-11, 16-18, 23; emphasis added).

Note that **Mormon had not been carrying all the Records**, for they must have been very great in number. When he saw that he would soon be cut off from access to the place where the remainder of the Records were buried, he decided to take the Records with him.

Mormon Gave the Records to His Son, Moroni

Mormon, seeing the precarious state of his people, tried to preserve most of the plates in a hill. He gave his compiled record to his son Moroni.

And now **I finish my record** concerning the destruction of my people, the Nephites. And it came to pass that we did march forth before the Lamanites.

And it came to pass that when we had gathered in all our people in one to the land of Cumorah, behold I, Mormon, began to be old; and knowing it to be the last struggle of my people, and **having been commanded of the Lord that I should not suffer the Records which had been handed down by our fathers, which were sacred, to fall into the hands of the Lamanites, (for the Lamanites would destroy them) therefore I made this record out of the plates of Nephi, and hid up in the hill Cumorah all the Records which had been entrusted to me by the hand of the Lord, save it were these few plates which I gave unto my son Moroni** (*BofM: Mormon* 6:1, 6; emphasis added).

Mormon Again Took Up the Sword In Defense of His People

The Nephite nation was surrounded and far outnumbered. Mormon, "knowing it to be the last struggle" of his people, took up the sword, in **defense** of his people.

And it came to pass that I did go forth among the Nephites, and did repent of the oath which I had made that I would no more assist them; and **they gave me command again of their armies, for they looked upon me as though I could deliver them from their afflic-**

tions.

But behold, I was without hope, for I knew the judgments of the Lord which should come upon them; for they repented not of their iniquities, but did struggle for their lives without calling upon that Being who created them (*BofM: Mormon* 5:1-2).

Mormon: An Example of the Dynamics and of Loving One's "Enemies"

Even after being wounded in battle, and after having seen so many thousands of his people destroyed by the enemy, Mormon's thoughts turned to helping the descendants of these Lamanites. Mormon wrote of his concern for the welfare of their future descendants as well as the descendants of the Nephites who had survived by joining the Lamanites.

Mormon had tried to help the people of his own time. When his contemporaries rejected his help completely, Mormon helped the only people he could—those of the future.

In this way, he was much like Enos. We have cited Enos as an example of one who was concerned about later people, and other dynamics. Here are some of Mormon's words to those of future generations:

> And now, behold, **I would speak somewhat unto the remnant of this people** who are spared, if it so be that God may give unto them my words, that they may know of the things of their fathers; yea, I speak unto you, ye remnant of the house of Israel; and these are the words which I speak:
>
> Know ye that ye must come to the knowledge of your fathers, and **repent of all your sins and iniquities, and believe in Jesus Christ, that he is the Son of God,** and that he was slain by the Jews, and by the power of the Father he hath risen again, whereby he hath gained the victory over the grave; and also in him is the sting of death swallowed up—
>
> And **he bringeth to pass the resurrection of the dead,** whereby man must be raised to stand before his judgment-seat.
>
> And **he hath brought to pass the redemption of the world,** whereby he that is found guiltless before him at the judgment day hath it given unto him to dwell in the presence of God in his kingdom (*BofM: Mormon* 7:1; 5-7; emphasis added).

MORMON'S RECORD

Mormon's Final Words Were a Testimony of the Power of God, of His Records and a Plea to Follow the Savior's Example

Mormon's last message contained a testimony of the truth of *The Book of Mormon*. He also testified of *The Holy Bible* calling it: "the Record which shall come...from the Jews." Mormon concluded his Record with a plea for his readers to follow "the example of the Savior". Here are Mormon's final words:

> Therefore **repent, and be baptized in the name of Jesus, and lay hold upon the gospel of Christ, which shall be set before you, not only in this record [*The Book of Mormon*] but also in the Record which shall come unto the Gentiles from the Jews [*The Holy Bible*],** which record shall come from the Gentiles unto you.
>
> For behold, **this [*The Book of Mormon*] is written for the intent that ye may believe that [*The Holy Bible*]; and if ye believe that [*The Holy Bible*] ye will believe this [*The Book of Mormon*] also; and if ye believe this ye will know concerning your fathers, and also the marvelous works which were wrought by the power of God among them.**
>
> And ye will also know that ye are a remnant of the seed of Jacob; therefore ye are numbered among the people of the first covenant; and if **it so be that ye believe in Christ, and are baptized, first with water, then with fire and with the Holy Ghost, following the example of our Savior, according to that which he hath commanded us, it shall be well with you in the day of judgment.** Amen (*BofM: Mormon* 7:8-10; emphasis added).

Mormon outlined the relationship of *The Book of Mormon* and *The Holy Bible* as joint witnesses of the Savior. These scriptures each bear record to us of the "power of God". Jesus Christ has made the power of God available to help us. If we believe in Him; repent; are baptized; receive the Holy Ghost **and follow His example, it will be well with us in the day of judgment.**

Again, following the Savior's example is equivalent to following the principle of **Power Change** with Him. Following Him not only leads us to be **where** He is, following Him also leads us to be **like** He is.

Mormon and the Principles of Spiritual Non Existence and of the Spiritual Power Change Formulas

These were the last words of Mormon before he was killed. Although he was writing mainly to descendants of the Lamanites, these truths apply to all of us. Mormon's concluding message taught the principles described previously as the **Spiritual Non Existence** and **Power Change Formulas**.

> ...and if it so be that ye **believe in Christ, and are baptized, first with water, then with fire and with the Holy Ghost,** [spiritual rebirth or **Spiritual Non Existence Formula**] following the example of our Savior, according to that which he hath commanded us, [**Power Change Formula**] it shall be well with you in the day of judgment. Amen (*BofM: Mormon* 7:10 emphasis added).

We have previously considered the steps of the **Formula** for coming out of **Spiritual Non Existence**. These steps include:

1) Faith in Jesus Christ;
2) Repentance;
3) Baptism;
4) Receiving the gift of the Holy Ghost.

These are the steps which lead to spiritual rebirth. This spiritual rebirth is equivalent to finding out what is needed and expected of us by the Lord. In other words, following these principles allows us to come out of a **Condition of Spiritual Non Existence** in our relationship to God. In doing so we become aware of our true identity as the spirit children of God.

After we come out of the **Condition of Spiritual Non Existence**, by being born of God, what should be our goal? You will recall that the Savior set our goal with these words:

> ...be perfect even as I, or your Father who is in Heaven, is perfect" (*BofM: 3 Nephi* 12:48).

We could describe this goal as the **Condition of Spiritual Power**. How do we arrive at this condition? We do so by following a **Spiritual Power Change Formula**. Mormon outlined this formula in the very last sentence he engraved. He concluded that we should follow:

> ...the example of the Savior, according to that which he hath commanded us..." (*BofM: Mormon* 7:10).

May we **not** forget Mormon's final testimony of the power of God, and his testimony of the truthfulness of the Lord's records. May we heed Mormon's plea to follow "the example of the Savior. Thereby, it be well for us in the day of judgment" (*BofM: Mormon* 7:10).

Chapter 16

Moroni Finished the Record of His Father

Moroni's Grief, an Internal Evidence of the Truthfulness of the Record

With the death of Mormon, his son Moroni became the final Record Keeper. As we read his opening lines we are touched by the sorrow and loneliness that Moroni was feeling following the death of his father, and the destruction of his nation. See if you don't **feel** Moroni's underlying sadness as he engraved this portion of his record:

> Behold **I, Moroni, do finish the Record of my father, Mormon. Behold, I have but few things to write, which things I have been commanded by my father.**
>
> And now it came to pass that after the great and tremendous battle at Cumorah, behold, the Nephites who had escaped into the country southward were hunted by the Lamanites, until they were all destroyed.
>
> And **my father also was killed by them, and I even remain alone to write the sad tale of the destruction of my people. But behold, they are gone,** and I fulfill the commandment of my father. And whether they will slay me, I know not.
>
> Therefore I will write and hide up the Records in the earth; and **whither I go it mattereth not.**
>
> Behold, my father hath made this record, and he hath written the intent thereof. And behold, **I would write it also if I had room upon the plates, but I have not;** and ore I have none, **for I am alone. My father hath been slain in battle, and all my kinsfolk, and I have not friends nor whither to go; and how long the Lord will suffer that I may live I know not** (*BofM: Mormon* 8:1-5; emphasis added).

Moroni's Words Reflected His Emotional Tone at the Time He Was Writing

Here we have another internal evidence of the truthfulness of *The Book of Mormon*. These are the words of a man who had experienced the tragedy of seeing the great destruction which Moroni had seen. **Did you notice above how Moroni told us twice that his father had died. Why would he do this?**

Also, as Moroni engraved these words, his thoughts and his writing was turned inward influenced by how he was feeling. This is why he used the personal pronoun "I" so often in these verses (16 times in 5 verses).

When Moroni mentioned the death of Mormon twice and as he wrote of his feelings about his loss, it was because **this was a reflection of Moroni's emotional tone at the time he wrote these words.** Moroni was experiencing **sorrow and grief**, and these emotions impacted his writing. There is even a hint of **apathy** in his words "...whither I go, it mattereth not."

How could a young man, such as Joseph Smith, who had not experienced such great losses, have written with these feelings and perspectives. In fact, it reminds one of earlier portions of *The Book of Mormon* which could have also only been written by men who had experienced things which the prophet Joseph Smith had not experienced at the time *The Book of Mormon* was published.

Examples of these experiences are: Jacob's sorrow for his brother's rebellion; Alma's[2] experiencing the pains of hell; and the joy of forgiveness; Ammon and his brothers discouragements and joys and love felt while serving as missionaries; the missionary enthusiasm of Alma, and Mormon's expression of the sorrows and horrors of war.

Moroni was a Witness to the Truthfulness of Mosiah's Prophecy of Great Destruction When a Nation Chooses Iniquity

You will recall that king Mosiah had prophesied that a free people would not long survive if their majority chose iniquity over right. The Nephites were about to experience a terrible fulfillment of Mosiah's prophecy. Here again, are Mosiah's words of warning:

> Now it is not common that the voice of the people desireth anything contrary to that which is right; but it is **common for the lesser part of the people to desire that which is not right;** therefore this shall ye observe and make it your law—to **do your business by the voice of the people.**
>
> **And if the time comes that the voice of the people doth choose iniquity, then is the time that the judgments of God will come upon you; yea, then is the time he will visit you with great destruction even as he has hitherto visited this land** (*BofM: Mosiah* 29:26-27; emphasis added).

The Nephite nation demonstrated the truth of Mosiah's prophecy. Moroni[2] was left as a witness of their terrible fulfillment of this warning. This principle is still true, and this warning still applies.

Moroni's Name, Another Internal Evidence of the Truthfulness of the Record

Another internal evidence of the truthfulness of *The Book of Mormon* is the **name** that Mormon gave his son. As noted earlier, Mormon was a great general, and he wrote extensively about war. As one reads Mormon's writings about war, it becomes obvious that he had a great deal of respect for a previous Nephite general, Moroni[1].

This Moroni had lead the Nephite forces during the great war with the Lamanites in the time of Helaman[2] (about 72 B.C.). This was about 450 years before Mormon's time. In his abridgement of Alma, Mormon spent nearly a full page describing the virtues of this great general. Among his words were these:

> And Moroni was a **strong and a mighty** man; he was a man of a **perfect understanding**; yea, a man that **did not delight in bloodshed**; a man whose soul did **joy in the liberty and the freedom of his country**, and his brethren from bondage and slavery;
>
> Yea, **a man whose heart did swell with thanksgiving to his God**, for the many privileges and blessings which he bestowed upon his people; a man **who did labor exceedingly for the welfare and safety of his people.**
>
> Yea, and he was a man who was **firm in the faith of Christ, and he had sworn with an oath to defend his people, his rights, and his country, and his religion, even to the loss of his blood.**
>
> **Yea, verily, verily I say unto you, if all men had been, and were, and ever would be, like unto Moroni, behold, the very powers of hell would have been shaken forever; yea, the devil would never have power over the hearts of the children of men** (*BofM: Alma* 48:11-13,17; emphasis added).

Mormon not only had great respect for Moroni[1], he also identified with this great Nephite general. Although Mormon would never use such praise in describing himself, it is obvious that Mormon had many of these same traits which Moroni demonstrated.

Mormon and Moroni[1] had many things in common, both of them became the military leader of their people at a very young age. Mormon commented about Moroni[1] being, **"only twenty and five years old when he was appointed chief Captain over the armies of the Nephites."**

> Now, the leader of the Nephites, or the man who had been appointed to be the chief captain over the Nephites—now the chief captain took the command of all the armies of the Nephites—and his name was Moroni;

And Moroni took all the command, and the government of their wars. And he was only twenty and five years old when he was appointed chief captain over the armies of the Nephites (*BofM: Alma* 43:16-17; emphasis added).

As noted earlier, Mormon became the leader of the Nephite armies at an even younger age than Moroni[1]. Mormon was appointed to be the leader of the Nephite armies when he was only in his "sixteenth year" (*BofM: Mormon* 2:1-2).

Another thing that Mormon and general Moroni[1] had in common was that they each lead a defensive struggle against a superior force. These wars were also fought in the same geographic location. The war that Mormon was involved in occurred nearly 500 years after the war that Moroni fought. However, the circumstances of these wars, including weapons and defensive tactics, were probably quite similar.

Put yourself in Mormon's place for a moment. His assignment to lead the defense of his nation must have been an overwhelming burden upon his young shoulders. Who could he turn to for training? We know that he turned to the Lord. He also gained strength and insight from general Moroni's great example.

Moroni[1] was probably Mormon's role model as a righteous, and courageous defender of his people. In fact, it could be said that in reading of Moroni[1] and his military leadership techniques, Mormon found a **Power Formula** for the post of supreme commander of the Nephite nation's military forces. Also, by following this example, it could be said that Mormon did **Power Change** with Moroni[1] for this post.

When Mormon had a son, is it any wonder that he named this son Moroni? Perhaps this is a coincidence, but probably not. **It would be unlikely** for a modern writer like Joseph Smith to have incorporated a detail such as this in a fictitious book. It is far more likely that Mormon named his son after a man he greatly admired, and identified with. It is also far more likely that *The Book of Mormon* was a record made by the ancient prophet and military leader, Mormon, rather than any modern writer.

Moroni First Finished His Father's Personal Record

Now, let us look back to the lonely years of Moroni[2] to see how he took care of the Records and secured them for future generations. You will recall that Nephi, in the first verse of *The Book of Mormon*, told us that he was going to **"make a record"** (*BofM: l Nephi* 1:1).

As he engraved his inspired work of abridgment and compilation, Mormon also wrote that he was going to **"make a record"** (*BofM: 3 Nephi* 5:14-15). In addition to his abridgment of the engravings of earlier writers, Mormon also wrote a first person record. We have noted earlier how Mormon began his personal book. Here is **his** declaration about **making a record** of the things he had "seen and heard."

And now I, Mormon, **make a record** of the things which I have both seen and heard, and call it *The Book of Mormon* (*BofM: Mormon* 1:1; emphasis added).

It is fascinating that these two authors, who are the primary first person authors in *The Book of Mormon*, used this same phrase: "make a record." In Chapter 1 of this book, we noted how this phrase had also been used by L. Ron Hubbard in the **Power Formula**.

As you will recall, Mormon lost his life while trying to defend his people. Therefore, he could not finish the Record. This holy calling, and responsibility of preserving and completing the Record fell to his son, Moroni. This is why Moroni wrote that he was going to **"finish the Record"** of Mormon.

Moroni Also Abridged the Record of an Earlier Group, the Jaredites

Like his father, Moroni became an editor who abridged older records, and then included them with the plates. Specifically, Moroni abridged the Record of an earlier people, the Jaredites.

The Book of Mormon tells of three separate immigrations to this land. These three groups were:

1) The people of Jared at about the time of the tower of Babel, more than 1000 years B.C.;
2) Lehi and his party in about 600 B.C.; and
3) Another group of Israelites led by a man named Mulek, also around the year 600 B.C.

We know very little about of the people of Mulek, prior to the time when they were discovered by the Nephites. We can see a great contrast between these two groups, because the Mulekites did not bring **records** to guide them. The Mulekites were discovered by the people of king Benjamin's **father, Mosiah**[1].

> Behold, it came to pass that Mosiah discovered that the people of Zarahemla **came out from Jerusalem at the time that Zedekiah, king of Judah, was carried away captive into Babylon.**
> And they journeyed in the wilderness, and were brought by the hand of the Lord across the great waters, into the land where Mosiah discovered them; and they had dwelt there from that time forth.
> And at the time that Mosiah discovered them, they had become exceedingly numerous. Nevertheless, they had many wars and serious contentions, and had fallen by the sword from time to time; and **their language had become corrupted; and they had brought no records with them; and they denied the being of their Creator; and**

Mosiah, nor the people of Mosiah, could understand them.

But it came to pass that Mosiah caused that they should be taught in his language. And it came to pass that after they were taught in the language of Mosiah, Zarahemla gave a genealogy of his fathers, **according to his memory;** and they are written, but not in these plates (*BofM: Omni* 1: 15-18; emphasis added).

In this description of this group, we can see the great importance of the Record. Mulek and his followers came from the same area as Lehi and his family. Also, they came at about the same time. However, Lehi and his family brought the sacred scripture record with them, and this other group did not.

Because "they had not brought sacred records with them", these people had "corrupted" their language, and they were denying "the being of their Creator". We can see why the Lord inspired Lehi and Nephi to bring the Record of the scriptures contained on the brass plates.

Fortunately, these two peoples merged under the leadership of king Mosiah[1]. The Mulekites then received the blessing of having access to the Lord's records and the leadership of living prophets.

The Jaredites, and Moroni's Abridgement of Their Record

The earliest migration discussed in *The Book of Mormon* is the migration of the people of Jared. These people had crossed the ocean after the Lord confounded the language of the people who were building a tower to get to heaven. This tower is described in *The Holy Bible* in *Genesis*, Chapter 11. These people developed a great culture upon the American continent. They also kept a record.

Unfortunately, their society did not survive its own internal problems and civil wars. Twenty-four gold plates containing the Jaredite record were found by a group of Nephites led by a man named Limhi. He turned the plates over to king Mosiah[2].

The language of these plates was not familiar to the Nephites nor the Mulekites. Mosiah[2] was able to translate these records in the same way that Joseph Smith later translated the plates he received. Here is Mormon's account of how these twenty-four Jaredite plates were found and interpreted:

> Therefore he [Mosiah[2]] took the Records which were engraven on the plates of brass, and also the plates of Nephi, and all the things which he had kept and preserved according to the commandments of God, after having translated and caused to be written the Records which were on the plates of gold which had been found by the people of Limhi, which were delivered to him by the hand of Limhi;
>
> And this he did because of the great anxiety of his people; for they were desirous beyond measure to know concerning those people who

had been destroyed.

And now he translated them by the means of those two stones which were fastened into the two rims of a bow.

Now these things were prepared from the beginning, and were handed down from generation to generation, for the purpose of interpreting languages;

Now after Mosiah had finished translating these records, behold, it gave an account of the people who were destroyed, from the time that they were destroyed back to the building of the great tower, at the time the Lord confounded the language of the people and they were scattered abroad upon the face of all the earth (*BofM: Mosiah* 28:11-14,17; emphasis added).

Like Joseph Smith, Mosiah Used a Urim and Thummim to Help Translate Ancient Records

This device, which had been prepared for "the purpose of interpreting languages," was called a Urim and Thummim. There is also mention of a Urim and Thummim in *The Old Testament*. One of *The Old Testament* references is in the book of Exodus.

> And thou shalt put in the breastplate of judgment the Urim and the Thummim; and they shall be upon Aaron's heart, when he goeth in before the LORD: and Aaron shall bear the judgment of the children of Israel upon his heart before the LORD continually (*OldT: Exodus* 28:30).

When Joseph Smith was given the golden plates to translate, he was also given a Urim and Thummim. He used this instrument to translate the plates he received. He also gave us a partial description of the Urim and Thummim:

> Also, that there were two stones in silver bows—and these stones, fastened to a breastplate, constituted what is called the Urim and Thummim—deposited with the plates, and the possession and use of these stones were what constituted "seers" in ancient or former times; and that God had prepared them for the purpose of translating the book.[101]

These stones were clear and served as lenses, like eyeglasses. The prophet who used these lenses to look at the ancient records, which were written in a language he did not understand, could read them in his own language to translate the Record.

THE POWER FORMULAS

The Origin of The Book of Ether

The name of this Jaredite record is *The Book of Ether*. This may be getting a little confusing, so let's summarize. Ether was a Jaredite who engraved a record of his people on golden plates. These plates were later found by the Nephites and translated by Mosiah[2]. Moroni[2] later abridged Mosiah's translation, and added a commentary of his own. Moroni prefaced his abridgement in this way:

> And now I, Moroni, proceed to give an account of those ancient inhabitants who were destroyed by the hand of the Lord upon the face of this north country.
> And I take mine account from the twenty and four plates which were found by the people of Limhi, which is called the book of Ether.
> But behold, I give not the full account, but a part of the account I give, from the tower down until they were destroyed.
> And on this wise do I give the account. He that wrote this record was Ether...(*BofM: Ether* 1: 1-2, 5-6).

As mentioned previously, this Record deals with a people who were led by a man named Jared. These people had left the old world at the time when the Lord confounded the languages while the people were building the tower of Babel. These people had great prophets among them.

Their final prophet was named Ether. He was the prophet who recorded their revelations and their history on these twenty-four plates. Ether may have also been abridging from a larger set of plates made by earlier Jaredite prophets.

After arriving in the new world, the Jaredites divided into factions and rejected the words of the prophets. This eventually led to great civil wars, and finally to the destruction of the Jaredite nation.

The Book of Ether contains one of the great chapters of *The Book of Mormon*. This is the twelfth chapter of Ether. In this chapter the Lord taught many great lessons, through Moroni. These lessons included **how we can overcome our weaknesses (verses 23-28) and the great importance of faith, hope, and charity, or love, in our lives** (*BofM: Ether* 12:3-22, 32, 33-36).

Moroni Originally Planned to End His Record with the Abridgment of Ether's Record

Moroni must have considered finishing his Record, for he made a farewell statement at the end of this twelfth chapter of Ether. Here is an excerpt from Moroni's first farewell statement:

> And now **I, Moroni, bid farewell** unto the Gentiles, yea, and also unto

my brethren whom I love, **until we shall meet before the judgment-seat of Christ,** where all men shall know that my garments are not spotted with your blood.

And **then shall ye know that I have seen Jesus, and that he hath talked with me face to face,** and that he told me in plain humility, even as a man telleth another in mine own language, concerning these things;

And **only a few have I written, because of my weakness in writing.**

And now, **I would commend you to seek this Jesus** of whom the prophets and apostles have written, that the grace of God the Father, and also the Lord Jesus Christ, and the Holy Ghost, which beareth record of them, may be and abide in you forever. Amen (*BofM: Ether* 12:38-41; emphasis added).

Moroni's plan was to finish translating the remainder of the plates of Ether, and then to bury the Record. He may have been being pursued at this time by the Lamanites, and he was probably greatly concerned that the sacred records might fall into their hands. We shall see later however, that he decided to add more to the Record, as he continued to survive.

Also, a careful reading of *Mormon*, Chapter 8 indicates that Moroni may have even considered ending the Record when he finished Mormon's Record. He was running out of room on these plates, and he probably did not feel like writing at this time. Here is that reference.

And my father also was killed by them, and I even remain alone to write the sad tale of the destruction of my people. But behold, they are gone, and I fulfill the commandment of my father. And whether they will slay me, I know not.

Therefore I will write and hide up the Records in the earth; and whither I go it mattereth not.

Behold, my father hath made this Record, and he hath written the intent thereof. And behold, **I would write it also if I had room upon the plates, but I have not;** and ore I have none, for I am alone. My father hath been slain in battle, and all my kinsfolk, and I have not friends nor whither to go; and how long the Lord will suffer that I may live I know not (*BofM: Mormon* 8:3-5; emphasis added).

It is probable that Moroni was able to find more plates or to fashion new plates. This allowed him to do an abridgement of Ether's Record. He later decided to add a record of his own: *The Book of Moroni*.

THE POWER FORMULAS

Similarities Between Ether and Moroni

Although Ether, lived about 2,000 years prior to Moroni's time, he had many things in common with Moroni. Both of these men were the last survivors of their nation. Like Moroni, Ether survived to see the final destruction of his nation. They both chronicled these events as a warning to future peoples. Also, both men took steps to preserve the Records that they might come forth to later generations. These are the final thoughts engraved by Ether:

> And the Lord spake unto Ether, and said unto him: Go forth. And he went forth, and beheld that the words of the Lord had all been fulfilled; and he finished his record; (and the hundredth part I have not written [Moroni's commentary]) and **he hid them in a manner that the people of Limhi did find them.**
>
> Now the last words which are written by Ether are these: Whether the Lord will that I be translated, [changed instantly from mortality to immortality] or that I suffer the will of the Lord in the flesh [die], **it mattereth not, if it so be that I am saved in the kingdom of God. Amen** (*BofM: Ether* 15:33-34; emphasis added).

Please note the similarity of Ether's words to the following words of Moroni.

> And my father also was killed by them, and I even remain alone to write the sad tale of the destruction of my people. But behold, they are gone, and I fulfill the commandment of my father. And whether they will slay me, I know not.
>
> **Therefore I will write and hide up the Records in the earth; and whither I go it mattereth not** (*BofM: Mormon* 8:3-4; emphasis added).

Both Ether and Mormon seemed to be relatively unconcerned about their physical survival. This may seem like a strange attitude, but it was not an expression of giving up. Rather, both Ether and Moroni realized that their **Condition** in the next life was much more important than how or when their mortal life ended. Also, both of these men knew that they had finished their work, and had completed the Records that the Lord had assigned to them.

Ether and Moroni, Two Witnesses That Ethical Deterioration Brings National Destruction

In *Chapter 13*, we reviewed the Lord's principle of witnesses. You will recall that the Records of Third Nephi in *The Book of Mormon* and Matthew in *The New Testament* of *The Holy Bible*, both witness to the reality of others being resurrected following the Savior's resurrection (see *NewT: Matthew* 27:2-53; *BofM: Helaman* 14:21-26; *3 Nephi* 23:7-13).

In this chapter, we have reviewed Moroni's witness of the truthfulness of the principle taught by Mosiah. Here again is that prophecy:

> **Now it is not common that the voice of the people desireth anything contrary to that which is right;** but it is common for the lesser part of the people to desire that which is not right; **therefore this shall ye observe and make it your law — to do your business by the voice of the people.**
>
> **And if the time comes that the voice of the people doth choose iniquity, then is the time that the judgments of God will come upon you;** yea, then is the time he will visit you with great destruction even as he has hitherto visited this land (*BofM: Mosiah* 29:26-27 emphasis added).

You will note that Mosiah referred to "great destruction" which had "hitherto visited this land." This is a reference to the Record of Ether which he had translated (see *BofM: Mosiah* 29:23, 28:8-11).

In Ether and Moroni, we have two witnesses that *freedom to choose also brings a burden of responsibility*. If "the voice" or majority of the nations' people use their freedom to choose evil, and they then refuse to repent, they will eventually bring upon themselves destruction. Moroni and Ether both lived to chronicle the downfall of their nations, brought on by their ethical deterioration, and their falling **Spiritual Condition**.

Mormon knew that this warning also applied to the people of future generations. While he was abridging king Mosiah's record, Mormon made this commentary regarding the importance of our receiving an account of Ether's Record:

> Now after Mosiah had finished translating these records, behold, **it gave an account of the people who were destroyed,** from the time that they were destroyed back to the building of the great tower, at the time the Lord confounded the language of the people and they were scattered abroad upon the face of all the earth, yea, and even from that time back until the creation of Adam.
>
> Now this account did cause the people of Mosiah to mourn exceedingly, yea, they were filled with sorrow; nevertheless it gave them much knowledge, in the which they did rejoice.
>
> **And this account shall be written hereafter; for behold, it is expedient that all people should know the things which are written**

in this account (*BofM: Mosiah* 28: 17-19; emphasis added).

The final verse above gives an interesting insight into a possible reason why Moroni decided to abridge and include Ether's writing to the Record. It is possible that Moroni included Ether's account because Mormon felt that it was important to do so. Here are four possible ways Moroni could have been influenced to add *The Book of Ether*:

1) He may have heard his father Mormon speak of it, and Moroni may have known that Mormon wanted to include Ether, but that he did not have time to do so himself;
2) Moroni may have been given an assignment by Mormon to add *The Book of Ether*, (see *BofM: Mormon* 8:1);
3) Moroni may have also learned of his father's wish to include Ether's account by reading Mormon's commentary in *Mosiah* 28:17 (see above).

4) It is also possible that Moroni was independently inspired by the Spirit of the Lord, to insert Ether's Record.

In any case, Mormon's comment about the significance of "all people" receiving this Record gives us an insight into why Moroni engraved an abridgement of King Mosiah's translation of *The Book of Ether* on the plates.

At first glance, it may even seem unusual that Moroni would insert this ancient account between his completion of his father's record and his own book. However, with the insight of Mormon's placing a high value on the Record of the Jaredites, it becomes very understandable and logical for Moroni to add Ether's writings.

In fact, **when The Book of Ether is seen in this light, it demonstrates the consistency and thoroughness of the Record Keepers.** Thus, Ether's Record is actually another internal witness of the truthfulness of *The Book of Mormon*.

Ether's Record Became a Power Formula for Moroni

Perhaps the Lord saved this Record for Moroni to abridge for a reason. It is possible that Mormon could have made this abridgment himself. However, the similarity between the roles of Ether and Moroni could help prepare Moroni for his task. No doubt Moroni took some solace and strength from his study of Ether's experience.

We could consider Ether's record a **Power Formula** for the final Record Keeper. How appropriate that Moroni, the final Record Keeper for his people, should be the one to abridge the Record of Ether, who was the final Record keeper of the Jaredite nation.

Moroni's Second Great Project: Adding His Testimony to the Record

After completing his abridgement of Ether, Moroni originally had decided to end his writings. Here is Moroni's account of why he later decided to continue writing:

Now I, Moroni, after having made an end of abridging the account of the people of Jared, I had supposed not to have written more, but I have not as yet perished; and I make not myself known to the Lamanites lest they should destroy me.

> For behold, their wars are exceedingly fierce among themselves; and because of their hatred they put to death every Nephite that will not deny the Christ.
> And I, Moroni, will not deny the Christ; wherefore, I wander whithersoever I can for the safety of mine own life.

Wherefore, I write a few more things, contrary to that which I had supposed; for I had supposed not to have written any more; but I write a few more things, that perhaps they may be of worth unto my brethren, the Lamanites, in some future day, according to the will of the Lord (*BofM: Moroni* 1:1-4; emphasis added).

Moroni's Two Endings are Another Internal Evidence of the Truthfulness of the Record

Here is another internal evidence of the truthfulness of *The Book of Mormon*. Why would a modern author, such as Joseph Smith, have left two endings to *The Book of Mormon*? The fact that there are these two farewell statements by Moroni is another evidence that the book is true. *The Book of Moroni* was written by an ancient prophet who was living in constant danger, of being captured by his enemies.

These two endings are an indication that the Record was made by someone who was actually experiencing the events he wrote about.

Here is an excerpt from Moroni's second farewell:

> And now I bid unto all, farewell. I soon go to rest in the paradise of God, until my spirit and body shall again reunite, and I am brought forth triumphant through the air, to meet you before the pleasing bar of the great Jehovah, the Eternal Judge of both quick and dead. Amen (*BofM: Moroni* 10:34);

Moroni Finished the Record by Adding Many Important Teachings

The Book of Moroni contains truths which are of great worth to each of us. He commented on such topics as;

1) How ordinations to the priesthood were to be performed (Chapter 3);
2) How the sacrament of the Lord's supper was to be administered (Chapters 4 and 5);
3) How new members are to be admitted to the church by repentance and baptism (Chapter 6); and
4) How Church meetings are to be conducted under the direction of the Holy Ghost (Chapter 6).

Moroni Also Added the Teachings of His Father, Mormon, to the Record

In *Chapters 7* through *9*, Moroni added some of the teachings of his father, Mormon. Here is another example of the Lord adding teachings to the Record which He knows to be vital, and which had not yet been included. You will recall that in *The Book of Third Nephi*, the Savior Himself instructed Nephi[3] to add the fulfillment of Samuel's prophecy of the resurrection of the saints to the Record. In a like manner, Moroni was inspired to add some important teachings of his father.

Chapter 7 includes some of the greatest words ever written about the subject of charity. Moroni was quoting from a letter by his father, Mormon, on this subject. Mormon wrote:

> But **charity is the pure love of Christ**, and it endureth forever; and whoso is found possessed of it at the last day, it shall be well with him.
>
> Wherefore, my beloved brethren, **pray unto the Father with all the energy of heart, that ye may be filled with this love, which he hath bestowed upon all who are true followers of his Son, Jesus Christ;** that ye may become the sons of God; that **when he shall appear we shall be like him,** for we shall see him as he is; **that we may have this hope; that we may be purified even as he is pure. Amen** (*BofM: Moroni* 7:47-48; emphasis added).

Chapter 8 of *The Book of Moroni* also came from a letter, or epistle, written by Mormon to his son, Moroni[2]. Mormon had written this letter "soon after my [Moroni's] calling to the ministry" (*BofM: Moroni* 8:1). In this letter, Mormon taught that the doctrine of infant baptism was not correct. It is apparent, from the letter, that there were some people during the time of Mormon and Moroni, who were practicing infant baptism. Mormon had inquired of the Lord about the correctness of this practice.

In answer to this prayer, Mormon received a revelation. This revelation was very significant for our times as well. Moroni was inspired to include this epistle in his book. Here is an excerpt from this epistle, a letter, written by Mormon to his son, Moroni:

> And now, my son, **I desire that ye should labor diligently, that this gross error should be removed from among you;** for, for this

intent I have written this epistle.

For immediately after I had learned these things of you I inquired of the Lord concerning the matter. And the word of the Lord came to me by the power of the Holy Ghost, saying:

Listen to the words of Christ, your Redeemer, your Lord and your God. Behold, I came into the world not to call the righteous but sinners to repentance; the whole need no physician, but they that are sick; wherefore, **little children are whole, for they are not capable of committing sin...**

Behold I say unto you that this thing shall ye teach—repentance and baptism unto those who are accountable and capable of committing sin; yea, **teach parents that they must repent and be baptized, and humble themselves as their little children, and they shall all be saved with their little children.**

And **their little children need no repentance, neither baptism...**(*BofM: Moroni* 8:6-8, 10, 11 emphasis added).

Moroni Also Added Mormon's Summary of How We Progress in Our Spiritual Condition

In this letter, Mormon also gave perhaps the finest summary in all scripture of how the Savior is able **to turn us from** our iniquities and **turn us to His Father. Here is Moroni's summary of the steps in the sanctification process:**

And the **first fruits of repentance is baptism; and baptism cometh by faith** unto the fulfilling the commandments; and **the fulfilling the commandments bringeth remission of sins;**

And the **remission of sins bringeth meekness,** and lowliness of heart; and **because of meekness and lowliness of heart cometh the visitation of the Holy Ghost, which Comforter filleth with hope and perfect love, which love endureth by diligence unto prayer, until the end shall come, when all the saints shall dwell with God** (*BofM: Moroni* 8:25-26; emphasis added).

If we look at this closely, we see a progression of virtues which can occur in our the lives. Indeed, this is how we are able to improve our **Spiritual Conditions** until we are able to live with our Father in Heaven. This is the essence of the gospel of Jesus Christ:

1) We must have faith in Jesus Christ;
2) We must repent and fulfill the Lord's commandments;
3) The initial commandment we are to fulfill after repentance is baptism for the

remission of sins;
4) The remission of sins next brings meekness and lowliness of heart, which is humility, and because of our humility, we are prepared to receive the gift of the Holy Ghost;
5) The Holy Ghost will begin to be fill us with hope and perfect love as we continue to live worthily;
6) Our next duty is to see that this Christ-like love (or charity) "endureth by diligence unto prayer";
7) When we have obtained this perfect love and have endured to the end, the time will come when we will "dwell with God".

Mormon explained how to obtain this love in an epistle we cited earlier. These words were quoted by Moroni:

> Wherefore, my beloved brethren, **pray unto the Father with all the energy of heart, that ye may be filled with this love, which he hath bestowed upon all who are true followers of his Son, Jesus Christ; that ye may become the sons of God; that when he shall appear we shall be like him,** for we shall see him as he is; that we may have this hope; that we may be purified even as he is pure. Amen (*BofM: Moroni* 7:48; emphasis added).

The reason that we will be able to dwell with God is that, because of our Savior's atonement, or suffering for our sins in our place, we will have been "purified as He is pure," and "we shall be like Him [Jesus Christ]". The way we can eventually become like Him is by loving like He loves.

His atonement was the ultimate act of love. The Savior taught:

> ... greater love hath no man than this, that a man lay down his life for his friends (*NewT: John* 15:13).

Also, the apostle John taught that:

We love him, because he first loved us (*NewT: 1 John* 4:19).

Elder Max C. Caldwell, a member of the Council of Seventy of The Church of Jesus Christ of Latter-day Saints, has given us an excellent definition of what is meant by "the love of Christ". His address was given at the November 1992 General Conference of the Church.

> ...I wondered why charity [out of the qualities of faith, hope and charity] should be the greatest. **Charity was a word I did not understand.** Part of the reason for my dilemma was that the common use of

the word charity did not seem to be consistent with the doctrinal or scriptural use.

As I searched the pages of *The Book of Mormon*, **I gained a new view. Mormon, an ancient prophet of the Americas, connected the word charity to the Savior. He declared that "charity is the pure love of Christ and it endureth forever"** (*BofM: Moroni* 7:47; emphasis added).

...How deeply do we love him? Does our love depend on favorable environments? Is it diminished or strengthened by our experiences? Is our love for Him evident by our behavior and our attitude? Charity, or **love for Christ** sustains us in every need and influences us in every decision.

A second dimension of the meaning of charity is **love from Christ**. From a prophet of *The Book of Mormon* comes and inspired explanation. Speaking to the Lord, Moroni declared: **"Thou hast said that thou hast loved the world, even unto the laying down of thy life for the world..."**

This love which thou hast had for the children of men is charity (*BofM: Ether* 12:33-34; emphasis added).

Through His compliance with the severe requirements of the Atonement, the Savior offered the ultimate expression of love. **"Greater love hath no man than this, that a man lay down his life for his friends"** (*NewT: John* 15:13). **And by permitting his Son to make such a selfless and suffering sacrifice, the Father provided us with an ultimate expression of His love as a gift to the rest of His children.**

...The gift of charity is to be received. The Savior's act of redemption for our sins is of no effect without our willingness to comply with the conditions of his atonement.

A third perception of charity is to possess **a love that is like Christ**. In other words, **people are the object of Christ-like love**. Nephi said, "I have charity for my people...I have charity for the Jew...I also have charity for the Gentiles" (*BofM: 2 Nephi* 33:7-9).

...Jesus' love was inseparably connected to and resulted from His life of serving, sacrificing, and giving in behalf of others. We cannot develop Christ-like love except by practicing the process prescribed by the Master.

Charity is not just a precept or a principle, nor is it just a word to describe actions or attitudes. Rather **it is an internal CONDITION that must be developed and experienced in order to be understood.** We are possessors of charity when it is part of our nature. **People who have charity have a love for the Savior, have received of His love,**

and loves others as He does.[102]

When this inspired Church leader described Christ-like love, or charity, he discussed it as not just a principle, but as an internal **Condition**. We could go further, and when we think in terms of the **Spiritual Conditions**, the **Condition** of Christ-like love is also the **Spiritual Condition of Power**. This also helps us to understand the meaning of the last sentence of the *Preface* of this book: "It is by gaining perfect love that we will find true and lasting **Power**."

Mormon's Final Epistle and His Farewell to Moroni

Moroni chapter 9, is another epistle of Mormon to his son Moroni. This letter was written during the last days of the great war. Mormon could see that his people were going to be destroyed. He knew that recounting of these tragic circumstances would be depressing to his son, and did not want to leave this final impression upon him. Therefore, he finished with these encouraging words:

> My son, be faithful in Christ; and **may not the things which I have written grieve thee, to weigh thee down unto death; but may Christ lift thee up, and may his sufferings and death, and the showing his body unto our fathers, and his mercy and long-suffering, and the hope of his glory and of eternal life, rest in your mind forever** (*BofM: Moroni* 9:25; emphasis added).

Mormon's Power Formula and Transfer of the Record to Moroni

In the above verse, Mormon made his written farewell to his son Moroni. Mormon also gave the final instructions on record keeping in *The Book of Mormon*. Here is Mormon's account of these instructions, and of his intent to transfer the Record to Moroni:

> But behold, my son, I recommend thee unto God, and I trust in Christ that thou wilt be saved; and I pray unto God that he will spare thy life, to witness the return of his people unto him, or their utter destruction; for I know that they must perish except they repent and return unto him.
>
> **And if they perish it will be like unto the Jaredites, because of the willfulness of their hearts, seeking for blood and revenge.**
>
> And if it so be that they perish, **we know that many of our brethren have deserted over unto the Lamanites,** and many more will also desert over unto them; **wherefore, write somewhat a few things,** if thou art spared and I shall perish and not see thee; but I trust that I may see thee soon; for **I have sacred records that I would de-**

MORONI'S RECORD

liver up unto thee (*BofM: Moroni* 9:22-24; emphasis added).

Mormon also wrote his small book, *The Words of Mormon*, at about the same time he wrote this epistle to Moroni. In this book, **he wrote of his intention to give the Record to Moroni.** Mormon was hopeful that Moroni would add to the Record.

> And now **I, Mormon, being about to deliver up the Record which I have been making into the hands of my son Moroni,** behold I have witnessed almost all the destruction of my people, the Nephites.
> And it is many hundred years after the coming of Christ that **I deliver these records into the hands of my son;** and it supposeth me that he will witness the entire destruction of my people. But may God grant that he may survive them, that **he may write somewhat concerning them, and somewhat concerning Christ, that perhaps some day it may profit them** (*BofM: Words of Mormon* 1:1-2; emphasis added).

Mormon did deliver the Record to Moroni. Moroni later added: the abridgement of Ether's record, writings of his own, and these epistles from his father. The Lord wanted His Record to be complete; and He used Mormon's son to finish it.

Moroni, by inspiration, included these letters from Mormon. Is it not likely that the Lord inspired Mormon to write these letters, so that Moroni could include them on the plates? Thus, we see that the ultimate Abridger or Editor of this Record was the Lord, Himself.

Revelation and *The Book of Mormon*

The words of *The Book of Mormon* Record came to these ancient prophets by revelation. The Record was translated by Joseph Smith through revelation. It is only fitting then, that those who read it, can learn of its truthfulness, only by revelation.

Those Who Read the Record are Promised a Revelation

The last chapter of Moroni's book, contains a wonderful promise. This promise is shared by every missionary of the Church of Jesus Christ of Latter-day Saints, and with every willing student of the gospel. This is **a promise of a revelation from God to those who read *The Book of Mormon*.** Here is that promise:

> And I seal up these records, after I have spoken **a few words by way of exhortation unto you.**
> Behold, I would exhort you that **when ye shall read these things**...that ye would **remember how merciful the Lord hath been unto the children of men,** from the creation of Adam even down unto

the time that ye shall receive these things, **and ponder it in your hearts [think about what you have read, and about how you have felt while reading** *The Book of Mormon*].

And when ye shall receive these things, **I would exhort you that ye would ask God, the Eternal Father, in the name of Christ, if these things are not true; and if ye shall ask with a sincere heart, with real intent, having faith in Christ, he will manifest the truth of it unto you, by the power of the Holy Ghost.**

And by the power of the Holy Ghost ye may know the truth of all things (*BofM: Moroni* 10:2-5; emphasis added).

How to Obtain a Revelation of the Truthfulness of *The Book of Mormon*

In order to receive a revelation, the reader must be prepared. This preparation includes:

1) Remembering how merciful the Lord has been, which implies an attitude of humility and gratitude;
2) Pondering, or thinking about, what you have read, and how you have felt while reading *The Book of Mormon*;
3) Praying with a sincere heart, with real intent and with faith in Jesus Christ about the truthfulness of *The Book of Mormon*;
4) Receiving your Father in Heaven's revealed answer to your prayer, by the Power of the Holy Ghost. This comes as a sure knowledge in your mind and an emotional witness to your heart that *The Book of Mormon* is truly and undeniably the Word of God.

What it Means To Read *The Book of Mormon* "With a Sincere Heart and With Real Intent"

The Lord expects certain actions from those who receive a revelation confirming the truthfulness of *The Book of Mormon*. These actions include: exercising faith in Jesus Christ by repenting, being baptized, and receiving the gift of the Holy Ghost, and thus becoming a member of His Church.

The revelation that *The Book of Mormon* is true will come to you, if you really want to know, and if your intent is to act upon the revelation you receive. Recently, watching a PBS Masterpiece Theater entitled *Lark Rise to Candleford*, one of the characters uttered these words: "Before you can know, you must be willing to know." This truth applies to gaining a knowledge of the truthfulness of *The Book of Mormon*. Not only must we be willing to know, we must also be willing *to do*. We must be willing *to act*! We act by joining His Church and keeping His commandments, and by following His example for the rest of our lives. This is the meaning of real intent, and this is a description of the actions of the **Spiritual Non Existence** through **Spiritual Power Change Formulas**.

Denying the Undeniable

Also, a word of warning: when the revealed answer from God was described above as being undeniable, this means it is undeniable at *the time it is received*. However, if we fail to act, or fail to continue to act upon this knowledge from God of what He wants us to do, we can deteriorate to the point that we will deny the revelation we have received. In terms of the **Conditions Formulas**, this means that if we fail to act, our **Condition** will not improve, and we will not achieve the **Spiritual Condition of Power**. Rather we will fail in our **Spiritual Condition** to **Doubt**, and, possibly, even lower.

Please don't let this happen to you! Make sure that your actions follow your "real intent".

THE POWER FORMULAS

Chapter 17

Moroni's Farewell Advice to Us: Become "Perfect In Christ" and "Deny Not His Power"

Moroni's First Farewell to His Readers

As noted previously, Moroni ended his Record twice. He had decided to conclude the Record at the end of his abridgement of Ether's writings (see *BofM: Ether* 12:38-41). When he continued to survive, he decided to engrave more on the plates. Eventually, he concluded the Record with his final farewell.

Moroni's Second Farewell: A Plea for Us to Not Deny the Power of Christ

In his last chapter, Moroni made his second farewell. As part of this farewell, he encouraged those who would receive the Record to not deny the power of God. These words have special significance to those who accept the **Conditions Formulas** as taught by L. Ron Hubbard. Those who have an understanding of the **Conditions Formulas** will recognize the importance of finding out Who is in **Power**.

For instance, if we were to embark upon a new job, we would first need to find out who is in charge. Otherwise, we could not find out what is needed and wanted of us. By doing this, we can do the **Non Existence Formula**, and with persistent effort, we can steadily improve our **Conditions**.

Those who understand the **Conditions Formulas** should have the highest **Condition of Power** as their goal. We can achieve a **Condition of Power** as we receive a record or **Power Formula** from someone who is already in that **Condition**. Next, we must become familiar with this record. Then we need to follow the example of the one in power, thus accomplishing **Power Change**. In order to do **Power Change**, it is necessary to know who to receive the **Power Formula** from.

This same reasoning holds true for our **Spiritual Condition. In order to achieve the highest Spiritual Condition possible, we need to identify Who is in Power, and find Their Power Formula**. Once we have identified Who is in Power, and obtain a copy of Their **Power Formula**, then, and only then, can we follow this **Formula**. We can now understand why Moroni taught that recognizing the **Power** of God is **essential**. Moroni stated it this way:

> Yea, **Come unto Christ, and be perfected** in him, and deny yourselves of all ungodliness; and if ye shall deny yourselves of all ungod-

liness and **love God with all your might, mind and strength, then is his grace sufficient for you, that by his grace ye may be perfect in Christ;** and if by the grace of God ye are perfect in Christ, **ye can in nowise deny the power of God.**

And again, if ye by the grace of God are perfect in Christ, and deny not his power, then are ye sanctified in Christ by the grace of God, through the shedding of the blood of Christ (*BofM: Moroni* 10:32-33; emphasis added).

Why it is Important That We Not Deny the Power of God?

While preparing to write about these verses, a friend taught me about the subject of denying the **Power** of God. His comments helped to shed light upon the meaning of why we must not deny the **Power** of God. He spoke about the many good people in the world who were each trying to live correctly.

These people, **in their own way**, are trying to help others, and to better the world. However, he saw a potential tragedy in this. This potential tragedy is that as people find some success in their activities, they may become so satisfied that they stop looking for the higher law.

This man then quoted a scripture which explained why is it so important that we not deny the **Power** of Christ. This scripture comes from a revelation to Joseph Smith. You will recall that when Joseph Smith was a young man, he prayed to find out which church to join. In answer to his prayer, the Father and the Son appeared to him. Joseph was instructed to join none of the churches.

In addition, Jesus Christ told him **why** he should not join any existing church. Here is Joseph's question, and the Lord's response:

>...When the light rested upon me **I saw two Personages**, whose brightness and glory defy all description, standing above me in the air.
>
>One of them spake unto me, calling me by name and said, pointing to the other—**This is My Beloved Son. Hear Him!**
>
>My object in going to inquire of the Lord was to know which of all the sects [churches] was right, that I might know which to join. No sooner, therefore, did I get possession of myself, so as to be able to speak, than I asked the Personages who stood above me in the light, which of all the sects was right (for at this time it had never entered into my heart that all were wrong)—and which I should join.
>
>I was answered that I must join none of them ... "They draw near to me with their lips, but their hearts are far from me, **they teach for doctrines the commandments of men, having a form of godliness, but they deny the power thereof**" (*PofGP*: Joseph Smith-History 1:17-19; emphasis added).

If We Deny the Power of Jesus Christ, We Deny Ourselves Access to God's Forgiveness and Power Formula

The reason people have only a form of godliness is because they deny His power. **As we deny the Savior's Power, we are denying ourselves access to His Power Formula.** We also deny ourselves access to the only means of obtaining forgiveness of our sins. Without **His Power Formula**, men can devise plans and philosophies, and accomplish much. However, these accomplishments will not change us so that we become like God. Only His power can produce this great change in our hearts.

To become a son or daughter of God, means to become like God, or "perfect in Christ". This can only come about by His **Power**.

If we deny His **Power**, we cut ourselves off from the means of being made perfect. The reason why the Savior has this ability to purify and perfect us is because of His atonement. Only Jesus Christ has the **Power** to perfect us. **Jesus Christ obtained the Power to give us these blessings by doing His Father's will, or in other words, by accomplishing the actions of the Power Change with His Father.**

The Father covenanted with us and with His Son, Jesus Christ, to accept the Savior's offering, or atonement as the means of giving us a remission of our sins. The **Savior holds the Power whereby our unforgiven sins can become forgiven sins. Also, He holds the Power to make our mortal bodies perfect and immortal.** Thus, the **Power** of Jesus Christ is our bridge across the abyss of sin and death.

What Can We Say When We Are at the Judgment Bar?

The scriptures teach that the day will come when each of us will stand at the judgment bar of God, to be judged, "according to their works" (see *NewT: Revelation* 29:12 and *BofM: Alma* 11:42-43). Each of us will be confronted with the facts that some of our actions have hurt others, and have hurt ourselves. This is a definition of sin, and none of us will be free of sin. What do we say when this moment comes? A Christian song writer has written that this is what he will say: "I trust in Jesus [Christ], my strong Deliverer, my Great Redeemer, the Son of God!"

We May Become Perfect Only in Christ (by the Power of Christ)

We may be very honest, sincere, hard-working and productive people, but this is not enough. We are expected to become **perfect** (see *NewT: Matthew* 5:48; and *BofM: 3 Nephi* 12:48). The fact is, **we cannot** make ourselves perfect. However, **we can become perfect in Christ. Becoming perfect in Christ means adding the Savior's grace (or Power) to our efforts. His Power makes up for all that we cannot do.**

To become perfect in Christ means to be made perfect by the Power of Jesus Christ. Joseph Smith learned, by revelation, that those who receive the highest degree of glory are those who have been **made perfect through Jesus Christ.**

>These are they who are **just men made perfect through Jesus the mediator of the new covenant, who wrought out this perfect atonement through the shedding of his own blood.**
>
>**These are they whose bodies are celestial, whose glory is that of the sun, even the glory of God, the highest of all**, whose glory the sun of the firmament is written of as being typical (*D&C* 76:69-70; emphasis added).[103]

The Grace of Jesus Christ is the Enabling Power to Perfect Us

These blessings that come from the Savior to us, and which we could not obtain without Him can be called by another name: **grace**. In his book: *The Broken Heart*, author Bruce C. Hafen gives an excellent description of grace. In the following quote he also explained how the Savior can perfect us. We also looked at this reference in the Chapter titled "Bridges."

>The Dictionary in the 1979 edition of the King James Bible, under the heading "Grace," suggests that grace is needed not only because of our sins, but also because of our weaknesses and shortcomings: "It is through the grace of the Lord Jesus, made possible by his atoning sacrifice, that...individuals thorough faith in the atonement of Jesus Christ and repentance of their sins, receive strength and assistance to do good works...**This grace is an enabling power**...[that is needed] in consequence of the fall of Adam and also because of man's weaknesses and shortcomings. However, **grace cannot suffice without total effort on the part of the recipient...**"

Bruce C. Hafen also wrote:

>Not long before he passed away, Elder Bruce R. McConkie [who was one of the twelve apostles of The Church of Jesus Christ of Latter-day Saints] visited Ricks College to deliver a devotional talk. As we drove together toward the campus from the airport, I asked Elder McConkie if he thought the concepts of grace and the Lord's Atonement had anything to do with the affirmation process of perfecting our nature—apart from the connection of those concepts with forgiveness of sin.
>
>He said that is what the scriptures teach. Turning to the Doctrine and Covenants, he read aloud from Joseph Smith's description of those in the celestial kingdom: "These are they who are just men **made perfect** through Jesus the mediator of the new covenant, who wrought out

this perfect atonement through the shedding of his own blood" (*D&C* 76:69; emphasis added).

The Atonement in some way, apparently through the Holy Ghost, makes possible the infusion of spiritual endowments that actually change and purify our nature, moving us toward that state of holiness or completeness we call eternal life or Godlike life. At that ultimate stage **we will exhibit divine characteristics not just because we think we should but because that is the way we are.**

The bestowal of the gift of charity is the clearest illustration of this process, as king Benjamin's phrase, "full of love," suggests. This love, the very "love which [the Lord] hast had for the children of men" (*BofM: Ether* 12:34), is not developed entirely by one's own power; even though our faithfulness is a necessary qualification to receive it. Rather, as Mormon so eloquently tells us in *Moroni* 7, charity is **"bestowed upon" the "true followers"** of Christ. Its source, like all other blessings of the Atonement, is the grace of God.

The purpose of the endowment of charity is not only to cause an unselfish motivation for charitable acts toward other people, although that is a most valuable result. The ultimate additional purpose is to make Christ's followers like him: "...he hath bestowed [this love] upon all who are true followers of his Son, Jesus Christ; that ye may become the sons of God; that when he shall appear **we shall be like him**..."(*BofM: Moroni* 7:48; emphasis added).

And charity is only part of the total blessing. In its fullness, this "gift" of grace is eternal life—being fully like God—"the greatest of all the gifts of God" (*D&C* 14:7). The term "at-one-ment" thus seems to mean not only being with God, but being like God (emphasis added).[104]

Our Part in the Perfection Process

What is our part in this perfection process? First, we must be willing and desirous to accept His power in our lives. Second, we must choose to follow Him to the best of our ability. Nephi put it this way:

> For we labor diligently to write, to persuade our children, and also our brethren, to believe in Christ, and to be reconciled to God; for we know that **it is by grace that we are saved, after all we can do** (*BofM: 2 Nephi* 25:23; emphasis added).

Jesus Christ has walked the path and built the bridge to perfection, but we must choose to walk across it.

THE POWER FORMULAS

What the Savior's Grace or Power Includes

In review, the grace of Jesus Christ includes these powers, among others:

1) **The power to resurrect our bodies** (see *BofM: Jacob* 4: 11);
2) The power to **forgive our sins**, which comes because of His **perfect atonement** (see *BofM: 2 Nephi* 10:25; also see the sections which speak about **Christ being our bridge back to our Father in Heaven);**
3) **His power to turn us from our iniquities and to change our hearts** including the power to overcome addiction (see *BofM:3 Nephi* 20:26, *Alma* 5:6-14, *Mosiah* 5:1-2);
4) **His power to heal us emotionally**, and spiritually thereby raising our emotional tone and **Spiritual Condition** (see *BofM: 3 Nephi* 9:13, *Alma* 36:1-18);
5) **The gift of perfect love or charity** which is given to those who are true followers of Jesus Christ (see *BofM: Moroni* 7:48).

It is through His application of these powers in our lives that He is able to make us perfect! The Savior has the Power, and He is the Power. There is no other Power, no other way, no other means for us to fulfill our potential, and no other person who has the power to perfect us. He is our Measure and our Standard. We are to pattern our lives after His. We are expected to become "even as" He is, and He is "even as" the Father (see *BofM: 3 Nephi* 27:27).

We must accept that **He is the way, the truth and the life.** Then we can follow **His way**, learn **His truth** and be born of the spirit so that we can **live His type of life**. Until we acknowledge His **Power**, the best we can hope for is a "form of godliness." With His **Grace, meaning His Power** added to our own, we can be "made perfect through Jesus the Mediator...".

Why the Commandment to be Perfect is Not Unfair

Some may think it unfair that the Lord expects, and even commands us, to become perfect. Here again is the Savior's commandment to reach our potential:

> Therefore I would that ye should be perfect even as I, or your Father who is in heaven is perfect (*BofM: 3 Nephi* 12:48; see also *NewT: Matthew* 5:48).

This commandment **would** be unfair if He expected us to do this on our own. However, He has provided the "capability of doing or accomplishing" this lofty goal. You will recall that one of the definitions of *Power* referred to in the first chapter is the "capability of doing or accomplishing something."

This commandment to "be perfect" is not unfair, for He has provided us with the **Power** to accomplish it. We can become perfect, but not of ourselves. If we are to become perfect, we will be **"perfect in Christ"**. Again, this phrase, "becoming perfect in Christ," really means being made perfect **by the Power of Christ.**

It is obvious that we cannot be perfected by a power which we deny. This is why Moroni emphasized that we could be perfected by Jesus Christ if we "deny not his power".

Is it Blasphemy to Think That We Can Become Perfect, "...Even As I, or Your Father in Heaven is Perfect"? (3rd Nephi 12:48)

There are some who might say that it is presumptuous and even blasphemous to believe that we can ever become perfect, and like our Savior, and like our Father in Heaven. However, **it is much closer to blasphemy to believe that God has insufficient power to perfect us.** Also, why would the Savior give us the commandment to "...be ye therefore perfect..." if the achievement of perfection is not possible?

Moroni and Jacob's Two Farewells are Internal Evidences of the Truthfulness of *The Book of Mormon*

We considered how Moroni's two farewells are an internal evidence of the truthfulness of *The Book of Mormon* in the previous chapter.

Moroni's farewell and his instructions to "deny not the power of God", bring to mind an earlier prophet's similar testimony. Jacob, like Moroni, actually made two endings to his writings. The first ending came at the end of the sixth chapter of his book. We must conclude that, like Moroni, Jacob had intended to finish his Record, and then he changed his mind. We read that "after some years had passed away" Jacob decided to add to his account (see *BofM: Jacob* 6:13, 7:1). Jacob's second farewell is found in the final verses of his book.

Both Jacob's and Moroni's two farewells are internal witnesses to the truthfulness of *The Book of Mormon*. Why would a modern writer end the story of two of his characters, twice? It is much more likely that this would have been written by ancient writers, who actually made an inspired decisions to add to their records, after further experiences.

Jacob Also Cautioned Against Denying the Power of God

In the sixth chapter, Jacob, while engraving his first farewell, made a plea for us to **not "deny the good word of Christ, and the power of God."**

Here, once more, is Jacob's testimony and summation:

Wherefore, my beloved brethren, **I beseech of you in words of soberness that ye would repent, and come with full purpose of heart, and cleave unto God as he cleaveth unto you.** And while his arm of mercy is extended towards you in the light of the day, harden not your hearts.

Yea, today, if ye will hear his voice [by learning from Him, and by feeling His Spirit], harden not your hearts; for why will ye die?...

...**Behold, will ye reject these words? Will ye reject the words of the prophets; and will ye reject all the words which have been spoken concerning Christ, after so many have spoken concerning him; and deny the good word of Christ, and the power of God, and the gift of the Holy Ghost, and quench the Holy Spirit, and make a mock of the great plan of redemption, which hath been laid for you?**

Know ye not that if ye will do these things, that **the power of the redemption and the resurrection, which is in Christ,** will bring you to stand with shame and awful guilt before the bar of God?...

...O then, my beloved brethren, repent ye, and enter in at the strait gate, and continue in the way which is narrow, until ye shall obtain eternal life.

O be wise; what can I say more?

Finally, I bid you farewell, until **I shall meet you before the pleasing bar of God,** which bar striketh the wicked with awful dread and fear. Amen (*BofM: Jacob* 6:5-6, 8-9, 11-13; emphasis added).

Our Future Meeting with Jacob, Moroni, and Nephi

In addition to teaching us to not deny the power of God, the farewell statements of both Jacob and Moroni have something else in common. Both of these Record Keepers testified that they would **meet those of us who have read their testimonies** on the day of judgment. According to Jacob, this meeting will take place at the "bar of God" (*BofM: Jacob* 6:13).

Moroni wrote that he would meet us at "the judgment seat of God" (see *BofM: Ether* 12:38). Moroni also wrote these words concerning our meeting with him:

And **then shall ye know that I have seen Jesus, and that he hath talked with me face to face,** and that he told me in plain humility, even as a man telleth another in mine own language, concerning these things (*BofM: Ether* 12:39; emphasis added).

You will recall that the first Record Keeper of *The Book of Mormon* was Nephi. He also prophesied that he would meet those who had read his words in the day of judgment. Here is that prophecy:

And now, my beloved brethren, and also Jew, and all ye ends of the earth, hearken unto these words and believe in Christ; and if ye believe not in these words believe in Christ. **And if ye shall believe in Christ**

ye will believe in these words, for they are the words of Christ, and he hath given them unto me; and they teach all men that they should do good.

And if they are not the words of Christ, judge ye—for Christ will show unto you, with power and great glory, that they are his words, at the last day; and **you and I shall stand face to face before his bar; and ye shall know that I have been commanded of him to write these things,** notwithstanding my weakness (*BofM 2 Nephi* 33:10-11).

Whether our meeting with Jacob, Moroni, and Nephi, and possibly other Record Keepers, at the bar of God is a "pleasing" one, or a meeting which causes us to have "awful dread and fear", depends on us.

Although we may deny His **Power**, we will not be able to avoid the effect of His **Power**. For example, we will all be resurrected by that **Power**. Jacob taught that, if we:

...deny the Power of God, the Power of the redemption and the resurrection which is in Christ, will bring you to stand with shame and awful guilt before the bar of God (*BofM: Jacob* 6:9).

If we deny the **Power** of God, then we make it impossible for us to become changed and perfected by His **Power**.

Now, perhaps, we can see why the Lord associates denying "the good word of Christ [meaning the scriptures, including *The Book of Mormon*] with denying the **Power** of God. **When we deny His Record and His Power Formula, we prevent His Power from changing our lives!**

The Book of Mormon **contains the Power Formula of God. It is up to us to receive this Power Formula and to follow the Savior's teachings. As we follow Him, we are given the great opportunity of doing Power Change with Him, thereby becoming like Him.**

Dear Reader, Here Are Some Personal Thoughts About These Last Pages

While reviewing the manuscript in 2012 it occurred to me that these words of warning may be offensive to some readers. Perhaps these words need to b removed, or softened somewhat. However as these thoughts were considered, it became apparent, that it was not my right to change the message that the Lord conveyed through these of His ancient prophet record keepers.

The message is too important to soft pedal. Some of you by now will have felt the promptings of the Lord's Spirit to read *The Book of Mormon* with real intent. However, the fact that you are still reading this book, instead of reading *The Book of Mormon*, may indicate that you are still skeptical about *The Book of Mormon*, and more importantly, that some of you are still skeptical about *The Book of Mormon*'s central message, that Jesus is the Christ, the Son of God and that He alone is our Savior. You may be tempted to turn away and not grow in your faith in Jesus Christ. If you do this, you are passing by the Treasure and the Peal of Great Price that the Savior described in His beautiful parable (see *NewT: Matthew* 13:44-46).

The Power Formulas, Part Three contains a section titles "God is [Tough] Love". Here is a short excerpt from that section:

> Let us step aside for a minute to look at an example of how these books have been written. One morning, a thought occurred in my mind: "...God is love" (*New Test. 1st John* 4:8, 16). Then another thought came to mind, that sometimes, when He needs to be for our benefit, God is *tough love*! Of course this is a metaphor. God is not just Love, He is a Person who has, as one of His attributes, Perfect Love. *To be perfect, love must also, when necessary, be tough.* If we will listen for what He wants to communicate to us, *He will tell us what we need to know and do, and not just what we want to hear.*
>
> Okay, so these ideas came into my consciousness. How should this information be used? Should it be part of these books or not? If so, where should it be placed? Then later that day, while reviewing this manuscript, and specifically this section on "What Think Ye of Christ", and how we will die in our sins if we don't believe in and follow Jesus Christ, it became apparent that *here* is where this idea fits.
>
> When Jesus Christ made this statement, He was speaking to those who were rejecting Him, and who were even trying to find a way to suppress His work and destroy Him. Even though they were doing so, He still loved them. After all, He is their older Brother, as He is ours. Because of His desire to help them, and to help us, He has to say it like it is, and at times, He has to use tough love to get our attention.

It is not my intention to offend anyone. Especially, it is not my intention to offend the Lord or His prophets by watering down these message they have given to rouse those who have not yet paid attention. Their messages are serious, and these messages cannot be ignored with impunity. To do so is to cause harm to yourself and to others you could have helped learn of, believe in and follow Jesus Christ.

The Most Correct Book

In the Introduction to *The Book of Mormon* is this statement by Joseph Smith regarding what reading *The Book of Mormon*, and abiding by its precepts, can do for us.

> I told the brethren that ***The Book of Mormon* was the most correct of any book on earth,** and the keystone of our religion, and **a man**

would get nearer to God by abiding by its precepts, than by any other book (*BofM: Introduction* 2:6; emphasis added).

According to the Prophet Joseph Smith, if we follow the teachings of *The Book of Mormon*, we grow "...nearer to God..., meaning more like God", and more in communication with Him than we can by reading any other book.

You may wonder "what about *The Holy Bible*?" Joseph Smith wrote:

> We believe *The Bible* to be the word of God as far as it is translated correctly; we also believe *The Book of Mormon* to be the word of God...[105]

The Book of Mormon was translated by a prophet, under the inspiration and power of God. *The Holy Bible* was not translated by a prophet. This shows why *The Book of Mormon* is "the most correct book" (see *Introduction to The Book of Mormon*). One of my purposes for writing this book was to show that, **also from the stand point of God's Power Formulas, *The Book of Mormon* is the most correct Book**.

Could Joseph Smith Have Written *The Book of Mormon*?

Here is a great question which confronts all who learn of *The Book of Mormon*. Also, another question has special meaning for those who believe in the **Power Formula** and **Power Change Formulas**: How could Joseph Smith have known and taught these great ideas? Moreover, how could he have woven such teachings into a narrative historical, and religious account of a group of people in ancient America? Even further, how could he have added emotions, and events with which he had no first-hand experience.

If we will honestly consider these questions, the answers are clear. Joseph Smith had no knowledge of the **Power** and **Power Change Formulas**. Indeed these formulas would not even be discovered by L. Ron Hubbard until more than 100 years after Joseph's time.

He also had no leadership experience when *The Book of Mormon* was published. The Church of Jesus Christ of Latter-day Saints was organized after *The Book of Mormon* was published. He also had no experience in battle, or in missionary work. Yet *The Book of Mormon* contains the writings of men who obviously had experienced these events.

Please think of your own experience. Could you write such a book, and publish it when you were twenty-seven years of age?

Could you have done so, if you had only the equivalent of a 5th grade education? *The Book of Mormon* could not have been written by Joseph Smith or any other individual or group. *The Book of Mormon* must be the revealed word of God.

THE POWER FORMULAS

As We Come to Know That the Record is True, We Also Come to Know Three Other Truths

Through study, prayer and personal revelation, we can know for ourselves that *The Book of Mormon* is true. In doing so, we will also know other truths. The following quote, from the Introduction page to *The Book of Mormon*, lists what these other truths are:

> Those who gain this divine witness from the Holy Spirit will also come to know by the same power **that [1] Jesus Christ is the Savior of the world, that [2] Joseph Smith is his revelator and prophet in these last days, and that [3] the Church of Jesus Christ of Latter-day Saints is the Lord's kingdom,** once again established on the earth, preparatory to the second coming of the Messiah (*BofM: Introduction*).

It only makes sense that if we know, by personal revelation, that *The Book of Mormon* is true, we then know that its central message, that Jesus is the Christ, is also true. Additionally, we know that the Book's translator, Joseph Smith, must be a prophet, and the Church restored through this prophet must be the Lord's own true Church.

A Second Witness of the Power of Jesus Christ

It would not do to state the issue with any less clarity or directness. In fact, it would be doing the reader a disservice to allow him to consider *The Book of Mormon* as only another religious book. The issue is clear, and the evidence overwhelming, for those who understand the **Power Formulas. God's Power Formula is the gospel of Jesus Christ. The Record portion of the Power Formula is contained in *The Book of Mormon*.**

To do **Power Change** with Him, we must have His record and follow it. We have *The Holy Bible,* and now we have a second witness of the **Power** of Jesus Christ. This witness is *The Book of Mormon*.

The Book of Mormon is the Savior's Record to direct our lives. Jesus Christ inspired His servants to make this Record, to protect it, and to pass it on. He personally reviewed the Record, and added new teachings to it. The Lord also called a modern prophet to translate and publish the Record to the world.

If Men do Power Formulas to Help One Another, Can We Expect the Lord to do Less?

People can help others in their occupations by doing a **Power Formula** for those who follow them. **Can we expect the Lord to do any less to help us in our greatest occupation: life? Please ask yourself this question: would our loving Father in Heaven leave us here without a Power Formula for our lives? The answer seems obvious, He would not!**

Our Father has prepared a Power Formula for us. He has made a Record for us. He has, and is, getting the Record into our hands, and He is doing everything to help us occupy the post of becoming His heirs. That Record is *The Book of Mormon*. We need not be confused. We have His Record, and we now need to follow it.

The Purposes of This Book

In the introduction, one purpose of this book was explained. This was to encourage you to read *The Book of Mormon*. Please do so, and study it prayerfully, with real intent.

As you study and pray "with real intent" **your faith in Jesus Christ and in His Power will grow. This faith will lead to a desire to obtain the blessings of repentance and baptism for the remission of sins. You will then receive the gift of the Holy Ghost.**

Other important purposes of this book are to bear testimony of Jesus Christ and of His Record, *The Book of Mormon*. In addition, this book bears testimony that Joseph Smith, and those who have followed him as leaders of the The Church of Jesus Christ of Latter-day Saints, are prophets of God.

Jesus Christ loves us with all of His heart. His goal and work is to perfect us. His joy comes as we return to live with Him and His Father. His love for us, and His perfection and **Power** are absolute reflections of His Father's love, perfection and **Power**.

My testimony is that our Father in Heaven lives and that He has great concern and love for each of us. His love is so great that He prepared His Son, and empowered Him to be able to lead us back into His presence.

Only the **Power** of Jesus Christ can bring us to the Father. Also, only the **Power** of Jesus Christ can perfect us so that we can become like the Father.

The Ultimate Purpose of *The Book of Mormon*

The most important purpose of *The Book of Mormon* is to bring us back into the presence of our Father in Heaven. This occurs as we read *The Book of Mormon*, become converted to Jesus Christ, and follow Him.

The Path, the Gate, the Guide, the Bridge, the Goal and the Record

The Path
The Savior has prepared **the Path of His example and teachings** for us to follow.

The Gate
The **Gate** to this path is spiritual rebirth through **faith,** our **Heavenly Father** and **Jesus Christ, repentance, water baptism** and **receiving the Gift of the Holy Ghost.**

The Guide
The **Guide** along this path is the Holy Spirit, Who is also known at the Holy Ghost.

The Bridge
The Savior's power of resurrection and atonement provide the **Bridge** across the abyss of death and sin, which blocks our path back to our Father in Heaven's presence.

The Goal
With the help of the Holy Ghost, we can follow the Savior for the rest of our lives. If we do this, we will eventually return to the presence of our Brother Jesus Christ and of our loving Father. **With Them, we will receive a fullness of Joy, and we will receive a fulness of Their Power to do good. This is the goal of our existence! May we reach this goal!**

The Record
When we reach this goal, may we realize that it is through the power and love of Jesus Christ that we are able to do so. May we be thankful for His love, and for His **Power Formula Record**:

The Book of Mormon!

APPENDIX I

Appendix I

Power Formulas and Record Transfers Between *The Book of Mormon* Record Keepers

In the previous chapters, we have seen how *The Book of Mormon* plates were kept and passed on from one Record Keeper to the next. In this appendix, we will review all of the references about these transfers and the instructions between these Record Keepers. We will look at the **Power Formula-** like actions for each Record Keeper of *The Book of Mormon*. We will also see that these new Record Keepers used actions that are consistent with the principles of **Power Change**.

This review starts with Nephi's passing of the Record to Jacob, and ends with Moroni's transfer of the plates to the prophet, Joseph Smith.

Power Formula #1, Nephi to Jacob

It was Jacob who recorded Nephi's instructions rather than Nephi himself. Also, Jacob indicated later, that the instructions he received from Nephi, were actually meant for subsequent Record Keepers as well. We should understand that it was not necessary to make major changes in these instructions from generation to generation. Most of the Record Keepers were asked to **carry out** the instructions, not to change them. When a change in instructions did come, after Enos, we shall review the reasons for this change.

These repeated cycles of action are, as shown previously, wonderful examples of **Power Formula**-like actions followed by **Power Change Formula**-like actions. Here is the first of a continuing set of instructions, or **Power Formulas**, for those who were to be entrusted with protecting, engraving and eventually transferring the sacred Record:

> For behold, it came to pass that fifty and five years had passed away from the time that Lehi left Jerusalem; wherefore, **Nephi gave me, Jacob, a commandment concerning the small plates,** upon which these things are engraven.
>
> And he gave me, Jacob, a commandment that **I should write upon these plates a few of the things which I consider to be most precious;** that I should not touch, save it were lightly, concerning the history of this people which are called the people of Nephi.
>
> For he said that the history of his people should be engraven upon his other plates, **and that I should preserve these plates and hand them down unto my seed, from generation to generation.**

And if there were **preaching** which was sacred, or **revelation** which was great, or **prophesying, that I should engraven the heads of them upon these plates, and touch upon them as much as it were possible, for Christ's sake, and for the sake of our people.**

...I, Jacob, take it upon me to fulfill the commandment of my brother Nephi (*BofM: Jacob* 1:1-4, 8; emphasis added).

A consideration of these verses yields the realization that, in transferring the Records, Nephi employed the same four steps which are in the **Power Formula**. These same steps were used repeatedly as the plates were passed from one Record Keeper to another. We shall review these four steps, as we consider the second transfer of the Records.

Power Formula #2, Jacob to Enos

Jacob's instructions to his son, Enos, are found in the last verse which Jacob recorded. Here is how Jacob transferred the Record, and how he instructed his successor:

And I, Jacob, saw that I must soon go down to my grave; wherefore, **I said unto my son Enos: Take these plates. And I told him the things which my brother Nephi had commanded me, and he promised obedience unto the commands.** And I make an end of my writing upon these plates, which writing has been small; and to the reader I bid farewell, hoping that many of my brethren may read my words. Brethren, adieu (*BofM: Jacob* 7:27; emphasis added).

Please note that Jacob rehearsed to Enos, "...the things which my brother [Nephi] commanded me..." Therefore, Jacob was passing on the same instructions, or **Power Formula**, which he had received from Nephi. Also, like Jacob, Enos accepted the challenge. Just as Jacob was willing to "...take it upon me to fulfill the commandments of my brother Nephi, 'Enos'...promised obedience unto the commands," regarding record keeping (see *BofM: Jacob* 1:1-8, 7:27).

These instructions actually fulfill the first through fourth steps of the **Power Formula**. These steps, paraphrased, were to: 1) maintain contact or communication; 2) make a Record; 3) get it into the hands of the person who will be filling your position; and 4) do all you can to help the one taking over the responsibility and succeed. Jacob accomplished these same actions, as he made a Record, preserved it, and communicated with his son, Enos, teaching him the gospel and instructing him to "...take these plates...".

Thus, we can see that the actions of the first two Record Keepers of *The Book of Mormon* fulfilled perfectly all of the **Power Formula** steps.

Also as Jacob and Enos followed the instructions of the previous Record

APPENDIX I

Keeper, Nephi, they actually fulfilled the actions described in the **Power Change Formula**, as well.

Power Formula #3, Enos to Jarom

It is important to recall that the Record we are currently discussing is the small plates of Nephi. You may want to review Chapter 2 regarding the difference between the two sets of plates that Nephi made. In brief, the large plates contained mostly the secular history of the Nephites, and their contacts with the Lamanites.

The small plates were meant to contain "...preaching which was sacred, or revelation which was great, or prophesying..." (*BofM Jacob* 1:1-4). By the time the small set of plates got to their fourth Record Keeper, Jarom, they were nearly full. Therefore, at that time, there was a change in the **Power Formula** instructions to the next Record Keeper.

Jarom did **not** indicate that he received the same instructions which had been followed by his father, Enos and his grandfather, Jacob. Rather, he tells us that he had received a **"...commandment of my father, Enos, that our genealogy may be kept"**. Jarom also mentioned that there was very little space left on the plates. Here are the verses which tell of Enos' instructions to Jarom regarding his responsibilities as Record Keeper:

> Now behold, I, Jarom, **write a few words according to the commandment of my father, Enos, that our genealogy may be kept.**
>
> And as **these plates are small**, and as these things are written for the intent of the benefit of our brethren the Lamanites, **wherefore, it must needs be that I write a little; but I shall not write the things of my prophesying, nor of my revelations. For what could I write more than my fathers have written? For have not they revealed the plan of salvation? I say unto you, Yea; and this sufficeth me** (*BofM: Jarom* 1:1-2; emphasis added).

Note how Enos' instructions differed from instructions of his predecessors. Enos commanded only that a genealogy be kept. However, Jarom did find room to express his testimony that the record he had received from his fathers, "...revealed the plan of salvation". In the last verse of Jarom's Record, we learn that he had also been instructed to preserve and pass the Record on.

> **And I deliver these plates into the hands of my son Omni, that they may be kept according to the commandments of my fathers** (*BofM: Jarom* 1:15 emphasis added).

In these verses, we see no indication that Jarom was to write of "... preaching which was sacred, or revelation which was great or prophesying..." (*BofM: Jacob* 1:4), as had Nephi, Jacob and Enos. Rather, Jarom informs his readers that "...I shall not write the things of my prophesying, nor of my revelations...".

Jarom gave two reasons why he did not record his revelations and prophesying. First, he was running out of room on this small set of plates: "and as these plates are small...wherefore it must needs be that I write a little...". The second reason he cited for not writing of spiritual things was because Nephi, Jacob and Enos' writing must have already fulfilled the Lord's purpose for this small set of plates. Again, Jarom stated it this way:

> **...For what could I write more than my fathers have written? For have not they revealed the plan of salvation? I say unto you, Yea; and this sufficeth me** (*BofM: Jarom* 1:2; emphasis added).

There is one other reason why Jarom didn't write as his predecessors. This is because **he was not instructed to do so.** Jarom was following the instructions which he had received from Enos. Thereby, Jarom completed the action we now call the **Power Change**.

Power Formulas #4 Through #9: Jarom to Omni, to Amaron, to Chemish, to Abinadom, to Amaleki, and to King Benjamin

Jarom's instructions to his son Omni appear to be the same as he had received from Enos. Omni was to keep a genealogy, preserve the Record and pass it on.

> Behold, it came to pass that I, Omni, **being commanded by my father, Jarom, that I should write somewhat upon these plates, to preserve our genealogy—** (*BofM: Omni* 1:1; emphasis added).

Omni preserved the Record and passed it on. As noted in the chapter about Omni and his descendants, they lived in a time of war and great danger. These Record Keepers mentioned very little about themselves or their spiritual experiences. However, from one of these men, Chemish, we gain an important insight into how the Record Keepers trained their successor by engraving or making a Record as their successor watched.

> Now I, Chemish, write what few things I write, in the same book with my brother; for behold, **I saw the last which he wrote, that he wrote it with his own hand; and he wrote it in the day that he delivered them unto me. And after this manner we keep the Records,** for it is according to the commandments of our father. And I make an end (*BofM: Omni* 1:9; emphasis added).

APPENDIX I

From this verse, we learn that Omni engraved his final words on the plates **as his successor, Chemish, observed**. It was possibly at this same time the **Power Formula**-like instructions to preserve the Record, and keep a brief genealogy and to then pass the Record to someone else were rehearsed with the successor.

Chemish made it clear that this process was not unique to himself: "...and after this manner *we* keep the Records, for it is according to the commandments of our fathers." Therefore, the Record Keepers not only told their successor how to keep the Record, they actually **showed them how to do it,** as well!

Each of these Small Plate Record Keepers engraved brief accounts which included their genealogy, communicated with their successors, and then passed the plates to their successors. These actions are comparable to the steps of the **Power Formula**.

The Brevity of the Records of Jarom Through Amaleki is an Internal Evidence to the Truthfulness of *The Book of Mormon*

By the time the plates were given to Amaleki, they were nearly full. In fact, Amaleki's last engravings upon the plates were these words:

> **...And I am about to lie down in my grave; and these plates are full. And I make an end of my speaking** (*BofM: Omni* 1:30; emphasis added).

These final Record Keepers of the small plates of Nephi knew that they were running out of room to engrave their portions of the Record. Therefore, they kept their entries as short as possible. We do see a trend to shorter and shorter accounts, as the space available on the set of plates becomes smaller and smaller. This topic was also addressed in Chapter 5.

As we look at the shortening lengths of each Record Keeper's writings **in the context that they were engraving on a set of plates that were nearly full, it makes sense that each writer would be brief.** In this, we see another internal evidence of the truthfulness of *The Book of Mormon*, for why would a modern writer have incorporated these patterns into a fictional narrative? **It is much more likely that this pattern of compacted writings would come from a group of ancient writers, each with less and less room to record their genealogy.**

Amaleki had no children, so he decided to pass the completed small plates of Nephi to king Benjamin for preservation. This decision to give the plates to Benjamin was surely inspired. Amaleki must have known that Benjamin had possession of the brass plates, and the large plates of Nephi. He also observed that Benjamin was a "...just man before the Lord...". Therefore, Amaleki decided to "...deliver these plates unto him...".

> And it came to pass that I began to be old; and, having no seed, and knowing king Benjamin to be a just man before the Lord, wherefore,

I shall deliver up these plates unto him... (*BofM: Omni* 1:25).

Because Benjamin had possession of at least two other sets of plates, he must have been following a Record Keeper's **Power Formula** also. Nephi had seen to it that the kings would keep "...the history of his people..." upon the larger set of plates that he had made (*BofM: Jacob* 1:1-3).

From the time of Nephi, two records had been kept. The large record contained the history of people, and "...the Record of our wars..." (*BofM: Jarom* 10). The small record contained the preaching, revelations and prophesying of these early Nephite spiritual leaders.

The last six keepers of the small record engraved only brief genealogies. When Amaleki gave the completed plates, to Benjamin, there was no need for him to instruct him in record keeping. Benjamin would have already received his instructions or **Power Formula** for record keeping from his father, king Mosiah[1]. This would have occurred as Mosiah[2] gave Benjamin the Brass Plates and the Large Plates of Nephi.

Power Formula #10, Benjamin to Mosiah[2]

In *Chapter 2*, we reviewed three instances in which Benjamin used actions like those of the **Power Formula**. You will recall that he used two **Power Formula**-like actions for his son, Mosiah. These were: 1) for his responsibility as the spiritual leader and Record Keeper, and 2) for the office of king.

Benjamin also gave a long farewell address to his people. He had his remarks recorded and distributed to them. We would say that these teachings constituted a **Spiritual Power Formula** for his people.

Here is a brief look at Benjamin's instructions and **Power Formula** for the next king and Record Keeper, Mosiah[2].

> And he [Benjamin] also taught them [his sons, including Mosiah[2]] concerning the Records which were engraven on the plates of brass, saying: My sons, **I would that ye should remember that were it not for these plates, which contain these records and these commandments, we must have suffered in ignorance**, even at this present time, not knowing the mysteries of God.
>
> O my sons, **I would that ye should remember that these sayings are true, and also that these records are true**. And behold, also the plates of Nephi, which contain the Records and the sayings of our fathers from the time they left Jerusalem until now, and they are true; and we can know of their surety because we have them before our eyes.

APPENDIX I

And now, my sons, I would that ye should remember to search them diligently, that ye may profit thereby; and I would that ye should keep the commandments of God, that ye may prosper in the land according to the promises which the Lord made unto our fathers.

And it came to pass that after king Benjamin had made an end of these sayings to his son, that he gave him [Mosiah²] charge concerning all the affairs of the kingdom.

And moreover, he also gave him charge concerning the Records which were engraven on the plates of brass; and also the plates of Nephi...(*BofM: Mosiah* 1:3, 6-7, 15-16; emphasis added).

Benjamin's mentioning of "...the plates of brass..." in these verses is another internal evidence of the truthfulness of *The Book of Mormon*. These brass plates had no direct bearing on the Record of the plates of Nephi that Benjamin had been keeping, and was soon to pass on to his son Mosiah.

How astute would a fiction writer need to be to remember to insert references to a different set of plates, that had no direct tie in to the immediate information that king Benjamin was sharing with his successor. In other words, the existence of this peripheral set of plates would be important for a king to discuss with his successor. This is because he would be getting more than one set of Records "...into the hands of the guy who is going to take care of it [his son, Mosiah]...".

However, this would be a very unlikely detail for a fiction writer to remember to include in his narrative! This is especially true for a first-time fiction writer, in his mid twenties, who had received little formal education. This episode is an example of the internal consistency of *The Book of Mormon*.

Power Formula #11, Mosiah² to Alma²

The first translated portion we now have of the large plates is the Record of Mosiah². Perhaps you asked yourself this question, why isn't the first part of Mosiah called the *Book of Benjamin*, since it records his teachings. One possible answer is that Benjamin's teachings were actually being recorded by his son Mosiah.

This seems likely, because Benjamin was quite advanced in age, when we first learn of him. Therefore, the *Book of Mosiah* begins with Mormon's abridgement of Benjamin's teachings which were probably being recorded for him, by his son Mosiah.

We do know that when Benjamin gave his final address as king, "...he caused that the words which spoke should be written and sent forth...". We know then that someone else actually wrote his words for the people, and that these words were eventually engraved upon Nephi's large plates.

We also know that Mosiah received the Records from his father, Benjamin. Thus, it is probable that it was Mosiah who recorded Benjamin's teachings upon the plates.

Also, there are precedents for this type of Record Keeping in *The Book of Mormon*. The prophet Nephi's recorded teachings of his brother Jacob, (see *2 Nephi* Chapters 6-10). Also, Mosiah recorded the teaching of a prophet named Abinadi (see *Mosiah* Chapter 11-17).

Many wonderful things occurred during the reign of Mosiah, who was the last Nephite king. First, he changed the government from a monarchy to a representative type. Second, the Lord's Church was organized among the people, and Alma was named to lead the Church. Thereby, Mosiah accomplished a separation between the Church and the State. Third, Mosiah's sons, along with Alma's son, Alma^2, had a miraculous conversion. This led to a great missionary effort among the Lamanites and Nephites.

Following a successful 27-year reign, Mosiah turned the Record over to the next Record Keeper. It is interesting to note that he did not turn it over to any of his four sons. Perhaps this was because they were on missions to the Lamanites.

More likely, however, Mosiah turned the Records over to Alma^2 by inspiration, for Alma^2 would shortly follow his father as the leader of the Church.

In these instructions to Alma^2, note how Mosiah made reference to the **consistent pattern of record preservation and transmission.** Mosiah directed Alma^2 to continue, **"...handing them down from one generation to another...even as they had been handed down from the time that Lehi left Jerusalem."**

> And now, as I said unto you, that after king Mosiah had done these things, **he took the plates of brass, and all the things which he had kept, and conferred them upon Alma, who was the son of Alma; yea, all the Records, and also the interpreters, and conferred them upon him, and commanded him that he [1] should keep and preserve them, and [2] also keep a record of the people, [3] handing them down from one generation to another, even as they had been handed down from the time that Lehi left Jerusalem** (*BofM: Mosiah* 28:20; emphasis added).

Here again, we see that Mosiah used all of the steps in the **Power Formula**. In brief, these are: 1) Maintaining contact/communication with his successor, Alma; 2) Making a Record; 3) bring him the Record; 4) Help Alma to succeed as the next Record Keeper through training him in his duty to preserve the previous Records, add his teachings to the Record, and eventually pass the plates to the next Record Keeper.

Power Formula #12, Alma^2 to Helaman^2

The transfer of records from Alma^2 to Helaman^2 was preceded by the most com-

APPENDIX I

plete set of instructions in the entire *Book of Mormon*. The other Record Keepers probably also went into detail with their successors about the care and precautions they should take with the sacred Record.

However, only Alma's account included those instructions in such depth. We shall not review all of it now, and the reader is referred to Chapter 37 of Alma for the full instructions and **Power Formula** between these men. Here are a few highlights from these instructions:

> And now, my son Helaman, **I command you that ye take the Records** which have been entrusted with me;
> And I also command you that ye **keep a record of this people, according as I have done,** upon the plates of Nephi, and **keep all these things sacred** which I have kept, **even as I have kept them**; for it is for a wise purpose that they are kept (*BofM: Alma* 37:1-2; emphasis added).

Alma cautioned Helaman against personal unrighteousness. In fact, Helaman was told that if he were to "...transgress the commandments of God, behold these things [the Records] shall be taken away from you by the power of God...".

> And now remember, my son, that **God has entrusted you with these things, which are sacred, which he has kept sacred, and also which he will keep and preserve for a wise purpose in him, that he may show forth his power unto future generations.**
> And now behold, I tell you by the spirit of prophecy, that **if ye transgress the commandments of God, behold, these things which are sacred shall be taken away from you by the power of God,** and ye shall be delivered up unto Satan, that he may sift you as chaff before the wind (*BofM: Alma* 37: 14-15; emphasis added).

On the other hand, if Helaman, and probably any other Record Keeper were to remain faithful, the Lord would help them to protect and hold onto the plates.

> **But if ye keep the commandments of God,** and do with these things which are sacred according to that which the Lord doth command you, (**for you must appeal unto the Lord for all things whatsoever ye must do with them) behold, no power of earth or hell can take them from you,** for God is powerful to the fulfilling of all his words (*BofM: Alma* 37:16; emphasis added).

Another great thing about Alma's instructions to Helaman is that these instructions reveal some of the Lord's purposes in making this Record. One purpose of *The Book of Mormon* Records was to produce change in the lives of people. These changes occur as people are brought to Christ through reading, and then living by the true principles contained in the Records.

> For he will fulfill all his promises which he shall make unto you, for he has fulfilled his promises which he has made unto our fathers. For **he promised unto them [previous Record Keepers] that he would preserve these things for a wise purpose in him**, that he might show forth his power unto future generations.
> And now behold, one purpose hath he fulfilled, even to the restoration of many thou**sands of the Lamanites to the knowledge of the truth; and he hath shown forth his power in them, and he will also still show forth his power in them unto future generations; therefore they [the Records] shall be preserved** (*BofM: Alma* 37:17-19; emphasis added).

Many people have experienced a great change in their life as a result of reading the Record. The Lord has, and **will continue**, to show His power by the changes brought about in His children's lives as they read *The Book of Mormon*.

In the final verse of this chapter, Alma again emphasized the need for Helaman to "...take care of these sacred things [meaning the Record]".

> And now, my son, **see that ye take care of these sacred things**, yea, see that ye look to God and live. Go unto this people and declare the word, and be sober. My son, farewell (*BofM: Alma* 37:47 emphasis added)

Record Transfer #13, Alma² and Helaman² to Shiblon

Helaman became an important military leader, and a great missionary. He was also the Record Keeper for about ten years. Shiblon was one of Helaman's brothers. Mormon does not include any instructions from Helaman to his brother Shiblon about the responsibility of record keeping. However, in this case, **it probably was not necessary since Shiblon had access to his father, Alma's² detailed instructions to Helaman!**

In effect, Alma probably was doing a Power Formula for both his sons at once. Also, later generations of Record Keepers would have access to Alma's instructions, as well. Here is Mormon's account of how Shiblon became the Record Keeper:

> **...because of so many wars and contentions, it had become expedient that a regulation should be made again in the church.**

APPENDIX I

Therefore, Helaman and his brethren went forth, and did declare the word of God with much power unto the convincing of many people of their wickedness, which did cause them to repent of their sins and to be baptized unto the Lord their God.

And it came to pass that **they did establish again the Church of God, throughout all the land.**

And it came to pass that all these things were done. And Helaman died, in the thirty and fifth year of the reign of the judges over the people of Nephi.

And it came to pass in the commencement of the thirty and sixth year of the reign of the judges over the people of Nephi, that **Shiblon took possession of those sacred things [the Records]** which had been delivered unto Helaman by Alma.

And he was a just man, and he did walk uprightly before God; and **he did observe to do good continually, to keep the commandments of the Lord his God; and also did his brother** (*BofM: Alma* 62:44-46, 52; 63: 1-2; emphasis added).

Helaman's Mission to Regulate the Church and Its Similarity to Modern Events is Another Internal Evidence of the Truthfulness of *The Book of Mormon*

Here we find another internal evidence of the truthfulness of *The Book of Mormon*. After World War II, The Church of Jesus Christ of Latter-day Saints found that its membership in Europe was in great need of assistance and reorganization. Therefore, the Church sent one of its Twelve Apostles to aid the saints in these war torn nations. Elder Ezra Taft Benson, who later served as the prophet and president of the Church, was sent on this great mission.

With the Lord's help, much relief was administered to these Church members. Their congregations were reorganized. New leaders were ordained, just as in the time of Helaman. Also, communications were reestablished with the leadership of the Church.

While making revisions in Part One, it was my privilege to meet an elderly Latter-day Saint woman from Germany. She testified of how she and her family had been helped by this living apostle of Jesus Christ after the war in Europe. Also, in addition to the meeting the survival needs of these people, Elder Benson and others were able to "... establish again the Church..." just as Helaman[2] and his brethren had done about 2,000 years before.

And thus ended the thirty and first year of the reign of the judges over the people of Nephi; and thus they had wars, and bloodsheds, and famine, and affliction, for the space of many years.

> But behold, because of the exceedingly great length of the war between the Nephites and the Lamanites many had become hardened, because of the exceedingly great length of the war; and **many were softened because of their afflictions, insomuch that they did humble themselves before God, even in the depth of humility.**
>
> And Pahoran did return to his judgment-seat; and **Helaman did take upon him again to preach unto the people the word of God; for because of so many wars and contentions it had become expedient that a regulation should be made again in the church.**
>
> **And it came to pass that they did establish again the church of God, throughout all the land** (*BofM: Alma* 62:39, 41, 44, 46).

It wasn't until World War II that the need of helping the Latter-day Saints in Europe became apparent, and then the Lord inspired His prophet to send a modern "Helaman" to help these people.

Please consider this question; how could a modern writer, such as Joseph Smith, have been able to foresee this necessity of establishing again the Church after a great war like the one between these Nephite and Lamanite nations? **Is it not much more likely that such an event could only have been recorded by ancient writers, who had actually experienced a war and its aftermath!**

Stepping Stones or Stumbling Blocks

Also, in the preceeding verses, it was remarkable to find how living through this war had two totally opposite effects in these people. Some people became "hardened" "...because of the exceeding great length of the war...". While others "...were softened because of their afflictions, insomuch that they did humble themselves before God...". Why the difference? The answer is simple. Some chose to have faith and trust in God, while others chose not to. The choice to have faith in God, or not, will determine whether the difficulties and afflictions of our lives will become stepping stones or stumbling blocks.

Power Formula #14, Shiblon to His Brother Helaman[2]'s Son, Helaman[3]

After keeping the Records for about three years, Shiblon transferred the plates to his nephew, Helaman[3]. A careful reading indicates that Helaman[3], after receiving the Records, also followed his grandfather Alma's instructions, or **Power Formula**.

> Therefore it became expedient for Shiblon **to confer those sacred things, before his death, upon the son of Helaman, who was called Helaman,** being called after the name of his father.
>
> Now behold, all those engravings which were in the possession of

APPENDIX I

Helaman were written and sent forth among the children of men throughout all the land, **save it were those parts which had been commanded by Alma** should not go forth.

Nevertheless, **these things [the Records] were to be kept sacred, and handed down from one generation to another;** therefore, in this year, **they had been conferred upon Helaman, before the death of Shiblon** (*BofM: Alma* 63:11-13; emphasis added).

Please note Mormon's reference to how Helaman[3] published and distributed the Record, except for those parts of it which **Alma** had commanded to be reserved. It had only been twenty years previous to this time, when Alma gave the Records to Helaman[2]. It is even possible that his grandson, Helaman[3] may have heard these instructions directly from Alma. At the very least, Helaman[3] must have read Alma's instructions, or how else would he know which sections of the Record that Alma did not want to be sent forth?

It is becoming increasingly clear that Alma's wonderful and lengthy **Power Formula** had become a standard for his brother, and for his own descendants who became the next eight Record Keepers. Alma, Helaman[2], Shiblon, and possibly even Helaman[3], were all contemporaries. Therefore, all of them could have been trained by Alma.

Those who were not directly trained by Alma were probably trained in Alma's instructions, by their predecessors. Another thing that is clear is that it is not always necessary for a Record Keeper to re-do the **Power Formula** they give to their successors. Alma's **Power Formula** was so detailed, and so complete that His successors only needed to follow it, and pass it on. Alma's **Power Formula** was really not his own. It came by way of inspiration, for he was a prophet of God.

There was no need to change it until the Conditions of the people determined significantly during this time of Ammaron and Mormon, many years later.

Just as the Lord's **Power Formula** given through Alma became the standard for future Record Keepers, Jesus Christ has given us a **Power Formula** that is a standard, even the scriptures of The Church of Jesus Christ of Latter-day Saints. These four books: T*he Book of Mormon, The Holy Bible, The Doctrine and Covenants of the Church of Jesus Christ of Latter-day Saints,* and *The Pearl of Great Price* are known as *The Standard Works*.

These, plus the words of the living apostles and prophets, are the Standard, or **Power Formula** for us from our Father in Heaven, and His Son Jesus Christ. We should not seek to make changes in these, rather, we should do **Power Change** with God, by following the directions for our lives which these, The Records of God, contain.

THE POWER FORMULAS

Power Formula #15, Helaman³ to His Sons, Nephi and Lehi

Helaman³ wore more than one hat. In addition to being the Record Keeper, he was also elected to be the chief judge of the Nephite government. Mormon gives this account of Helaman³'s death, and of Helaman³'s son, Nephi² filling the judgment seat "...in his stead...".

> And it came to pass in the fifty and third year of the reign of the judges, Helaman died, and his eldest son **Nephi began to reign in his stead.** And it came to pass that he did fill the judgment-seat with justice and equity; yea, **he did keep the commandments of God, and did walk in the ways of his father** (*BofM: Helaman* 3:37; emphasis added).

Mormon does not, in this case, make a separate reference to Nephi² becoming the Record Keeper. However, he did tell us that Nephi did, "keep the commandments of God, and did walk in the ways of his father." This is a perfect description of actions like **Power Change**. Therefore, we can assume that he received instructions from his father, Helaman³. These instructions were both his father's example, and by the written instructions from Alma².

We do know that Nephi² received the Record, for he later passed it on to his own son. When he transferred the Record on, Nephi² gave instructions to his son Nephi³. This indicates that Nephi² **had received similar training himself**.

We shall turn to that reference shortly. However, before doing so, we need to look at one more reference from Mormon's last commentary about this period.

> And thus ended the book of Helaman, according to **the Record of Helaman and his sons** (*BofM: Helaman* 16:25; emphasis added).

Helaman³ had two sons who were mentioned in the Record. These were Nephi² and his brother Lehi⁴. Both of these men became great missionaries, and although Nephi succeeded his father as chief judge and Record Keeper, Lehi was equal to his brother in righteousness.

> And behold, the people did rejoice and glorify God, and the whole face of the land was filled with rejoicing; and they did no more seek to destroy Nephi, but they did esteem him as a great prophet, and a man of God, having great power and authority given unto him from God.
>
> **And behold, Lehi, his brother, was not a whit behind him as to things pertaining to righteousness** (*BofM: Helaman* 11:18-19; emphasis added).

APPENDIX I

From Mormon's comment about "**...the Record of Helaman and his sons**" (*BofM: Helaman* 16:25), we learn that it is possible that Lehi wrote some of this book also. It is possible that Lehi engraved the sermons of his brother Nephi upon the plates.. He may have also recorded the prophecies of Samuel the Lamanite. However, the Record Keeper, or possessor, was Nephi, for he passed the Record on later.

Power Formula #16, Nephi² to His Son, Nephi³

Mormon gave us this abridged account of the transfer of the Records from Nephi², to his son:

> Now it came to pass that the ninety and first year had passed away and it was six hundred years from the time that Lehi left Jerusalem; and it was in the year that Lachoneus was the chief judge and the governor over the land.
> **And Nephi, the son of Helaman, had departed out of the land of Zarahemla, giving charge unto his son Nephi, who was his eldest son, concerning the plates of brass, and all the Records which had been kept,** and all those things which had been kept sacred from the departure of Lehi out of Jerusalem.
> Then he departed out of the land, and whither he went, no man knoweth; and **his son Nephi did keep the Records in his stead, yea, the Record of this people** (*BofM: 3 Nephi* 1:1-3; emphasis added).

In his abridgement of the Records, Mormon, on more than one occasion, wrote that the next Record Keeper did keep the Record "...in his stead...". According to Noah Webster, the meaning of *stead* is: "Place or room which another had...noting substitution or filling the place of another."[106]

Could we not also say that when one acts in the stead of another, they are "...filling the place [or post] of another"?

Here for the sixteenth time in *The Book of Mormon* we have evidence of a transfer of records from one person to another. These previous Record Keepers had remained in contact, or kept connected to, his successor. Also, he did "...make a record...", and "...get it into the hands of the guy who is going to take care of it...". Also, the previous Record Keepers did all they could to "...make the post occupiable" for their successors. These actions are identical with those contained in the **Power Formula**.

In this case, Nephi³ kept the Record in his father's "stead". In doing so, Nephi³ fulfilled his father's wishes, and thus accomplished the actions we now know as **Power Change**.

Nephi³ became a great teacher of the gospel (*3 Nephi* 1:23-24); He also became the earthly leader of Christ's Church (*3 Nephi* 18:27). He even raised his brother, Timothy, from the dead (*3 Nephi* 19:4). Both Nephi³ and Timothy were selected and

THE POWER FORMULAS

ordained by the Savior to be members of His leading twelve disciples over His Church in the Americas.

The Lord Jesus Christ Took Possession of the Record to Review It

For a short period during Nephi's[3] time as Record Keeper, he actually gave the Records to the Savior for His evaluation. This occurred during the Savior's visit to the people on the American continent.

> Therefore give heed to my words; **write the things which I have told you...**
> And now it came to pass that when Jesus had said these words he said unto them again, after he had expounded all the scriptures unto them which they had received, he said unto them:
> **Behold, other scriptures I would that ye should write, that ye have not.**
> **And it came to pass that he said unto Nephi: Bring forth the Record which ye have kept.** And when Nephi had brought forth the **Records** and laid them before Him [Jesus Christ], He cast His eyes upon them..." (*BofM: 3 Nephi* 23:4-8; emphasis added).

Jesus Christ then had Nephi[3] add the fulfillment of a prophecy made by Samuel the Lamanite. He also had His own teachings and some of the prophecies of Isaiah and Malachi added to the Record. Therefore, we can include the Savior's name to those who had custody of the Record.

After reviewing the Records, Jesus gave them back to Nephi[3], who then engraved those teachings which the Savior wanted him to add.

The lesson we learn from the Savior reviewing the Record, is that He maintained quality control, and responsibility for the Record. *The Book of Mormon* is not just the Record of Nephi or Helaman or Alma. In reality, Jesus Christ is the Source Author for the entire B*ook of Mormon* Record.

It is the **Record of Jesus Christ**. The Savior taught this truth through His final Record Keeper, Moroni.

> ...the time speedily cometh that ye shall know that I lie not, for ye shall see me [Moroni] at the bar of God; and **the Lord God will say unto you: Did I not declare my words unto you, which were written by this man...?** (*BofM: Moroni* 10:27 emphasis added).

APPENDIX I

Power Formulas #17 and #18, Nephi³ to His Son Nephi⁴, and Nephi⁴ to His Son Amos

Following the Savior's visit, these people experienced a great period of peace and righteousness. Eventually, the Record was passed to Nephi's³ son, Nephi². The first eighteen verses of the book of *Fourth Nephi* are Mormon's abridgement of Nephi⁴'s writings. Mormon's abridgement did not tell of the actual transfer of the Record to Nephi⁴. However, Mormon did write that the Record Keeper and author of the next book, *Fourth Nephi*, was "... the son of Nephi—one of the disciples of Jesus Christ" (see heading of the book of *Fourth Nephi*). When Nephi⁴ died, his son Amos became the next Record Keeper.

> And it came to pass that Nephi, he that **kept this last record,** (and he kept it upon the plates of Nephi) died, and his **son Amos kept it in his stead;** and he kept it upon the [large] plates of Nephi also (*BofM: 4 Nephi* 1:-19, emphasis added).

Power Formula #19, Amos to His Son, Amos²

Mormon then tells us of a transfer of the Records from father to son.

> And it came to pass that Amos died also, (and it was an hundred and ninety and four years from the coming of Christ) and **his son Amos² kept the Record in his stead;** and he also kept it upon the plates of Nephi; and it was also written in the book of [Fourth] Nephi which is this book (*BofM: 4 Nephi* 1:21; emphasis added).

During the time of Amos², the **Condition** of the people had greatly deteriorated. By the time Amos² gave the Records to his brother Ammaron, the **Spiritual Condition** of the people had dropped to the point that the Record had to be hidden for a time.

Power Formula #20, Amos² to Ammaron, His Brother

The following is Mormon's account of this transfer, and of Ammaron hiding the Record.

> And it came to pass that after three hundred and five years had passed away, (and the people did still remain in wickedness) **Amos died; and his brother, Ammaron, did keep the Record in his stead.**
> And it came to pass that when three hundred and twenty years had passed away, **Ammaron, being constrained by the Holy Ghost, did**

hide up the Records which were sacred—yea, even all the sacred records which had been handed down from generation to generation, which were sacred—even until the three hundred and twentieth year from the coming of Christ.

And he did hide them up unto the Lord that they might come again unto the remnant of the house of Jacob according to the prophecies and the promises of the Lord. And thus is the end of the Record of Ammaron (*BofM: 4 Nephi* 1:47-49; emphasis added).

Power Formula #21, Ammaron to Mormon

Although Ammaron had to hide the Records, he knew that this would be a temporary situation. Therefore, he selected, and trained a successor. He instructed a young man named Mormon, to eventually retrieve the plates. However, Mormon was to wait until he was older before taking possession of the Records. Here is Mormon's account of the instructions he received from his predecessor and teacher, Ammaron:

> And now I, Mormon, **make a record** of the things which I have both seen and heard, and call it The Book of Mormon.
>
> **And about the time that Ammaron hid up the Records unto the Lord, he came unto me,** (I being about ten years of age, and I began to be learned somewhat after the manner of the learning of my people) and Ammaron said unto me: I perceive that thou art a sober child, and art quick to observe;
>
> Therefore, **when ye are about twenty and four years old** I would that ye should remember the things that ye have observed concerning this people; and when ye are of that age go to the land Antum, unto a hill which shall be called Shim; and there have I deposited unto the Lord all the sacred engravings concerning this people.
>
> And behold, **ye shall take the [large] plates of Nephi unto yourself,** and the remainder shall ye leave in the place where they are; and ye shall **engrave on the plates of Nephi all the things that ye have observed** concerning this people.
>
> And I, Mormon, being a descendant of Nephi, (and my father's name was Mormon) **I remembered the things which Ammaron commanded me** (*BofM: Mormon* 1:1-5; emphasis added);

It is significant that Ammaron told Mormon to retrieve the plates of Nephi when he was **about** 24 years old. A great war was then brewing between the Nephites and Lamanites. Mormon would play a very important role in defending his country.

As noted earlier, Mormon became the leader of the Nephite armies at age 16. Like so many other young men, in all wars, when the conflict started, Mormon had to suspend other activities. He devoted himself to trying to defend and preserve his people. Because of his weighty responsibilities, it appears that Mormon may not have been able to remove the Records from hiding until he was well past the age of 24.

> And it came to pass that in the three hundred and forty and fifth year the Nephites did begin to flee before the Lamanites; and they were pursued until they came even to the land of Jashon, before it was possible to stop them in their retreat.
> And now, the city of Jashon was near the land where Ammaron had deposited the Records unto the Lord, that they might not be destroyed. And behold **I had gone according to the word of Ammaron, and taken the plates of Nephi, and did make a record according to the words of Ammaron** (*BofM: Mormon* 2:16-17; emphasis added).

If Mormon was eleven years old in 322 A.D. (see footnote, *BofM: Mormon* 1:6), then he would have been about 34 when he mentions retrieving the Record (see footnote, *BofM: Mormon* 2:16). It is possible that Mormon had possession of the Record, or a portion of the Record, prior to this time. Mormon may have removed the plates at about age 24, and re-deposited them for a period, during the fighting.

We cannot say for certain when he **first** took possession of the plates, but it is possible that Mormon had to postpone making his record because of his responsibilities during the war. As mentioned in the chapter on Mormon, much of the rest of his life was spent trying to help his nation survive. However, he did find time to **make a Record**, and eventually, Mormon turned the plates over to his son, Moroni.

Power Formula #22, Mormon to His Son Moroni

Near the end of his life, Mormon must have been separated from Moroni because of the war. He wrote an epistle to Moroni telling him of his intention to turn the Records over to him. Moroni later included his father's letter in his own record. Here is an excerpt from this letter:

> But behold, my son, I recommend thee unto God, and I trust in Christ that thou wilt be saved; and I pray unto God that he will spare thy life, to witness the return of his people unto him, or their utter destruction; for I know that they must perish except they repent and return unto him.
> And if they perish it will be like unto the Jaredites, because of the willfulness of their hearts, seeking for blood and revenge.
> And if it so be that they perish, we know that many of our brethren have deserted over unto the Lamanites, and many more will also desert

over unto them; **wherefore, write somewhat a few things, if thou art spared and I shall perish and not see thee; but I trust that I may see thee soon; for I have sacred records that I would deliver up unto thee** (*BofM: Moroni* 9:22-24; emphasis added).

Near the end of his life, Mormon also found time to write a brief explanation connecting the unabridged small plates of Nephi to his abridgement of the large plates. This section, known as *The Words of Mormon*, was an editor's note written by Mormon near the time he turned the plates over to Moroni.

> **And now I, Mormon, being about to deliver up the Record which I have been making into the hands of my son Moroni,** behold I have witnessed almost all the destruction of my people, the Nephites.
> And **it is many hundred years after the coming of Christ that I deliver these records into the hands of my son;** and it supposeth me that he will witness the entire destruction of my people. But may God grant that he may survive them, that he may write somewhat concerning them, and somewhat concerning Christ, that perhaps some day it may profit them (*BofM: Words of Mormon* 1:1-2; emphasis added).

Mormon and Moroni must have been reunited prior to the last battle, because Mormon did give the plates to his son.

> And it came to pass that when we had gathered in all our people in one to the land of Cumorah, behold I, Mormon, began to be old; and knowing it to be the last struggle of my people, and **having been commanded of the Lord that I should not suffer the Records which had been handed down by our fathers, which were sacred, to fall into the hands of the Lamanites, (for the Lamanites would destroy them) therefore I made this record out of the plates of Nephi,** and hid up in the hill Cumorah all the Records which had been entrusted to me by the hand of the Lord, save it were these few plates **which I gave unto my son Moroni** (*BofM: Mormon* 6:6; emphasis added).

It was probably after engraving these words, that Mormon engraved his final words, the seventh chapter of Mormon. Moroni was probably present, and he possibly observed these last engravings before he received the plates from his father.

Another Internal Evidence of the Truthfulness of *The Book of Mormon*

Also, it sounds like the large plates, which had been physically prepared by Nephi[1]

APPENDIX I

hundreds of years earlier, were nearly full with engravings. These remaining plates, which could still be engraved upon, were referred to as "those few plates". Moroni did engrave upon these plates, and eventually he made additional plates so that he could engrave his own Record. For further information on this, see Chapter 16 herein and *BofM: Mormon* 8:3-5.

This reference to the large plates of Nephi being nearly full reminds us of the words of the final Record Keepers of the smaller set of Nephi's plates (see Chapter 5 herein, and *BofM: Jarom* 1-2). Both of these references by the final Record Keepers of the small, and later the large plates of Nephi, are internal evidences of the truthfulness of *The Book of Mormon*.

The Records made by these men contained not only God's teachings and the history of their people; their Records also reflected the realities of their lives. This included the physical reality that they had no more room to engrave upon the plates they possessed. Thus, they had to conclude or "finish" the Records. These details of the realities of their lives are internal evidences that *The Book of Mormon* is a true Book of God's scriptures.

In terms of instructions, and a **Power Formula**, we should remember that like most of the Record Keepers, Moroni actually lived with the previous Record Keeper. It is probable that his father, Mormon, gave him **instructions and an example of how to keep the Record, over a period of many years!**

Moroni Actually Finished Two Records

The first thing Moroni wrote was that he was going to "...finish the Record of my father...". This indicates that he had been trained well by his father. Moroni must have had a great love and respect for his father, for it was Moroni who wrote the title page of the book. Moroni appropriately named the Record after the man who had abridged and compiled it into one set of plates. Moroni named the Record, *The Book of Mormon*, after his father.

Mormon had raised Moroni and trained him to be able to "... finish the Record...". Moroni finished both his father's personal Record which included Mormon's compilation of Records of the previous prophets. Moroni also wrote the abridgment of *The Book of Ether*. Moroni then finished his own Book to make what we now have as "Another Testament of Jesus Christ": *The Book of Mormon*.

Power Formula #23, Moroni to Joseph Smith

Moroni was the last person to actually **write** on the Record. However, he also **passed the Record to someone else.** When he finished his writings, Moroni placed the plates inside a box of stone, which he had buried in a hill near what we now know as Palmyra, New York. For nearly fourteen centuries, the Record lay undisturbed. In one of his psalms, David had testified that "truth shall spring forth out of earth..."

(*OldT: Psalms* 85:11). This prophecy was fulfilled in 1827. It was in that year, Joseph Smith was allowed to remove the Record from the hill.

For four years previous to this time Joseph had been receiving instruction from a heavenly messenger regarding the Record. This messenger was Moroni. How appropriate. Who else could better train the prophet Joseph Smith about his duty regarding the Record, than the **previous** Record Keeper?

In chapter one, we reviewed how, at age fourteen, Joseph had seen the Father and the Son in a glorious vision. In this vision, Joseph learned that he would be an instrument in the Lord's hands to restore The Church of Jesus Christ to the world. Part of this restoration was the translation and publication of *The Book of Mormon*.

Three years after the prophet Joseph Smith saw the Father and the Son, he was visited by Moroni. Joseph received training from this angel, meaning a messenger from God, as he prepared for his important mission. Here is the prophet's account of Moroni's first visit and instructions given in the year 1823:

> While I was thus in the act of calling upon God, I discovered a light appearing in my room, which continued to increase until the room was lighter than at noonday, when immediately a personage appeared at my bedside, standing in the air, for his feet did not touch the floor.
>
> Not only was his robe exceedingly white, but his whole person was glorious beyond description, and his countenance truly like lightning. The room was exceedingly light, but not so very bright as immediately around his person. When I first looked upon him, I was afraid; but the fear soon left me.
>
> He called me by name, and said unto me that he was a messenger sent from the presence of God to me, and that **his name was Moroni; that God had a work for me to do;** and that my name should be had for good and evil among all nations, kindreds, and tongues, or that it should be both good and evil spoken of among all people.
>
> **He said there was a book deposited, written upon gold plates, giving an account of the former inhabitants of this continent, and the source from whence they sprang. He also said that the fullness of the everlasting Gospel was contained in it, as delivered by the Savior to the ancient inhabitants** (*The Pearl of Great Price: Joseph Smith History* 1:30, 32-34; emphasis added).

Like Mormon, Joseph was instructed to wait until he was older to actually take possession of the Records. Each year, on the anniversary of Moroni's first visit, Joseph went to the place where the Record was buried. He was met there by Moroni on each of these occasions. During these visits Joseph was taught by Moroni. Joseph Smith described these visits in this way:

> Accordingly, as I had been commanded, I went at the end of each

APPENDIX I

year, and at each time **I found the same messenger there, and received instruction and intelligence from him at each of our interviews,** respecting what the Lord was going to do, and how and in what manner his kingdom was to be conducted in the last days (*The Pearl of Great Price: Joseph Smith History* 1:54; emphasis added).

On the fourth visit, Joseph was allowed to remove the plates and other items from the hill. These items included the Urim and Thummim, which was prepared by the Lord to help the prophet translate the Record. Joseph also received these instructions from Moroni concerning his responsibility to protect the Record:

> ...the same heavenly messenger [Moroni] delivered them up to me with this charge: **that I should be responsible for them;** that if I should let them go carelessly, or through any neglect of mine, I should be cut off; but that if **I would use all my endeavors to preserve them, until he, the messenger, should call for them, they should be protected** (*The Pearl of Great Price: Joseph Smith History* 1:59; emphasis added).

As we think back, we can recall that these instructions are very similar to those Alma[2] gave to Helaman. Here again is Alma's[2] warning:

> And now behold, I tell you by the spirit of prophecy, that **if ye transgress the commandments of God, behold, these things which are sacred shall be taken away from you** by the power of God, and ye shall be delivered up unto Satan, that he may sift you as chaff before the wind.
>
> **But if ye keep the commandments of God, and do with these things which are sacred according to that which the Lord doth command you,** (for you must appeal unto the Lord for all things whatsoever ye must do with them) behold, **no power of earth or hell can take them from you, for God is powerful to the fulfilling of all his words.**
>
> **For he will fulfill** all his promises which he shall make unto you, **for he has fulfilled** his promises which he has made unto our fathers (*BofM: Alma* 37:15-17; emphasis added).

The Record was Transferred for the 24th Time

Joseph did protect the plates. Also, he did translate the plates by the gift and **Power** of God. After finishing the translation, he returned the Record to Moroni. Here is the prophet's account of that transfer:

...The persecution became more bitter and severe than before, and multitudes were on the alert continually to get them from me if possible. But by the wisdom of God, **they remained safe in my hands, until I had accomplished by them what was required at my hand. When, according to arrangements, the messenger called for them, I delivered them up to him; and he has them in his charge until this day,** being the second day of May, one thousand eight hundred and thirty-eight (*The Pearl of Great Price: Joseph Smith History* 1:60; emphasis added).

The Book of Mormon was translated and published in the English language in 1830. It has since been fully translated into 82 languages and partially translated into 25 others (as of 1993). Also, it is likely that translations into additional languages are planned, are in process, or have been completed by the time of this revised edition of *The Power Formulas Part One* (2014).

In conclusion, we have a Record that was successfully preserved and passed on from one person to another 24 times. This Record, including *The Book of Ether*, covered a period of about 3,600 years.

Can we cite a better example of actions like the Power Formula being used and followed? Can we find any book which even comes close to being such an example of the principles of the Power Formula and Power Change Formula?

We can't find another book like *The Book of Mormon*. Not even *The Holy Bible* was made up of the writings of a **series** of Record Keepers, who each passed their cumulative records on to another Record Keeper.

Is the Record perfect? No. Even Moroni acknowledged as much. However, he also warned against our condemning it for its imperfections. He wrote:

And now, **if there are faults they are the mistakes of men;** wherefore, **condemn not the things of God,** that ye may be found spotless at the judgment-seat of Christ (*BofM: Introduction* 1:2 emphasis added).

Moroni also promised even greater knowledge to those who did not condemn the Record.

And whoso receiveth this record, and shall not condemn it because of the imperfections which are in it, the same shall know of greater things than these. Behold, I am Moroni; and were it possible, I would make all things known unto you (*BofM: Mormon* 8:12; emphasis added).

Although the Record was not perfect, it is, as Joseph stated: **"the most correct of any book on the earth..."** (see Introduction to *The Book of Mormon*). Before he buried the plates, Moroni commented about the worth of the Record. In this prophecy,

APPENDIX I

he also referred to the prophet Joseph Smith, although he doesn't mention him by name.

> And I am the same who hideth up this record unto the Lord; the plates thereof are of no [worldly or monetary] worth, because of the commandment of the Lord. For he truly saith that no one shall have them to get gain; but **the Record thereof is of great worth; and whoso shall bring it to light, him will the Lord bless [Joseph Smith].**
>
> For none can have **power** to bring it to light save it be given him of God; for God wills that it shall be done with an eye single to his glory, or the welfare of the ancient and long dispersed covenant people of the Lord.
>
> And **blessed be he that shall bring this thing to light;** for it shall be brought out of darkness unto light, according to the word of God; yea, **it shall be brought out of the earth,** and it shall shine forth out of darkness, and come unto the knowledge of the people; and **it shall be done by the power of God** (*BofM: Mormon* 8:14-16; emphasis added).

How appropriate it is that the Record we now call *The Book of Mormon* should come forth "...by the power of God ...". How else would we expect God's Power Formula to come forth?

In reviewing the transfers and instructions between these Record Keepers, we can find strong evidence that *The Book of Mormon* is God's **Power Formula** for our lives.

Also, in these transfers of the Record, we can find strong evidence that these Record Keepers used principles like those of the **Power** and **Power Change Formulas.** This is also another evidence of the truthfulness of *The Book of Mormon*, and a reason why each of us should have sufficient motivation to read the Record with real intent!

Power Formulas from *The Book of Mormon* Record Keepers to You

Thank you for the time and the effort you have given to reading *The Power Formulas Part One*. My hope is that you have an increased desire to read and study **God's Power Formula**, *The Book of Mormon*. So far, you have been only reading the menu. A spiritual feast now awaits you, as you read His Record with real intent!

One final thought about the **Power Formulas** in *The Book of Mormon*. Some of *The Book of Mormon* Record Keepers left a message to their future readers. These messages are usually located at the end of their Records. The parting words of these Record Keepers summarized and emphasized the central messages of their teachings.

These farewell messages actually represent **Spiritual Power Formulas** written

THE POWER FORMULAS

for us, the readers of the Record. In this way, these Record Keepers did a **Power Formula** on two levels: One for the next Record Keeper, and one for their readers. We have the opportunity of doing **Spiritual Power Change** with God as we follow the example, advice, and teachings of these prophets.

These farewells and **Power Formulas** can be found at the end of the Records of Nephi, Jacob and Moroni. Also, other **Spiritual Power Formulas** are located in *Jacob* 6; *Omni*: 25-26; and *Ether* 12. It is appropriate that we conclude with the final words of Mormon which are found in *Mormon* 7:8 and 10 (emphasis added). These instructions which constitute a spiritual **Power Formula** for all who read the book that bears his name. Here are Mormon's parting words, and his spiritual **Power Formula**, for you and I:

> Therefore repent and be baptised in the name of Jesus, and lay hold upon the gospel of Christ which shall be set before you, not only in this record [*The Book of Mormon*] but also in the record which shall come unto the Gentiles from the Jews [*The Holy Bible*]...
>
> ...and if it so be that ye believe in Christ, and are baptised first with water, then with fire and the Holy Ghost [receive the Gift of the Holy Ghost by the blessing of those holding God's priesthood authority] following the example of our Savior, according to that which He hath commanded us, [thereby doing **Power Change** with Him] it shall be well with you in the day of judgment.
>
> Amen.

APPENDIX II

THE FAMILY
A PROCLAMATION TO THE WORLD

THE FIRST PRESIDENCY AND COUNCIL OF THE TWELVE APOSTLES OF THE CHURCH OF JESUS CHRIST OF LATTER-DAY SAINTS

WE, THE FIRST PRESIDENCY and the Council of the Twelve Apostles of The Church of Jesus Christ of Latter-day Saints, solemnly proclaim that marriage between a man and a woman is ordained of God and that the family is central to the Creator's plan for the eternal destiny of His children.

ALL HUMAN BEINGS—male and female—are created in the image of God. Each is a beloved spirit son or daughter of heavenly parents, and, as such, each has a divine nature and destiny. Gender is an essential characteristic of individual premortal, mortal, and eternal identity and purpose.

IN THE PREMORTAL REALM, spirit sons and daughters knew and worshipped God as their Eternal Father and accepted His plan by which His children could obtain a physical body and gain earthly experience to progress toward perfection and ultimately realize their divine destiny as heirs of eternal life. The divine plan of happiness enables family relationships to be perpetuated beyond the grave. Sacred ordinances and covenants available in holy temples make it possible for individuals to return to the presence of God and for families to be united eternally.

THE FIRST COMMANDMENT that God gave to Adam and Eve pertained to their potential for parenthood as husband and wife. We declare that God's commandment for His children to multiply and replenish the earth remains in force. We further declare that God has commanded that the sacred powers of procreation are to be employed only between man and woman, lawfully wedded as husband and wife.

WE DECLARE the means by which mortal life is created to be divinely appointed. We affirm the sanctity of life and of its importance in God's eternal plan.

HUSBAND AND WIFE have a solemn responsibility to love and care for each other and for their children. "Children are an heritage of the Lord" (Psalm 127:3). Parents have a sacred duty to rear their children in love and righteousness, to provide for their physical and spiritual needs, and to teach them to love and serve one another, observe the commandments of God, and be law-abiding citizens wherever they live. Husbands and wives—mothers and fathers—will be held accountable before God for the discharge of these obligations.

THE FAMILY is ordained of God. Marriage between man and woman is essential to His eternal plan. Children are entitled to birth within the bonds of matrimony, and to be reared by a father and a mother who honor marital vows with complete fidelity. Happiness in family life is most likely to be achieved when founded upon the teachings of the Lord Jesus Christ. Successful marriages and families are established and maintained on principles of faith, prayer, repentance, forgiveness, respect, love, compassion, work, and wholesome recreational activities. By divine design, fathers are to preside over their families in love and righteousness and are responsible to provide the necessities of life and protection for their families. Mothers are primarily responsible for the nurture of their children. In these sacred responsibilities, fathers and mothers are obligated to help one another as equal partners. Disability, death, or other circumstances may necessitate individual adaptation. Extended families should lend support when needed.

WE WARN that individuals who violate covenants of chastity, who abuse spouse or offspring, or who fail to fulfill family responsibilities will one day stand accountable before God. Further, we warn that the disintegration of the family will bring upon individuals, communities, and nations the calamities foretold by ancient and modern prophets.

WE CALL UPON responsible citizens and officers of government everywhere to promote those measures designed to maintain and strengthen the family as the fundamental unit of society.

This proclamation was read by President Gordon B. Hinckley as part of his message at the General Relief Society Meeting held September 23, 1995, in Salt Lake City, Utah.

THE POWER FORMULAS

References

PREFACE

1. L. Ron Hubbard, *Modern Management Technology Defined* (Los Angeles: Bridge Publications, 1976), see *Power Formula*, p. 401.
2. *Random House Dictionary of the English Language*, 2nd Edition, Stuart Berg Flexner, Editor (New York: Random House, 1987), p. 1516.
3. L. Ron Hubbard, *Dianetics* (Los Angeles: Bridge Publications, 1950), pp. 557-559.
4. L. Ron Hubbard, *Modern Management Technology Defined* (Los Angeles: Bridge Publications, 1976), see *Power Change*, p. 400.
5. *The Pearl of Great Price, The Book of Moses* (Salt Lake City: Published by The Church of Jesus Christ of Latter-day Saints, 1986), See Chapter 5, verse 57, p. 15.
6. Subtitle of *The Book of Mormon* (Salt Lake City: Published by The Church of Jesus Christ of Latter-day Saints, 1986).
7. Joseph Smith, *The Teachings of the Prophet Joseph Smith*, compiled by Joseph Fielding Smith (Salt Lake City: Deseret Book Company, 1976), p. 313.
8. Brigham Young, as quoted in *The Journal of Discourses*, Vol 7. (Salt Lake City: Published by the Church of Jesus Christ of Latter-day Saints, 1967), p. 148.
9. John R. Talmage, *Life of James E. Talmage — Educator, Scientist, Apostle* (Salt Lake City: Book Craft, 1972), p. 240.
10. L. Ron Hubbard, *Organization Executive Course, Basic Staff Volume* (Los Angeles: Bridge Publications, 1986), see Important Note following title page.
11. *The Doctrine and Covenants of the Church of Jesus Christ of Latter-day Saints* (Salt Lake City: Published by the Church of Jesus Christ of Latter-day Saints, 1986), section 88, verse 33, p. 167.

CHAPTER 1

12. Joseph Smith, *The Teachings of the Prophet, Joseph Smith*, compiled by Joseph Fielding Smith (Salt Lake City: Deseret Book, 1976), p. 267.
13. Thanks to John E. Walker and his unpublished compilation, *Joseph Smith and The Isthmus of Darien*, for bringing this information to my attention.
14. *The Pearl of Great Price*, Joseph Smith's History (Salt Lake City: The Church of Jesus Christ of Latter-day Saints, 1986), pp. 47-49.
15. L. Ron Hubbard, *Introduction to Scientology Ethics* (Los Angeles: Bridge Publications, 1989), p. 38.
16. L. Ron Hubbard, *Modern Management Technology Defined* (Los Angeles: Bridge Publications, 1976), see *Condition*, p. 99.

17. L. Ron Hubbard, *Modern Management Technology Defined* (Los Angeles: Bridge Publications, 1976), see *Ethics*, p. 179.
18. L. Ron Hubbard, *Modern Management Technology Defined* (Los Angeles: Bridge Publications, 1976), see *Power Change*, p. 400.
19. See Chapter 9 herein, "Bridges."
20. See Chapter 9 herein, "Bridges."
21. See *The Holy Bible, New Testament:* John 1:12.
22. See *The Book of Mormon:* 1 Nephi 13:40-41.
23. See *The Book of Mormon:* Introduction.
24. *See The Book of Mormon:* 3 Nephi 18:32.
25. *See The Book of Mormon:* Alma 36:1-21.
26. *See The Book of Mormon:* Title Page.
27. *See The Book of Mormon:* Moroni 10:32-33.
28. *See The Book of Mormon:* Moroni 10:32-33.
29. *See The Book of Mormon:* 3 Nephi 27:20-21, 28:10.
30. *See The Book of Mormon:* Moroni 10:3-5.

CHAPTER 2

31. Spencer J. Condie, "Some Scriptural Lessons On Leadership," *The Ensign, of the Church of Jesus Christ of Latter-day Saints*, May 1990, p. 28.
32. Elder Boyd K. Packer, *The Things Of My Soul,* Video Tape (Salt Lake City: The Church of Jesus Christ of Latter-day Saints).
33. Joseph Smith, *The Teachings of the Prophet Joseph Smith,* compiled by Joseph Fielding Smith (Salt Lake City: Deseret Book Company, 1976), p. 151.
34. *Noah Webster, American Dictionary of the English Language* (originally published by S. Converse: New York, 1828. Republished in facsimile by the Foundation for American Christian Education: San Francisco, 1967), see "*Hearken.*" [Author's note: This dictionary was selected because it is the classic work of a genius, who was also a devout Christian. Also, the dictionary was published at the same time that the prophet Joseph Smith was translating the Record found on *The Book of Mormon* plates. Therefore, the word definitions found in Webster's 1828 Dictionary gave us an accurate and contemporary understanding of the American/English language that the prophet translated the Record into at that time].
35. Bruce R. McConkie, *Mormon Doctrine* (Salt Lake City: Bookcraft, 1966), p. 237.

CHAPTER 4

36. L. Ron Hubbard, *Dianetics* (Los Angeles: Bridge Publications, 1976), p. 48.
37. L. Ron Hubbard, *Introduction to Scientology* Ethics (Los Angeles: Bridge Publications 1989), p. 14.

REFERENCES

38. L. Ron Hubbard, *Modern Management Technology Defined* (Los Angeles: Bridge Publications, 1976), see *Dynamics*, p. 166.
39. L. Ron Hubbard, *Modern Management Technology Defined* (Los Angeles: Bridge Publications, 1976), see *Power Formula*, p. 401.
40. L. Ron Hubbard, *Organization Executive Course, Basic Staff Volume* (Los Angeles: Bridge Publications, 1986), p. 15.
41. *Noah Webster, American Dictionary of the English Language* (originally published by S. Converse: New York, 1828. Republished in facsimile by the Foundation for American Christian Education; San Francisco, 1967), see "*Dwindle*".
42. *Noah Webster American Dictionary of The English Language* (originally published by S. Converse, New York, 1828. Republished in facsimile by the Foundation for American Christian Education: San Francisco, 1967), see "*Charge*".
43. L. Ron Hubbard, *Dianetics* (Los Angeles: Bridge Publications 1986), p. 29.
44. Joseph Smith, *The Teachings of the Prophet Joseph Smith*, compiled by Joseph Fielding Smith (Salt Lake City: Deseret Book, 1976), p. 301.
45. Joseph Smith, *The Teachings of the Prophet Joseph Smith*, compiled by Joseph Fielding Smith (Salt Lake City: Deseret Book, 1976), pp. 355-356.
46. Joseph Smith, *The Teachings of the Prophet Joseph Smith*, compiled by Joseph Fielding Smith (Salt Lake City: Deseret Book, 1976), pp. 123-124.
47. Joseph Smith, *The Teachings of The Prophet Joseph Smith*, compiled by Joseph Fielding Smith (Salt Lake City: Deseret Book, 1976), p. 129.
48. L. Ron Hubbard, *Modern Management Technology Defined* (Los Angeles: Bridge Publications, 1976), see *Power Formula*, Step One, p. 401.
49. L. Ron Hubbard, *Modern Management Technology Defined* (Los Angeles: Bridge Publications, 1976), see *Power Formula, Step Two*, p. 401.
50. Dallin H. Oaks, *Pure in Heart* (Salt Lake City: Bookcraft, Inc., 1988), pp. vii, viii.
51. *Noah Webster, American Dictionary of the English Language* (originally published by S. Converse: New York, 1828. Republished in facsimile by the Foundation for American Christian Education: San Francisco, 1976), see "*Heart.*"
52. L. Ron Hubbard, *Organization Executive Course Basic Staff Volume* (Los Angeles: Bridge Publications, 1986), p. 583.
53. L. Ron Hubbard, *Modern Management Technology Defined* (Los Angeles: Bridge Publications, 1976), see *Power Formula, Step Four,* p. 401.

CHAPTER EIGHT

54. L. Ron Hubbard, *Modern Management Technology Defined* (Los Angeles: Bridge Publications, 1976), see *Power Change*, p. 400.
55. L. Ron Hubbard, *Modern Management Defined* (Los Angeles: Bridge Publications, 1976), see *Power Formula, Step One*, p. 401.
56. L. Ron Hubbard, *Modern Management Technology Defined* (Los Angeles: Bridge Publications, 1976), see *Power Formula, Step Two*, p. 401.

57. L. Ron Hubbard, *Modern Management Technology Defined* (Los Angeles: Bridge Publications, 1976), see *Power Formula, Step Three*, p. 401.
58. L. Ron Hubbard, *Modern Management Technology Defined* (Los Angeles: Bridge Publications, 1976), See *Power Formula, Step Four*, p. 401.
59. L. Ron Hubbard, *Modern Management Technology Defined* (Los Angeles: Bridge Publications, 1976), see *Power Change*, p. 400.
60. L. Ron Hubbard, *Introduction To Scientology Ethics* (Los Angeles: Bridge Publications, 1989), p. 349.
61. L. Ron Hubbard, *Modern Management Technology Defined* (Los Angeles: Bridge Publications, 1976), see *Non Existence Formula*, p. 349.
62. L. Ron Hubbard, *Modern Management Technology Defined* (Los Angeles: Bridge Publications, 1976), see *Non Existence Formula, Step Two*, p. 349.
63. *Noah Webster, American Dictionary of the English Language* (originally published by S. Converse: New York, 1820. Republished in facsimile by the Foundation for American Christian Education: San Francisco, 1967), see "Communication."
64. L. Ron Hubbard, *Modern Management Technology Defined* (Los Angeles: Bridge Publications, 1976), see *Non Existence Formula, Step Three*, p. 349.
65. L. Ron Hubbard, *Modern Management Technology Defined* (Los Angeles: Bridge Publication, 1976), see *Non Existence Formula, Step Four*, p. 349.
66. L. Ron Hubbard, *Modern Management Technology Defined* (Los Angeles: Bridge Publications, 1986), see *Cycle of Action*, p. 125.
67. L. Ron Hubbard, *Modern Management Technology Defined* (Los Angeles: Bridge Publications, 1976), see *Tone Scale*, pp. 526-27.
68. L. Ron Hubbard, *Scientology 0-8* (Los Angeles: Bridge Publications, 1988), p. 109.
69. L. Ron Hubbard, *Introduction to Scientology Ethics* (Los Angeles: Bridge Publications, 1989), pp. 103-104.
70. L. Ron Hubbard, *Modern Management Technology Defined* (Los Angeles: Bridge Publications, 1976), see *Stable Datum*, p. 491.
71. L. Ron Hubbard, *The Science of Survival* (Los Angeles: Bridge Publications, 1951), p. 18.
72. Bruce R. McConkie, *Mormon Doctrine* (Salt Lake City: Bookcraft, 1966), p. 237.

CHAPTER 9

73. J.R.R. Tolkien, *The Fellowship of the Ring* (New York: Ballentine Books Inc., 1965 edition), pp. 403-404.
74. J.R.R. Tolkien, *The Fellowship of the Ring* (New York: Ballentine Books, Inc., 1965 edition), pp. 427-430.
75. Noah Webster, *American Dictionary of the English Language* (originally published

REFERENCES

by S. Converse: New York, 1828. Republished in facsimile by the Foundation for American Christian Education: San Francisco, 1967), see "*Gulf.*"

76. *The Doctrine and Covenants of the Church of Jesus Christ of Latter-day Saints* (Salt Lake City: The Church of Jesus Christ of Latter-day Saints, 1986), Section 122, verses 1-9.

77. *The Doctrine and Covenants of the Church of Jesus Christ of Latter-day Saints* (Salt Lake City: The Church of Jesus Christ of Latter-day Saints, 1986), Section 18, verse 11.

78. James E. Talmage, *Jesus the Christ* (Salt Lake City: Deseret Book, 1915), p.613-614.

79. James E. Talmage, *Jesus The Christ* (Salt Lake City: Deseret Book, 1915), p.660, 661, 662.

80. *Noah Webster, American Dictionary of The English Language* (originally published by S. Converse, New York, 1820. (Republished in facsimile by the American Foundation for Christian Education: San Francisco, 1967), see "*Betwixt*".

81. *The Doctrine and Covenants of the Church of Jesus Christ of Latter-day Saints* (Salt Lake City: Deseret Book, 1986), Section 27, verse 12.

82. James E. Talmage, *Jesus The Christ* (Salt Lake City: Deseret Book, 1915), p. 23.

83. L. Ron Hubbard, *Dianetics* (Los Angeles: Bridge Publications, 1986), pp. 535-536, 542-543.

84. Bruce C. Hafen, *The Broken Heart* (Salt Lake City: Deseret Book, 1989), p.9, 19.

85. *Noah Webster, American Dictionary of the English Language*, (originally published by S. Converse, New York, 1828. Republished in facsimile by The Foundation for American Christian Education: San Francisco, 1967), see "*Way*".

CHAPTER ELEVEN

86. James E. Talmage, *Jesus The Christ*, (Salt Lake City: Deseret Book 1915), p. 36, 37.

87. James E. Talmage, *Jesus The Christ* (Salt Lake City: Deseret Book, 1915), p. 41.

88. James E. Talmage, *Jesus The Christ* (Salt Lake City: Deseret Book, 1915), pp.38, 39.

89. James E. Talmage, *Jesus The Christ*, (Salt Lake City: Deseret Book, 1915), p. 629.

CHAPTER THIRTEEN

90. James E. Talmage, *Jesus The Christ* (Salt Lake City: Deseret Book, 1915), p. 724.

91. *Noah Webster, American Dictionary of the English Language* (originally published by S. Converse, New York, 1828. Republished in facsimile by the Foundation for American Christian Education: San Francisco, 1967), see *"Suffer"*.
92. L. Ron Hubbard, *Modern Management Technology Defined* (Los Angeles: Bridge Publications,1976), see *Power Formula Step One*, p.40 1.
93. Robert J. Matthews, Editor, *The Book of Mormon: The Keystone Scripture* (Salt Lake City: Religious Studies Center, Brigham Young University, 1988), p. 31.
94. *Noah Webster, American Dictionary of the English Language* (originally published by S. Converse, New York, 1828. Republished in facsimile by the Foundation for American Christian Education: San Francisco, 1967), see *"Proud"*.
96. L. Ron Hubbard, *Modern Management Technology Defined* (Los Angeles: Bridge Publications, 1976), see *Power Formula Step Two*, p. 401.
97. L. Ron Hubbard, *Modern Management Technology De fined* (Los Angeles: Bridge Publications, 1976), see *Power Formula Step Three*, p. 401.
98. L. Ron Hubbard, *Modern Management Technology De fined* (Los Angeles: Bridge Publications, 1976), see *Power Formula Step Four*, p. 401).

CHAPTER FOURTEEN

99. L.Ron Hubbard, *Modern Management Technology Defined* (Los Angeles: Bridge Publications,1976), see *Power Formula Step One*, p. 401.
100. David B. Galbraith, "Orson Hyde's 1841 Mission to the Holy Land", *The Ensign of the Church of Jesus Christ of Latter-day Saints,* October 1991, p. 16-19.

CHAPTER SIXTEEN

101. *The Pearl of Great Price, Joseph Smith—History* (Salt Lake City: The Church of Jesus Christ of Latter-day Saints, 1986), verse 35, p. 52.
102. Max C. Caldwell, "Love of Christ", *The Ensign of The Church of Jesus Christ of Latter-day Saints*, November 1992) p. 29-30.
103. *The Doctrine and Covenants of the Church of Jesus Christ of Latter-day Saints* (Salt Lake City: The Church of Jesus Christ of Latter-day Saints, 1986), section 76, verse 69-70, p. 141.
104. Bruce C. Hafen, *The Broken Heart* (Salt Lake City: Deseret Book, 1989), pp. 9, 17, 18, 19.
105. Joseph Smith *The Pearl of Great Price, The Articles of Faith* (Salt Lake City: The Church of Jesus Christ of Latter-day Saints, 1986), verse 8, p.60.
106. *Noah Webster, American Dictionary of the English Language* (originally published by S. Converse, New York, 1828. Republished in facsimile by the Foundation for American Christian Education: San Francisco, 1967), see *"Stead"*.

www.ingramcontent.com/pod-product-compliance
Lightning Source LLC
Chambersburg PA
CBHW081345040426
42450CB00015B/3308